TRAIL TO THE INTERIOR

*Other books in the R.M. Patterson Collection
from Horsdal & Schubart*

FAR PASTURES

FINLAY'S RIVER

THE BUFFALO HEAD

TRAIL

TO THE

INTERIOR

by R.M. Patterson

Horsdal & Schubart

Horsdal & Schubart Ltd.
4252 Commerce Circle
Victoria, B.C., V8Z 4M2

Cover photograph by R.M. Patterson.
Text and photographs are reproduced from the first edition, published
in 1966 by Macmillan of Canada, Toronto, Ontario.

Maps by H.N. Davis, Victoria, B.C.

Printed and bound by Best Gagne Book Manufacturers,
Toronto, Ontario

Dedication: In tribute to the late T.F. Harper Reed, July 18, 1878, to
December 20, 1965, old-timer of the Stikine.

Canadian Cataloguing in Publication Data

Patterson, R.M. (Raymond Murray), 1898-1984.
    Trail to the Interior

Originally published: Toronto: Macmillan, 1966.
Includes bibliographical references.
ISBN 0-920663-18-4

1. Patterson, R.M. (Raymond Murray), 1898-1984—Journeys—Stikine
River Region (B.C. and Alta.) 2. Patterson, R.M. (Raymond Murray),
1898-1984—Journeys—British Columbia—Cassiar Mountains Region. 3.
Stikine River Regio (B.C. and Alta.)—Description and travel. 4. Cassiar
Mountains Region (B.C.)—Description and travel. 5. Stikine River Regio
(B.C. and Alta.)—History. 6. Cassiar Mountains Region (B.C.)—History.
FC3845.C35P38 1993   917.11'85   C93-091355-8
F1089.C35P38 1993

CONTENTS

Foreword

He came to our untamed frontier wilderness as a pioneer, took his lumps and bruises, became a skilled northern traveller and left a literary heritage. Those who delight in Canadian outdoor adventure will be pleased to learn that R. M. Patterson's finely crafted tales will be available to future generations, for as an author he was unique on several counts. His qualifications were remarkable. He had the advantage of an academic background, a great eye for country and a keen ear for dialogue. Through this he developed a writing style described by Bruce Hutchison as a "mixture of Thoreau and Jack London."

Born in the north of England on May 13, 1898, he was just old enough to serve as a gunner in World War I, 1917-18. Nine months of this was spent in Silesia as a guest of the Germans. Patterson recalled his prisoner-of-war experiences as simply another adventure. Following this, he took a degree in modern history at Oxford and tried to settle down to a career at the Bank of England. He suffered an attack of what he termed "claustrophobia" and "itchy foot" which brought him to Canada in the early 1920s.

Working his way west through jobs on farm and ranch, he discovered the prairies and mountains. In 1924 he decided to take the homesteader's gamble of a five-dollar filing fee with a vow to stick it out for three years, and struck out for the Peace River country to locate and stake out 320 acres that he could develop.

As one adventure led to another he wrote home regularly, and fortunately, his mother and a friend preserved every letter. He began describing the characters whose trails crossed his, and picked up the accents of natives, half-breeds, Scandinavians and Orientals who were struggling for a place in the vast sweep of country.

Until Patterson came along, Canadian history books highlighting adventure had been appearing and disappearing in three categories. There had been a succession of regional histories, in limited editions, culled from letters, diaries and photographs of pioneer families. University and trade presses had published important histories by academics, researched in the archives of governments and corporations. Then there was the professional adventurer, from "away", who sweeps through the country, often raising an expedition to power through dangerous waterways, or to challenge by ski or snowmobile perhaps, with radio and back-up. Following in the tracks of the early explorers, equipped as they never were, in six weeks or so they have enough material for a book. This was not the Patterson modus operandi.

Before putting pen to paper Patterson paid his dues. He learned how to fork a bronc, throw a diamond hitch, drive a dog team and read a river before running fast water. Then he wrote about these things, and his companions, with humour, style and remarkable dialogue.

He honed his writing style, patiently and laboriously, it seems, in this impatient age of computers and electronics. Writing in school copy-books in pencil, he scratched out many words. He was fussy about finding the right term, and strove to be literate but lucid, striking out a long word when a short one would do. He had tremendous admiration for the English author, Norman Douglas (1868-1952), and his style.

When his adventurous life began to seem noteworthy, he turned his longhand into typewritten manuscripts through the help of friends. His articles were published in *The Beaver* in Canada and *Blackwoods* in the United Kingdom. One of his exploits in the Northwest Territories brought him two letters from London publishers and he was on his way. His first book, *The Dangerous River* (1954), was published in London, New

York and Canada with translations in Spanish and Dutch, which brought him a world-wide readership. A lively correspondence built up with loyal fans and the result was a string of popular titles. Forty years in the western mountains led to *The Buffalo Head* (1961), *Far Pastures* (1963), *Trail To The Interior* (1966) and *Finlay's River* (1968). One reviewer commenting on *The Buffalo Head* wrote "... once again we accompany the author in his flight from the twentieth century." Patterson's reply is worth quoting: "But if the old times and the old ways are not worth keeping, they still may be worth recording for the benefit of the mechanized, enlightened posterity to whom a horse will have become a snob symbol and a canoe nothing but an unsafe craft...."

The pleasing thing about his life-style and narrative is the faithful way he kept in touch with, and maintained the friendship of, the rugged individuals he wrote about. From Gordon Matthews, his Nahanni partner, and Albert Faille, the prospector, to Paul Amos, the Stoney hunter, he managed to keep in lively contact. When Patterson ran the Buffalo Head ranch in the Alberta foothills, Paul would ride with him, checking the fences and cattle. From Paul he picked up native mountain lore and customs, and they became close, firm friends. In the evening of his life on Vancouver Island he enjoyed visits from a string of old-timers like Bert Sheppard, cattleman from High River, the McDougalls from Finlay Forks, and F. C. Swannell, the pioneer surveyor whose career had started in 1898.

His books are Patterson's living testimony and undying record of many known and unknown achievers who challenged an untamed frontier, helping to develop two western provinces and the Northwest Territories. "And so," he wrote, "in my character of unrepentant old-timer, I have arranged these word-pictures of the West."

Canada is enriched by keeping the memory green.

Gray Campbell, Deep Cove, 1993

Introduction

The history of the Cassiar district of British Columbia is a lively one, and I have been lucky enough to meet a few of the old-timers who knew that distant territory when it was still young, and when a man's ability to travel in it was still measured by his strength and endurance and his knowledge of the ways of the bush. Some of the tales that are told in this book have been given to me by those survivors from that earlier time, or else they have come to me in private letters from men who have lived, hunted and prospected in that empty land—and beyond its borders in Alaska, the Yukon and the North-west Territories. Back files of newspapers and magazines have also made their contributions, and a hitherto unpublished journal of the Klondike rush brings the events of that period to life again. For the rest, the adventures of the early explorers of the Hudson's Bay Company and of the later fur-traders, travellers and sportsmen are to be found scattered here and there: in deep volumes published for learned societies in limited editions or in books now long out of print—and in neither case easily available to the general reader. Some of these stories of bygone days I have tried to string together on the thread of my own experiences as I passed through the Stikine-Dease country by riverboat and canoe.

To the best of my belief, there has never been written any one book on this country; and here, for the first time, all this varied material is gathered together in one volume. The book does not pretend to be a complete history of that northern region: considerations of space make that impossible. But if it leaves the reader with a vivid picture of those splendid rivers and the mountains through which they pass, I shall be well content. Into that picture he should then be able to paint for himself, as I did, the persistent, determined men who pioneered those trails in days gone by.

One thing I should like to explain before I am hauled over the coals for it by some eagle-eyed perfectionist: in writing of olden times I have occasionally made use of the old-time spelling or phrasing of place names. Thus the river which we now call the Mackenzie may also be found in this book under its older appellation of "McKenzie's River" and Dease Lake may similarly change, with the period, into the original "Dease's Lake." This has been done deliberately and after due consideration, wherever it seemed necessary, in order to preserve the spirit of the time.

As for my own trip over that historic waterway, practically everything went wrong that could go wrong: the timing was bad—though that was unavoidable; the weather was often bad; mist drove in between myself and what may have been a record head of caribou; a painful injury made everything more difficult than it should have been; and even a despicable flu germ ranged itself against me. Only the canoe ran straight and never played me false. Yet all these mischances now count for little when weighed against the good days that country gave me and against the memory of old friends met with on the trail. My advice now to all who delight in northern travel is to see for themselves those rivers and the Dease Lake trail before the improvers and the planners—all those who would destroy, recklessly and wastefully, the fair places of the Northwest—change the Stikine-Dease watershed out of all recognition.

Acknowledgements

I am particularly obliged to Mr. George Kirkendale
for allowing me to reproduce much of his father's personal
record of the Trail of '98; to Mrs. George Ball for permission
to make use of her late husband's letters; to my daughter,
Janet Blanchet, for the extracts I have made from her diary
of 1946. The Hudson's Bay Record Society has allowed me to
quote from its Vol. XVIII, *Black's Rocky Mountain Journal,*
while the extracts from letters, now in the Hudson's Bay
Company Archives, regarding Alexandre "Buck" Choquette
are here published by the kind permission of the Governor
and Committee of the Hudson's Bay Company. Dr. W. Kaye
Lamb, Dominion Archivist, has been generous of his time in
his efforts to discover further detail regarding the wartime
freighting on the Dease River, and the Department of Transport Information Services have done likewise. To the Royal
Canadian Geographical Society I am indebted for permission
to use photographs from its article *Northwest Passage by Air*
(*Can. Geo. Journal,* March 1943), an article which appears to
be the sole printed Canadian record of that almost forgotten

episode of the last war. The assistance of the British Columbia Provincial Archives has been invaluable, and the Champlain Society's Vol. XXIV, *The Hargrave Correspondence*, has been, as always, a gold mine. Dr. Clifford Carl of the B.C. Provincial Museum and Mr. Davis Hancock, also of Victoria, have been forthcoming with regard to salmon, seals and eagles. Dr. Douglas Leechman, late Dominion Ethnologist, has patiently answered my many questions; and by the members of the late "Wiggs" O'Neill's family (of Smithers, B.C.) I have been given permission to make use of Mr. O'Neill's two books on the Skeena River. To all these, and also to Mr. A. C. McEachern of Vancouver, wartime superintendent of Whitehorse and Watson Lake airports, my sincere thanks.

And last, but by no means least, from among those who were on the spot and who saw things happen, I cannot thank sufficiently Captain and Mrs. Hill Barrington, Mr. S. C. Ells and Mr. T. F. Harper Reed for the time and the help they have so freely given.

R. M. PATTERSON

Victoria, B.C.
Sept. 1965

Part One

Prelude to a Journey

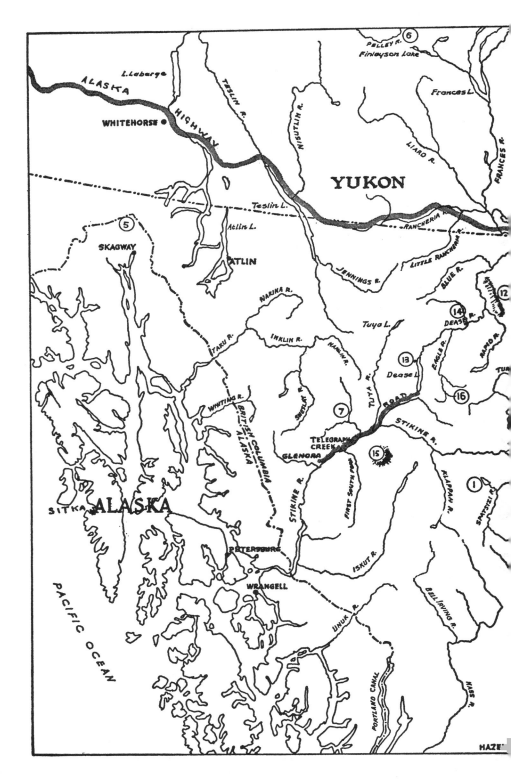

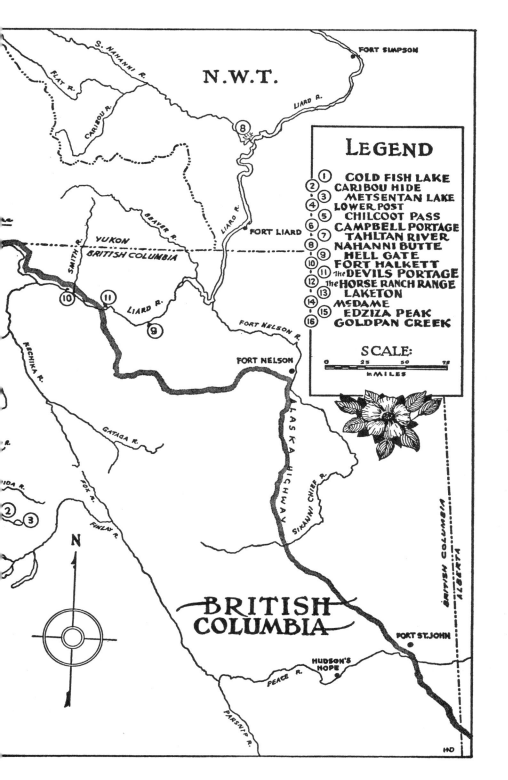

FORT SIMPSON

N.W.T.

S. NAHANNI R.

FLAT R.

CARIBOU R.

LIARD R.

⑧

LEGEND

① COLD FISH LAKE
② CARIBOU HIDE
③ METSENTAN LAKE
④ LOWER POST
⑤ CHILCOOT PASS
⑥ CAMPBELL PORTAGE
⑦ TAHLTAN RIVER
⑧ NAHANNI BUTTE
⑨ HELL GATE
⑩ FORT HALKETT
⑪ The DEVILS PORTAGE
⑫ The HORSE RANCH RANGE
⑬ LAKETON
⑭ McDAME
⑮ EDZIZA PEAK
⑯ GOLDPAN CREEK

SCALE:
0   25   50   75
in MILES

BEAVER R.

LIARD R.

FORT LIARD

SMITH R.

YUKON
BRITISH COLUMBIA

⑩   ⑪

LIARD R.

⑨

FORT NELSON R.

KECHIKA R.

FORT NELSON

GATAGA R.

FOX R.

IDA R.

② ③

FINLAY R.

N

ALASKA HIGHWAY

SIKANNI CHIEF R.

BRITISH COLUMBIA

FORT ST.JOHN

HUDSON'S HOPE

PEACE R.

PARSNIP R.

BRITISH COLUMBIA

ALBERTA

HD

Fᴏʀ the non-dedicated it would be easy to go quietly and hopelessly insane tending a garden and orchard on Vancouver Island. Seed-time, weed-time, drought and harvest: round and round the clock it goes, a habit-forming drug. Through early summer a man flails madly away at blackberries, thistles, plantains and their allies—a futile occupation if ever there was one, for they will all be there again next year, and with bells on. By August the grass, thank God, has turned a blistering yellow; it grows no longer and its capacity for harm is limited, except as a dangerous fire-hazard. But there still remain pampered bits of lawn and favoured plants to which the sweating gardener must drag hose and sprinklers. This ensures that these things—which are obviously unsuited to the climate, otherwise they would thrive of themselves—survive to trouble yet another summer. Then come the quiet days of autumn, when, far away in the North, the rivers run low and clear, the birches light the green woodlands with their golden fires, and the bull moose sound their challenge. These days the Island orchard owner spends perched precariously on top of a high pruning-ladder, reaching with the crook of a walking-stick for the scarlet apples that sway, just out of reach, in the tops of the lofty and long-neglected trees.

I owned just such an orchard. An inlet of the sea bounded it on three sides, and beyond the thick sea-hedge of snowberry and wild rose one would often hear small wavelets lapping softly on the beaches, the wash from some passing ship. It was a beautiful place; but at the end of a certain day's picking in the fall of 1947 I was, quite frankly, fed up with it. For the moment I hated apples; and, to make matters worse, there was a portent in the heavens: a wavering V of Canada geese was making its noisy way across the evening sky. The sound of the honking reached down, wild and stirring, into the orchard, and I watched the migrating birds with envy in my heart. Where had they come from? From the Yukon Flats? Or from some lonely lake-shore on the Dease? And where would be their journey's end?

Quite plainly, winter, with its storms, was coming close— a blessed season when nothing can grow and when a man can, with a clear conscience, slam the door and light the fire and reach for Sheldon's *Wilderness of the Upper Yukon* or War- burton Pike's *Through the Sub-Arctic Forest:* a time for arm- chair travel.

But why wait for winter? Why not now? For, with that haunting sound, there had come an inner vision of the snow- clad peaks of the Coast Range, cloaked in their dark rain- forest, split asunder by low-crawling glaciers, and pierced by a great river flowing swift and green under summer skies.

That vision, brought by the wild geese, marked the end of apple-picking for the day. Gingerly I climbed down the tall old ladder. Arrived at the foot of it, I dumped my load of apples into the pool of scarlet already on the grass. I had for- gotten all about the walking-stick; it was found the following season, hanging on the branch where I had last used it, weathered by a winter's rain. Turning my back upon the apples and the stack of apple-boxes, I walked absent-mindedly away through the "soft, sea-murmurous dusk" towards the house, muttering to myself about maps. A long-postponed decision had been made, and now there was a journey to think about and to plan: a journey to a far-off river—and, beyond that again, to other rivers, onwards into the country of an old and almost abandoned dream. New mountains, new horizons, new—

"New gardens, too, perhaps?" you may ask, smiling secretly.

A shrewd question. Yes, very likely new gardens, too—*but somebody else's!* And never an orchard for hundreds and hundreds of miles.

The green, ice-tinged river has a name: men call it the Stikine.

This was by no means a new idea. Almost twenty-five years had gone by since I had first read about the Stikine River. That was on winter nights in my homestead on Battle River in the Peace River country. I had got, from Ottawa, Dr. G. M. Dawson's famous *Report on an Exploration in the Yukon District, N.W.T., and adjacent northern portion of British Columbia*—a fine, resounding title, and one well in keeping with its period, for the year of that exploration was 1887. Beautiful river maps go with the 1898 reprint of that report. These maps, spread out on the table of my lonely cabin, held down by lamps and flickering candles in their wooden holders, together with that book by Dawson (after whom Dawson City is named) and his assistant, R. G. McConnell, were as a magic carpet to me on those stormbound winter evenings.[1] On those maps I travelled far from Battle River: I went with Dawson's party from Wrangell, Alaska, up the Stikine to Telegraph Creek, over the Pacific-Arctic Divide to Dease Lake, and down the Dease River to the Lower Post. There Dawson and Mc-Connell parted company—Dawson to travel on up the Liard and up the Frances to Frances Lake and by Campbell's Portage to the Pelly and the Yukon, while McConnell turned downstream towards the dangerous canyons of the Liard and towards the Mackenzie. Somewhere down on the Mackenzie he was to winter and then go on, in 1888, northwards, with an even vaster journey ahead of him before he would intersect Dawson's trail of 1887 at the mouth of the Pelly, and so close the circle. Then, like Dawson, he would follow what, in ten years' time, was to become world-famous as "the Trail of '98"—the way out by Lake Labarge and the Chilkoot Pass to the Taiya Inlet of the sea. Those two men, Dawson and Mc Connell, were of the select band of the explorer-surveyors, men to remember with honour. They were the men who reopened and mapped the trails and the uncharted river roads of the old fur-traders, so that those who came after them—the pathfinders of the Alaska Highway, perhaps—might find a framework waiting on which they could hang their more detailed surveys, made with the camera from the plane.

Research, especially when it is with a view to a journey, is a most absorbing pastime, and, as always, one discovery leads on to another. Delving after the relevant facts, I found that Dawson's *Report* was not the only book that could tell me things about the Stikine-Dease waterway into the Interior. I had other books in my own collection—and then, when those were drained dry, the B.C. Provincial Archives Library was laid under contribution, coming through with old government reports and books on fur-trade history. One way and another, that winter of 1947-48 was full of interest.

I was not without friends on the Stikine. I had first met George Ball on the South Nahanni River in 1928, together with Albert Dease, an Indian from Telegraph Creek reputed to have in his veins the blood of Peter Warren Dease, furtrader and arctic explorer, the man after whom Dease Lake and Dease River are named. George and Albert were acting as canoe men for Fenley Hunter, an American whose custom it was, whenever possible, to seek refuge from New York and from the cares of business in the wilds of the Canadian North-west, and who, that particular summer, had set his heart on seeing the Falls of the South Nahanni.

Well do I remember our first meeting and the look on the face of my partner, Gordon Matthews, as Fenley's outfit hove in sight, far away down a long reach of the Lower Canyon. Gordon was standing on the beach, gazing intently at this unexpected sight through my field-glass. We had not seen a human being for months—and yet Gordon's expression was not one of welcome. "My God!" he exclaimed. "A plane over Deadmen's Valley only three weeks ago—and now this! There's at least one white man in the party—possibly two. I'll tell you what it is: this blasted country's getting overrun. We might just as well have built our winter cabin in Piccadilly Circus!"

But we became friends with the newcomers, and in later years I stayed with Fenley at his house on Long Island and Gordon and I foregathered with George Ball and his wife, Agnes, on various occasions in Vancouver and Victoria. By this time George was the owner of the Diamond B Ranch on the Stikine, the most northerly dude and hunting ranch in B.C., ten miles or so below Telegraph Creek and opposite the old landing of Glenora. Hunting trips can be hard on horses, and in 1946 it happened that George needed a bunch of remounts for the outfit. He proposed to gather these horses at Hazelton in north-central B.C. and, from there, to drive them overland to the Stikine by way of the old Yukon Telegraph Trail—and so to find out if that worked out any cheaper and better than freighting them by sea from Prince Rupert to Wrangell and then to the ranch by scow up the Stikine. So he gathered together sixty-two head, mostly from the prairies around Edmonton, shipped them by rail to Hazelton and drove them north a few miles up the Kispiox valley. There, at the camp he had established, they were held by the six Indians who were to make the trip: four from Telegraph Creek and two from Kispiox. Two out of the six were boys of fifteen.

To help pay the expenses, George decided to let one or two dudes go in with the party at a nominal rate. Three went: my daughter, Janet, just out of school; a Miss Jean Davidson; and the M.L.A.* for the enormous constituency of Atlin, W. D. Smith. The whole outfit was in the care of Henry Gleisen, a Tahltan from Telegraph Creek. They left the Kispiox camp on July 8, and George himself, after seeing them off, departed by rail, sea and riverboat to his ranch on the Stikine.

The dust settled down again on the trail up the Kispiox valley, and George's sixty-two remounts and the nine human beings faded into the northern wilderness. Time went by— and at the other end of the trail, at the Diamond B, George and Agnes waited with growing impatience. A month passed, and now the remount cavalcade was overdue. Planes looked for them, but without success: as well hunt for the proverbial needle in its proverbial bundle of hay as hunt for sixty-two horses and a few people in that three-hundred-mile stretch of mountain and forest. So they gave that up; and then headlines began to appear in the Vancouver and Victoria papers: "Party Missing in the Wilds of Northern B.C." Kind friends asked us if we were not worried for the safety of our sixteen-year-old daughter. We were not, and we said just that—for, with capable guides, parties do not vanish into thin air. But, all the same, what in heaven's name *were* they up to?

They were having trouble. Information on the trails had been inaccurate and misleading, and the old Yukon Telegraph Trail was no longer kept open. They lost time getting over and around deadfall. The horses were strange to one another and not bunched, and they were apt to wander in different directions in search of feed; being prairie horses, they did not take at all kindly to this B.C. mountain stuff. The weather was bad. The people were soon out of meat, and other things ran low, and for four whole weeks they couldn't seem to get a sight of game. And so forth. Horses were lost

* M.L.A. Member of the Legislative Assembly.

fording dangerous rivers, over cliffs, and in muskegs, and some just plain strayed. The wolves probably got the strays. But let Janet's diary tell the tale:

On July 23 they passed Fifth Cabin,[2] and that meant a scant hundred miles in sixteen days' travel—a sufficient commentary on the state of the trail. "8 miles in 10 hours," Janet wrote one day. "It was often like that." On July 28 they tackled six-thousand-foot Groundhog Mountain. They stopped part way up on some open country "to give the horses a good feed—the first in ages," and themselves killed, cooked and ate ground-hog. Nelson Quock, the cook, by now was getting ornery. At this camp Janet inventoried the food in the pack boxes with a view to rationing. Of the horses, seven were gone, and they now had fifty-five.

Here they stayed three days to let the horses get filled up while the men went back over the trail to try to round up the strays. On August 1 they went on over the mountain, through snow. Janet's horse went lame, "so I walked 10 miles out of the 12. How do we estimate distance?"

August 5 was a red-letter day. They crossed Beirnes Creek and Jack Pete (the hunter) shot a big bull moose. They promptly camped and fell on the moose like a pack of wolves. In an incredibly short space of time they were all "sitting around the fire with half a rib each *to begin with.*" (The italics are mine.) Here, with the advent of the moose meat, Quock quit. No more cooking for him, "so from now on we all took a hand making bannock but Jack Pete did most. A quarter of a bannock was our lunch ration." They cut out all the bone they could and packed on with them 250 pounds of meat. From then on they saw game all the time.

They went on—to the very source of the Skeena, and then over the divide by Mount Gunanoot to the head of the Spatsizi, seeing goat and caribou. They were now on water that flowed to the Stikine. Then came another pass: "August 8th. Crossed the mountain in freezing rain and fog. Down over the snow to the head of the Little Klappan. Saw a grizzly and 11 caribou." They laid over there for a day to rest and graze the horses, and then went on, seeing goat and caribou and moose—forty-six goat on one hillside on Eaglenest Creek on August 12.

"Aug. 13th. Jack Pete out looking for meat again. *We* saw 4 moose and a grizzly."

"Aug. 14th. To Klappan Crossing. Fed up with everything today—want Daddy."

"Aug. 15th. The men built a raft of 6 logs roped together. Jack got a bear and cub—the bear charged him. In the evening we crossed the Klappan in two trips—and the horses were swum across."

"Aug. 17th. 15 miles to Grass Creek. The going is better but we are out of meat again. No more flour or baking powder, and we ate what we called slumgullion—cheese, macaroni and everything, all thrown into the same pot."

"Aug. 18th. Down the South Fork Valley and crossed the Second South Fork (of what?).* We now have 39 horses. Finished the coffee."

"Aug. 19th. No lunches today and only rice for breakfast. Used the last of the sugar. 15 miles to Ten Mile Flats. Had a cheese slumgullion and a bath—a freezing dip in a creek. Ate the last of the bannock."

"Aug. 20th. Rice and tea for breakfast. Now nothing in the grub box but barley and a little salt. 12 miles to Telegraph. Henry went ahead to get a boat and we finally ended up with 39 tired horses, in a corral opposite Telegraph Creek. We went down to the Stikine and were ferried across."

Forty-four days instead of about thirty, and twenty-three horses short: such was the overland route to the Stikine, and such the trials and hazards of dude-ranching in that far country. One man, however, came out of that picnic well ahead of the game: the Member for Atlin. He had seen a whole lot

* Of the Stikine.

more of his constituency than he had probably ever wished to see—though, of course, one could not say the same with regard to his constituents, for not a single one, white or Indian, had been met with in all those miles.

Janet was made an honorary member of the Ball family and had a marvellous time. So marvellous was it that she missed the last boat down the Stikine to Wrangell so as to be able to go on a sheep hunt with George Ball and F. Carrington Weems, a well-known sportsman and one of the leading authorities on the mountain sheep of North America. Georgiana Ball went, too, and the two girls cooked and kept camp for the two men. History does not relate what George and Weems got for breakfast and supper, and no tales were ever told. In the end it was beginning to look as if Janet would have to spend the winter at the Diamond B, when up to the ranch, one bright October morning, walked George Dalziel, the "Flying Trapper" of the thirties, in later years owner of the B.C.-Yukon Air Service. His plane was down on the Stikine at the ranch landing, moored to a tree; and now here he was, the very man who was needed! It was he who flew Janet out, down the Stikine and over the glaciers of the Coast Range, an hour and a half by air to Wrangell. "Dal would swoop down to show me goat and things, but I only had 2 exposures left on my film and he was quite cross with me when he found this out." Dalziel dumped Janet off at Wrangell, saw her through U.S. immigration, introduced her all round, got her a room—and then "in half an hour he was gone," leaving her to wait for the next boat home. "It was a *wonderful* summer— all in all the best I ever spent."

Old acquaintance on the South Nahanni, then Janet's visitation, and visits also to us at the Coast by George and Agnes Ball—one way and another the Diamond B was becoming almost part of our lives, and there was a standing invitation to visit the place. That now fitted in perfectly. As to the outfit, that was easy: mosquito net, eiderdown, rifle, tarpaulins. They had only to be extracted from their various cupboards and dark corners, checked and piled in the sun-room. The matter of a canoe seemed to present no difficulties: I had a fourteen-foot Chestnut "Prospector" lying, at the moment, on the Upper Columbia River in the East Kootenay. This canoe was thirty-four inches wide by thirteen inches deep and it weighed sixty pounds. It was just the thing—and I wrote up and asked a cousin of mine if he would be good enough to send it down to the Coast. "Pack it," I wrote, "with hay and burlap, the way the Chestnut people do."

A week or two later a large freight truck drove into the place. Two hefty-looking men got down, opened up the doors at the back and staggered out bearing a long, obviously heavy object, done up in burlap and much hay. "Where would you like your boat?" they said, and I pointed to a spot on the grass nearby. They set the canoe down carefully and straightened up with sighs of relief. The driver said, "Ouf!" And he mopped his head. His helper said, "Some boat! Where will you be taking that?"

"Telegraph Creek and the Yukon," I said, using names that they would know. They were impressed—though as they drove away, shouting to each other above the din of gears, I rather fancied I caught the words "a boat made of lead."

A boat made of lead! What on earth could have got into my little sixty-pound canoe that it made two strong men grunt when lifting it? I got a hunting knife and cut the sewing of the burlap. Then I rolled the burlap back, together with an outer packing of ten inches or so of hay, and the mystery was explained: my words, carelessly written, had been taken literally, and the canoe (which should have been empty) was wadded absolutely solid with good East Kootenay alfalfa hay—tramped down, rammed in, almost impossible to get out! "Thorough" was the word for that job—and the hay alone now represented quite an investment, for the whole thing had come down by express.

That was in June of 1948, and it remained only to get myself and the outfit to Wrangell so as to connect with a trip of the river boat *Hazel B 3* up the Stikine. That meant booking well ahead on an Alaska-bound boat—just exactly what I could not do until my wife returned from a visit to England . . . an indefinite date. Nor would it be seemly, or even particularly well-taken, if I were to rush straight off into the bush with a canoe the day after she arrived home. So in the end most of the essential month of July was lost; summer was slipping away and the trip I had planned was a long one.

The plan was to follow Dawson's trail of 1887 to Frances Lake, spending a week or so en route at the Diamond B Ranch in between trips of the *Hazel B*. This would involve a two-hundred-mile downstream run on Dease Lake and Dease River, and after that there would be about a hundred and fifty miles, with some portages, to pole and track up the Liard and up the Frances. At Frances Lake I would cache the canoe for the winter, having previously arranged with George Dalziel to come in with his plane and fly me out to Watson Lake Airport. In 1949 I would fly back in to Frances Lake with a fresh outfit, pick up the canoe and make my way from the West Arm of Frances Lake, by Finlayson River and Finlayson Lake, over Campbell's Portage to the Pelly, and then run down the three hundred and twenty miles of that river to the Yukon.

Part Two
Stikine River

Shortly before sunrise on July 30, 1948, the Alaska boat dumped two sleepy passengers, myself and one other, on to the dock at Wrangell, on Wrangell Island off the mouth of the Stikine. One equally sleepy U.S. Customs man appeared and seemed willing to take some interest in us until he found that we were not staying in the Alaska Panhandle but were merely in transit to Telegraph Creek. He gave our stuff a perfunctory going-over and then he departed, presumably to his bed again. The boat, too, departed, bound for Juneau and Skagway; and that left Stevens and myself alone on the plank wharf with the silence and the newly risen sun, and with a scatteration of stuff that included everything from my canoe and outfit to Stevens' carpenter's tools—with which he had been commissioned by a kindly government to build, at Telegraph Creek, a nice new jail for the accommodation of the local drunks and desperadoes.

Not a soul was about, so we piled the stuff in some sort of order and headed for the hotel at the far end of the wharf, hoping for coffee. But the hotel was asleep and so was all of Wrangell, including the Indian village, with the solitary exception of a raven which, rather surprisingly, swept down on silent wings to perch on Stevens' shoulder. It seemed to expect titbits, but we had nothing for it, since we were on the same errand ourselves and just as hungry as the raven. Yet the bird bore us no ill will and seemed happy to remain with Stevens. Balancing itself as he walked, it accompanied us back to the hotel, where we left it outside, croaking plaintively, while we went in to sleep through the sunrise hours in chairs in the deserted lobby.

Time went by, and life stirred in the hotel. Gradually even determined sleep became impossible, and I awoke to see George Ball coming down the stairs. "So you made it at last," he said as we shook hands. "Come on and let's get some breakfast." Magic words—and we roused Stevens and went in to the dining room.

That was the start of a three-day wait in Wrangell. "Getting out of the fort" was always the worst part of any trip in the North, whether by canoe, dogteam or riverboat, and this was to be no exception. The little twin-screw diesel—the *Hazel B 3*, passenger and freight—that ran the hundred and sixty-five miles up the Stikine to Telegraph Creek was more or less due to pull out as soon as the Alaska boat came in, but not a sign of pilot or crew was to be seen. One could ask, of course—no harm in that. But there seemed to be a conspiracy of silence. Then, gradually, it transpired that there had been a wedding the very night we landed; and, having once taken part in a wild wedding in Peace River town (upon which there also hinged the sailing of a riverboat), I understood. So George Ball came and went on his own business, and Stevens and I, often accompanied by "the Wrangell raven," walked and looked and slept and ate and read. We went north, through the almost tropical growth of the Coast rain-forest, to the northern point of the island, where we found the homestead of a man who bred malemutes and trained them as sled-dogs and who lived like this, far apart from his fellows, for the sake of peace in the canine world. We went south into the Indian village where the broad-shouldered, dark-faced

Tlingits lived—the dreaded "Kolosh" of Russian times—
where, as late as 1911, the Hudson's Bay Company post manager from Telegraph Creek would not let his Tahltan Indian
boat crew stray, since he knew they would be killed if they
ventured there. Then there was an enclosed space that was of
interest, where a carved notice-board was set up against the
neat, woven-wire fence:

> Site of Fort St. Dionysius. (*it said*)
> Built during Russian occupation by
> Dionysius Feodorovitch Zarembo.
> 1834.

And there was a queer sort of a half-island, approached by
a causeway; and on it was a Tlingit house, guarded by painted
totem poles and by a fearsome demon figure, which might
have stepped straight out of Aztec mythology (but which, for
all I know, could equally well have been some revered an-
cestor), painted on the rough wall of upright planks. Nearby
there was a small monument, a simple obelisk of carved mar-
ble, to the memory of Moses Shakes, son of Chief Shakes, who
was murdered on May 13, 1911. "A Christian," the carving
ran, "the Chief decide to be silenc and not go on warpath. I
live to pruve the guilty party."

Who were these people? I wondered. This Zarembo who
had named the fort after his own saint—was he some trader of
the Russian American Company? Or a Russian naval officer?
The fort, I knew, was built because of the oncoming threat of
the Hudson's Bay Company; but Zarembo's rank and func-
tions had escaped me. And Shakes . . . I had read of a Chief
Shakes who lived in 1838, "whose men were as numerous as
the grains of sand on a beach." Was this a family name? Or
a hereditary title?

Meanwhile the sun shone down out of a cloudless sky—an
unusual state of affairs on this humid coast—and the mountains, snow-streaked above their dark covering of forest, laid

shining paths of green and silver on the blue, tide-troubled
waters of Wrangell Sound. Conditions, in short, were ideal
for a visit to Wrangell. But it was Frances Lake that I was
thinking of, and now three full days had gone by since we
landed, and still the crew of the *Hazel B* coped, unseen by
mortal men, with what must surely have been the greatest
hang-over of all time. The *Hazel B* herself, we were told, was
also in distress, no doubt in sympathy. Engine trouble, they
called it—which, when you come to think of it, was just what
was wrong with her crew. I could see Frances Lake receding
into the far, dim distance; but it was no use worrying. The
North in summertime, with its long, light evenings and its
tendency to run day into night and night on into day, is
definitely the land of mañana. "We may not have done much
today," the motto runs, "but we'll give her hell tomorrow!"

The second of August came, and in the early afternoon
Stevens and I were taking a siesta in the cool of our rooms,
which overlooked the wharf and harbour. I was reading by
my window; and to Stevens' room, next door, the raven had
come as usual: it must have had a built-in clock, for its sense
of time was perfect. A friendship had sprung up between those
two; I could sometimes hear them talking together, and
Stevens never failed the bird: his pockets were always well
provided. But on this afternoon I was not interested in the
raven's antics. Two drunken Indians had teetered into view
down on the wharf beneath my window, dancing solemnly
and singing a dirge-like Tlingit song. They were appallingly
drunk and how they remained upright was a miracle. Soon
they fell; and they lay there for a while, flat on their faces,
continuing with their song. Then one of them staggered to his
feet. Lurching dangerously, he inspected the huge balks of
timber, twenty-four by twenty-four, that tied down, on each
side, the planks of the wharf. On one of these he laid himself
down with some difficulty and no little danger, tilted his hat
over his eyes to ward off the sun and went to sleep. He was a

strong, broad Indian and he filled that twenty-four inches full: there was nothing between him and the deep dark water where the rock ran down almost sheer, out of sight—nothing but one easy wriggle between that Indian and the crabs and the octopus and eternity!

The other Indian lay motionless for a while, watching the sleeper. Then he struggled to his feet and began again to dance, still hopelessly drunk but so light-footed that he never made the slightest sound. This time it was a different dance: with eyes gleaming fiercely and lips parted in soundless laughter, he would rush forward towards the sleeping man, whom the least touch would have tumbled over the fifteen-foot drop into the deep water. He danced as if in a war dance, crouched and with arms outstretched and fingers crooked like talons. He would come within inches and then back away with a rush so sudden that I expected him to go over back-wards from the opposite side of the wharf. But he never did—and, though he went through all the pantomime of throwing his friend overboard, he always checked himself at the last inch, to lurch away again in a whirling, drunken step-dance, as if to imaginary fiddles. I watched, fascinated and horrified, and feeling that there could only be one ending to it. . . . The place was deserted. Wrangell seemed to be again asleep, and no sound came, even from the dancer; only the cry of a passing gull broke the silence, or the genial croaking of the raven from Stevens' room next door. Quite plainly something had to be done by somebody or this madman would murder his partner for the sheer artistry of it—and I got up to go. And in the doorway I ran head on into George Ball.

"Get your stuff fixed up," he said. "We're off at four-thirty and there'll be Canadian Customs before we go. . . . What's that? A couple of drunken Siwashes? Let me have a look."

He watched for a while. Twice he gave a sudden movement, thinking that this time it was the real thing. Then he turned to me. "I wouldn't interfere if I were you," he said. "These

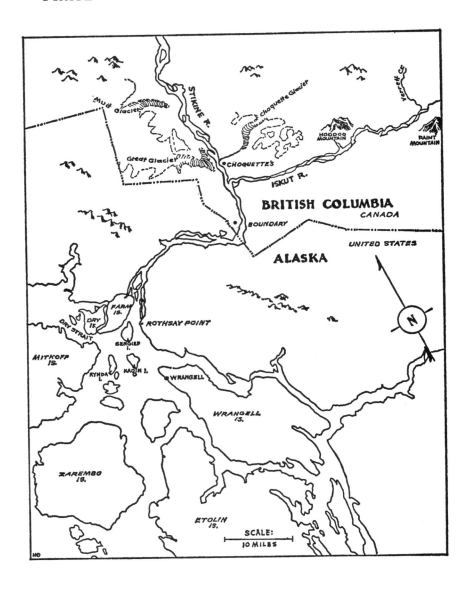

Coast Indians can be pretty savage at times, and that dancing fellow mightn't take it too kindly. Pretty soon he'll dance himself sober in that hot sun. No—stay out of it. We're not in our own country and there's no sense in getting into trouble in this one. Best get your stuff ready and we'll get everything down to the boat."

When I left that room for the last time, the one Indian was still asleep, motionless on his balk of timber and with certain death beneath him if he moved—while the other was still dancing, more nimbly now but with his dark face still distorted in the same savage, soundless laugh.

And that was Wrangell.

We tied up that night nearly thirty miles up the Stikine, a little below the mouth of its biggest tributary, the Iskut. We were beyond the boundary of the Alaska Coast Strip, back into British Columbia and almost into the heart of the Coast Range.

Starting from Wrangell in the late afternoon, the *Hazel B* had headed almost due north across the eight miles of sea that lie between Wrangell Island and Rothsay Point at the entrance to the river. The twisting currents of the rising tide showed clearly on the blue waters of the Sound—and then, across the shallows as we crept in close under the mountain to the east, came the milky flood of the Stikine. Across these flats and shoals of the delta there is scarcely a two-foot channel at low water, for here the river has been at work for millions of years, filling up and levelling off the lower part of its valley and pushing its delta out into the sea. The river was there before the Coast Range rose in its path—and, as the mountains rose, the river kept that path open, hammering away at the emergent barrier of rock with the tools it knew how to use: in flood-time with boulders it had fetched down from its upper reaches, from the Klappan, even from the Spatsizi—

from all that far upland where the Stikine and the Skeena and the Finlay take their rise; and in the spring break-ups with thousands of tons of grinding, pulverizing ice. And through the ice ages, when the river was silent and its sources lay frozen beneath the ice-caps, the glaciers crawled down this valley to the sea, scraping at the mountain flanks, dropping their loads of rock into the deep waters as a foundation for the delta of today.

In this monstrous battle (which continues even now, for the mountains are still rising) the rocks are ground to a fine sand and the sand is swept seaward by the victorious river. Islands are being built up and enlarged around their rocky cores: we had seen Kadin Island and Farm Island in the north-west as we crossed the Sound. Alluvial islands have been built up above high-water level—Dry Island and Sergiev Island— and on them there now are farms. The Stikine is filling the channels between these islands, slowly but surely making them into one; and beyond them, even now, it is possible to walk, at low tide, dryfoot across Dry Strait on to Mitkof Island with its four-thousand-foot mountains and its four hundred square miles of land. From north-west to south-east the front of that delta of the Stikine is twenty miles wide—and moving forward every year. Captain Vancouver came this way in 1793. He charted the shoals and marked the channels of the estuary; but, being a seaman and knowing little of the land, he seems not to have realized that all these sandbars and gravel-flats—and all the driftwood and uprooted, stranded trees—were the signs of a great river that reached far back beyond the mountains— signs of a waterway that might lead determined men deep into the heart of an unknown land.

From Rothsay Point the general course upriver, as far as the international boundary, is east. At that point the valley makes its great bend to the north, very much as the Fraser makes its northward bend at Hope. From the boundary the upstream course is north, and then slightly north-east, to Tele-

graph Creek—much as the same distance, following up the
Fraser and the Thompson, would take one north and slightly
east from Hope to Ashcroft. In each case the traveller has
penetrated clean through the Coast Range, passing from a
country of heavy rainfall into a dry belt. But the differences
vary. If you go, as most British Columbians do on some occasion in their lives, by road from the hemlock and vine maple
and the devil's-club of Hope to the cactus and the rattlesnakes
and the ponderosa pines of Ashcroft, you will have gone from
a rainfall and snowfall of almost sixty-two inches to one of
a little over seven. A big variation—but that between Telegraph Creek, with its yearly average of 13.57 inches, and the
abandoned post of Boundary, just above the big bend of the
Stikine, is bigger yet. At Boundary, on those flats in the deep
cut through the Coast Range, the annual precipitation is
around eighty-six inches. Ten feet of snow in wintertime on
the river flats is nothing out of the ordinary, whereas at Telegraph Creek or Tahltan people complain if they have eighteen inches—as well they may, for out on the range they have
horses that must rustle for their winter's feed.

Since 1861, when Buck Choquette and another miner,
Carpenter, discovered placer gold on the bars of the Stikine,
thousands of white men have used this river road from the
Coast to the Interior: fur-traders, prospectors, trappers, surveyors, freighters, sportsmen, police, and even a railroad crew
and a body of troops—all the motley personnel of the frontier,
the flotsam on the first lapping of the human tide. Many have
gone on—to the Yukon, to the Liard, to the Mackenzie—but
much of this human flood has returned by way of the Stikine,
bringing down its mineral samples, its reports and surveys,
its gold dust, trophies and furs. And for unnumbered generations the Coast Indians have passed this way in summertime:
upstream to the foot of the Grand Canyon to catch and smoke
their salmon in that drier climate, to pick berries, to trade
with the Indians of the Interior, to make war; downstream

with their dried salmon and berries and with the moosehide and the furs that they have got in trade. Whole communities have passed by in their migrations, driving their canoes ever southward in flight from the enemy that pressed them from behind. Yet man has left scarcely a mark on this deep valley of the Stikine. The cutline that marks the Alaska-B.C. boundary crawls painfully upward through the dark forest of the mountainside; but that is almost the only sign of human effort visible to the casual eye. No Tlingit or Tahltan or Nahanni ever made a home in this godforsaken country of rain-forest and deep snow. The islands and the flats support a stand of enormous cottonwoods with an undergrowth of devil's-club and willow, huckleberry and salmonberry. The Sitka alder reaches arboreal size. Hemlock and Sitka spruce climb the mountainsides in black, unbroken forest. A glance at the map shows that white men have tried here but have given up. "Boundary," the map says, and then in brackets "abandoned." "Fowler," too, is marked as abandoned—and who would wonder, for it was at the very tongue of the Great Glacier. Further upstream there is a notation even on Dawson's map of 1898: "H.B.Co.'s Post. (site of)." The hostility of this tremendous, overpowering country has been too much for the people in these places, and now they are gone, leaving the Stikine and its grim mountains to the bears, black and grizzly, and to the salmon and the bald eagles.[1] A Mr. Reeves, the officer in charge of Canadian customs and immigration, living alone at Boundary when that post was open, shot three black bears there in one morning—prowlers with designs on his larder.

Above timberline, in selected places, roam the mountain goats, alone with their natural enemies, which are few. Most of them must pass their entire lives up there without ever setting eyes on a human being, for few indeed are the men who would ram their way upwards through that appalling jungle for the sake of a problematical trophy or for goat meat when there is other and easier meat below.

The Coast and the islands are the home of the small Sitka deer, and behind the deer come the timber wolves. A University of California expedition, nosing about on Sergiev Island, saw in the long grass the bedgrounds of the wolves and talked with Mr. W. E. Parrott, who was farming there. They had noticed that Mr. Parrott always kept a ladder up against the roof of his house, and they questioned him about it. Oh, yes, he said, that was for the benefit of his cat, so that it could take refuge on the roof when he was away to Wrangell. Why, only the other morning the cat had rushed into the house in terror through the open door while he was at breakfast—and he had grabbed his rifle and shot a wolf in the garden. Farming amid hordes of wolves must keep a man on his toes: one hopes that Mr. Parrott was telling the truth, the whole truth, and nothing but the truth to the Californians.

It was that expedition that established, pretty much to its satisfaction, the fact that in the autumn the long north-south stretch of the Stikine is a flightway for migrating birds from the Interior and from the Yukon. The interesting thing about that flightway is that these birds do not seem to take the easy road round the big bend and westward to the Coast and the islands; instead they must turn eastward above the bend— eastward up the Iskut and then, by some easy pass, over to the headwaters of the Nass, and from there south-east inside the Coast Range. In other words, an Interior bird goes south by an Interior route, leaving the Coast flightway to the birds of the sea.

As it is to the migrating birds, so also to men the Stikine River has only rarely been an end in itself. Apart from the gold-miners of the early sixties and the age-old summer expeditions of the Tlingits to the great Indian rendezvous by the Tahltan River, most of the Stikine's travellers have used the navigable part of the river merely as a stage on the trail to places beyond—as a link in the chain of linked rivers that reaches from Wrangell on Wrangell Island to Fort Simpson

on the Mackenzie. Above Telegraph Creek the Grand Canyon
of the Stikine bars the way to the upper river. But nobody in
the old days ever came seeking a way around the canyon and
then onward by the river to its unknown headwaters. Rather
was it from the sources of Dease River that the Hudson's Bay
Company's explorers first came to the middle Stikine—from
the north-east, from the Mackenzie. They came in the 1830's,
up the Liard, up the Dease River and to the head of Dease
Lake. From there they followed the overland trail that today
is the road—down the Tanzilla and down the Stikine, close to
the rim of the Grand Canyon, to Shakes' camp by the Tahltan.
But they were not specifically looking for the Stikine; rather
they wanted a way to the Pacific and to get close in behind
the Russians and take their trade. The Stikine was an incident
—and when they came upon it they first called it the Pelly.
"Mr. Campbell was also on the Pelly's River (Russian
'Sticken') ." So wrote Chief Trader Murdock McPherson from
Fort Simpson in 1838 to his friend Hargrave at York Factory.[2]

The miners of the seventies, the men of the Cassiar rush,
came up the Stikine from Wrangell. To them again the river
was no end in itself: it was only a waterway that would give
them access, by way of seventy-odd miles of trail, to Dease
Lake and the famous placer creeks of Cassiar—Dease Creek,
Thibert and McDame. In fact, the less they saw of the Stikine
and the sooner they had it behind them, the better as far as
they were concerned.

It was the same with the men of 1898. All they wanted of
the Stikine was a trail to the Klondike that avoided Skagway
and the dreaded Chilkoot Pass. Such a trail was said to exist
from Glenora on the Stikine, ten miles down from Telegraph
Creek, to the head of Teslin Lake on Yukon water. The two
inseparables, the two Victoria newspapers, *The Daily British
Colonist* (as it then was) and *The Victoria Times,* quarrelled
furiously over this trail. On April 28, 1898, the *Colonist* pro-
nounced emphatically in favour of "Glenora, from which port

there is but a short portage before the chain of waters leading
to the Upper Yukon is reached," and flatly accused the *Times*
of lack of patriotism, treachery, ignorance and distortion of
the facts in backing the American routes. Neither newspaper
ever really knew what it was talking about when it came to
articles on the North, but in this case the *Times* was right:
the Glenora-Teslin Lake trail proved to be hell almost from
start to finish and its length was estimated at a hundred and
fifty miles. So much for the "short portage"! Nevertheless, up
the Stikine to Glenora in 1898 came hundreds of Klondikers,
dragging their outfits over the ice in the late winter, poling
and tracking upstream in summertime. Many also came the
easy way, by river steamer to Glenora. Of those who used their
own strength and skill, a number lost their lives on that
stretch of river: frozen or drowned, some through the ice
while sledding their outfits in wintertime, others by the
hazards of lining or poling up through the swift water. There
were other and stranger ways of getting killed: in June of that
tremendous year a young Nova Scotian by the name of
O'Brien, steering his canoe, which an Indian was tracking
from the steep bank, was killed instantly by a rock that was
loosed and crashed down from above. Yet, even with all the
effort and the hardship and the tragedy, the Stikine still remained only a stage on the long road to the Klondike and, as
usual, everybody was heartily glad when they saw the last of it.

And so—disregarding the Glenora-Teslin aberration—the
true function of this river in the history of the North has
been, till now, as a route to the Interior and to Arctic-flowing
waters. That it is a direct route can best be seen by taking a
map of British Columbia and drawing on it with a pencil a
straight line connecting Rothsay Point with the Lower Post
on the Liard at the mouth of the Dease. The length of that
line is 270 miles and its bearing is 30° east of true north. Now,
on the map, trace the course of the Stikine 156 miles upstream
to Telegraph Creek. From there go on over the 74 miles of

the portage road, which follows first the Stikine, then the Tanzilla, and then passes over the little gravelly hump which is the Pacific-Arctic Divide, to drop down at the finish through the trees to the head of Dease Lake. Dease Lake is 25 miles long; and beyond that come the windings of Dease River and its four little lakes—an estimated 180 river miles down to its meeting with the Liard. And on the far bank of the Liard, a little upstream and hidden from the mouth of the Dease by an island, are the old Log buildings of Sylvester's Lower Post. There you have it: 270 miles as the crow flies against 435 miles by river, road, lake and river.

The axis of the Coast Range at Boundary runs 30° west of true north, and the axis of the Cassiar Mountains, through which the Dease breaks, does much the same. The odd thing is that this way into the Interior, which has to penetrate these two formidable barriers and cross the intervening plateau, is so direct. Only in one place does the route deviate as much as fifteen miles from the pencil line on the map, and that is at the big bend below the Iskut. Nowhere else do trail and pencil line separate by more than ten miles. A royal road to the Liard—a road as straight as it is possible for a road to be in mountain country, and one that we shall travel. But not tonight, for it is already late and the *Hazel B* is still where we left her, safely moored to the bank of the Stikine below the Iskut River.

The others on board are already asleep: Al Ritchie in the pilot house; Betty Moore, our cook, somewhere down by the galley; and the two deckhands down amongst the freight. George Ball and Stevens, one prospector and one trapper— that completes the party. Nearby, in one of the little cabins, somebody is snoring gently.

Straight out of the north the river comes, lapping softly at the *Hazel B*—straight out of the lemon-coloured sky of the northern sunset—a moving flood of pale yellow, with every swirl and ripple outlined in deepest black, a pattern of coiled and twisting snakes. Night under the moon, or else in the last faint light of the sunset—those are the times to see and wonder at the power of a large river. In the flat light of day all these small, secret whirlpools and eddies are hidden; they throw no shadows and are lost in the moving mass of brilliant colour. But in that hour when evening deepens into night a river's secrets can no longer be concealed: it is then that they show, sweeping past at speed, a black, ever-changing pattern of arabesques on a driving flood of beaten gold.

Fascinated, I lingered on till the short northern darkness fell.

Life returned early to the *Hazel B*. The thudding of feet came from the pilot house and from down below. A slight vibration shook the boat as the engine turned over and settled down to a slow, rhythmical beat, warming up. Sleepily I considered the outlook through the mosquito-screen door: the sun had not yet risen, the mountains lay in shadow, the air was cool and fresh—and bed was very comfortable. Then I heard a voice and the rattle of a line flung from the shore on to the lower deck. That would be the stern line—and a minute or two later came a shout and the rattle of the forward line and then a thud. The man on shore had landed on the foredeck, and now he would be shoving out into the current with a pole. A bell sounded and the engine quickened to a steady roar: we were off. Bed might be warm and snug, but sleep had now become a waste of time, for one might never again get the chance of seeing the Stikine. I scrambled out and into my clothes.

The warmest place in the early hours before breakfast was the pilot house. There one could sit on Al Ritchie's bunk or stand behind him as he sat at the wheel, high above the river. From there one could read with him the swirling chart of the eddies and watch him take advantage of every weakness in the Stikine's defences.

For a while we remained in the morning shadow; but soon the light came flooding over the peaks and the snowfields on either side. From them it spilled slowly down over the glaciers and the dark forest, bringing to life the varied greens of the slides, gently touching the giant cottonwoods of the flats. Then a shaft of sunlight blazed over the mountains in the north-east and the river flashed into a dazzling mirror of silver. Right in our path the round, black outline of a seal's head broke the surface of the silver mirror. The seal looked at us for a moment and then sank again—and it was day.

Soon we were passing, on our right, the three-mile delta of the Iskut, the biggest tributary of the Stikine. Its wild, wide valley runs due east into the snow mountains, and from it there comes a story of a large nugget of pure gold. The story is current among the Indians and the old-timers of Telegraph Creek, and it goes back to the sixties of the last century, when the Tahltan Indians were enjoying a period of power and were able to maintain a village on the Iskut, below the first canyon and opposite Paint Mountain, about thirty miles up from the Stikine. At that time "Buck" Choquette had a trading post on the lower Stikine about five miles above the mouth of the Iskut, up on the hot-springs bench and below the tongue of the Choquette Glacier. This was the same Alexandre Choquette who first discovered placer gold on the bars of the Stikine. That was in 1861, and Choquette's Post was probably built soon afterwards, since, in March 1866, Chief Factor Roderick Finlayson wrote from Fort Victoria to London regarding "Alexr. Choquette, a Canadian, who has been for several years' back trading on the Stekine River and understands the native language there."

At that time the Hudson's Bay Company's district head-quarters was at Fort Stikine on Wrangell Island. This lasted till 1867, in which year Alaska passed from Russian to American rule and the Company's lease of the Coast Strip terminated. However, seeing possibly the writing on the wall, the Company had, in 1866, established a post at the mouth of the Anuk River on what came to be known as Hudson's Bay Flats. This was on the east side of the Stikine, about twenty-five river miles above the Great Glacier and well inside British territory. Choquette managed this post for the Company from 1866 to 1875, when the arrangement was terminated by Chief Factor Grahame of Victoria, "as I am led to believe that our agent on the Stekine River, A. Choquette, has been carried away by this mining excitement [the Cassiar gold rush] and wishes to leave us." This would seem to place the date of the following events somewhere between 1861, the year Choquette first hit the Stikine, and 1866, the year he became post manager for the Hudson's Bay Company.

The Tahltans, the story goes, came down the Iskut from their village and up the Stikine to Choquette's Post in the spring with their furs. After making the trade for their winter's hunt, they produced "a heavy rock which took two hands to hold easily," and Choquette, whose conception of mining had been, till then, chasing fine, and occasionally coarse, gold round a gold pan or sluicing it over a rocker, saw with staring eyes that the "rock" was nothing less than a golden nugget.

"Where you catch um?" demanded Choquette in the language of the Tahltans.

"Near camp."

"You show, I give you anything in store. I give you *all* store." Thus said Choquette, looking around at his depleted shelves. Later on he must have kicked himself for having appeared so eager.

After much talk a trip was arranged. But on the way up the Iskut a disagreement arose between the Indians and Choquette's party and the Indians became more and more silent and morose. By the time they reached the village they would neither talk nor show, and Choquette was obliged to return to the Stikine, not the least bit wiser with regard to the gold.

That fall the Indians came again to Choquette's Post for their winter debt and outfits. In some way the nugget changed hands—and then the row began. The Indians wanted more trade; they were dissatisfied and in an ill mood, and they threatened to use force. In the end they used it: they burnt the place down. Time and weather have left little to mark the site, but in the early 1900's the outlines and the charred remains of buildings were still plainly visible, up there on the hot-springs bench, where "millions of frogs" sing their deafening chorus to the summer sun.

As for the great nugget, it somehow found its way down "to Hudson's Bay headquarters at Wrangell," and there it vanishes from recorded history. The Company's Archives in London have no record of it—perhaps because it was wealth in too portable a form.

That was not the only indication of gold to come out of the Iskut. That country is highly mineralized, and during the course of the International Boundary Survey in the season of 1903 it became the custom for members of the party to produce, in camp after supper, any odd bit of interesting rock that might have caught their attention during the day. One evening, when they were somewhere near the divide between the Iskut and the Unuk rivers, various attractive fragments of galena and the gaudy ores of copper were set down on the square of canvas that was spread out by the fire. But one man waited till all the rest were done, and then he took out of the pocket of his mackinaw something that was wrapped up in a none-to-clean handkerchief. Slowly he undid the wrapping, and then he laid on the canvas, amid all the blues and greens and silvers, a piece of quartz about the size of a billiard ball, snow white and speckled with gleaming yellow—which was the free gold visibly showing—a find that, today, would start a stampede. He had picked this up on, of all places, the top of a high ridge, the one called 6,400, and he had not been able to find any outcrop or anything else like it lying around. They were on a survey, their time was not their own, the year was 1903, and there were no helicopters then to land men and equipment quickly and easily above timberline. The survey moved on—and now, today, which ridge of all the many ridges is the one that was 6,400 feet high?

But there is more than just stray auriferous quartz in that Iskut country: at the foot of Hoodoo Mountain, an extinct volcano with fantastic lava forms, placer gold has been found; and on Paint Mountain, across from the site of the old Indian village at Verrett Creek, there is a sort of a trench filled with liquid copper oxide. Shakes knew of this, and his people would be sent in to get it: they used it as an anti-fouling paint on their great dugout canoes. The mountain goat in that country are often red from rolling in the copper oxide dust on that mountain, ridding themselves in early summer of the fine wool of their winter undercoats. The belief that they deliberately redden themselves to camouflage their white coats in summertime is probably mistaken: they do exactly the same thing in early July far away down south in the East Kootenay, rolling there in the short, tough heather of the timberline country and becoming only mildly dusty in the process, but leaving behind handfuls of their fine, long-stranded wool for the passing mountaineer to gather.

Today, 1965, the silence of the Iskut is broken and helicopters flit around there in the summer months as thick as the little blue butterflies over a damp beach of river sand. And not only in summertime. Even now, in this hard winter of 1964-65, activity in the Iskut country has not been allowed to come to a standstill. Almost every helicopter that is based on the B.C. coast has been pressed into the race, and the work of staking and exploration is proceeding, in spite of the weather, in what may prove to be one of the great copper areas of North America, perhaps even of the world.

With that tremendous snowfall nothing is made easy for the working parties. The Iskut drains a tough country, clothed in the dense rain-forest of the Coast Range, capped by the glaciers that break the moisture-laden clouds. Indeed, so wet and snowy is the Iskut basin that at times it contributes as much as a third of the water in the Stikine in that river's last thirty miles or so down to the sea, thus making the Stikine in those lower reaches as large a river as the Skeena. There are plans afoot, even now, to harness the Iskut at the first canyon, and the day is close at hand when the mines that are in the making will look to the river for their power.

I looked over towards the Iskut with the glass; it was still a wild river then, and a black bear was ambling along the upstream edge of the delta. "How is that river?" I asked Ritchie. "Can a riverboat get up it?"

"Sydney Barrington got this same *Hazel B 3* about thirty miles up the Iskut in 1917," he replied. "Supplies to some prospecting, mining outfit. It took him eight hours to get up, using the line and everything, and two to get down. Shakes wouldn't let any boat or canoe of his go in, but Sydney Barrington took it on and made it. He'd tackle anything once, but even he didn't take the *Hazel B* up there a second time."

Somebody else told me that morning that the Iskut was fast and split into many channels, the intervening bars being heavily encumbered with dangerous drift piles. More than one boat had been wrecked there—and, thinking of the Splits of the South Nahanni, I could well believe that. An old Wrangell newspaper that I came across, years later, mentioned this Iskut venture of Sydney Barrington's and added that it was not only the dangers of the river that caused Shakes to forbid his people to make the trip. According to the Coast Indians, the paper said, an evil spirit dwelt up the Iskut beyond the canyon; it destroyed canoes and was apt to make a meal of their occupants. Could this belief (if it really existed) have been the

vague memory of some bygone massacre at the hands of the
Tahltans in the far reaches of that wild river?

The Barringtons have made history on the Stikine. The
family arrived in the North-west by a long, devious trail that
started in Ireland, where there has been a Viscount Barrington since the year 1720. A younger branch came from Ireland
to Nova Scotia, where they settled and held a grant of land
with a baronetcy. From Nova Scotia the most adventurous
Barrington of his generation, Edward Joseph, came west. He
ran away from home and shipped before the mast in a trading
vessel that was bound around the Horn for the California gold
rush. It was this young Barrington who founded the settlement of Oak Harbor on Whidbey Island in Puget Sound.
That was in 1852. Later, in the seventies, sons were born to
him there on that sparsely settled coast, where, in his early
days, the local Indians still watched with dread for the raids
of "King George's Indians" from Vancouver Island or the
Charlottes. And of these sons, Sydney and Edward Barrington
were the first to go north, leaving Oak Harbor in 1896 on the
stampede to Cook's Inlet, Alaska. At some Alaskan port, in
1897, they saw a south-bound ship that had "a couple of tons
of gold on board from the Klondike."

Whether it actually had or not makes no matter. There was
something magnificent in the idea of "tons of gold," and the
young Barringtons promptly hit for Dyea and the Chilkoot
Pass. The scene is familiar from old photographs: the trail
up that last pitch, seemingly almost vertical, and the men,
struggling upward or standing to one side in the resting
places, like a line of black ants against the snow. "I often
looked back down at the hundreds of men with packs," said
Sydney Barrington, years afterwards, "and wondered what the
hell we were all doing it for." He soon found out, for, arriving
with the earlier stampeders at Dawson, he and his brother
were in time to stake themselves a good claim on Boulder
Creek.

His younger brother, Hill Barrington, had been down in California at Cooper Medical, studying with a view to becoming a doctor, when the news of the Klondike broke. It was too much for Hill, and he closed his books and hit the trail—a most fortunate occurrence, for doctors are many but river captains of the caliber of the Barringtons are few. Hill went over the Chilkoot Pass in 1898. He joined Sydney and Edward, who, by this time, were well down into the pay-streak—better than well, in fact, for the Barringtons, when they really got going, took out something over $70,000 in five or six days. This got around, and the Guggenheims' agent offered them $300,000 for the claim. Sydney Barrington did some figuring, and it seemed to him that, at $12,000 to $15,000 a day, they could get that much themselves in about a month and still have the claim; so they turned the Guggenheims' offer down. This proved to be not the most fortunate decision, for a day or two later, and just where they thought the pay-streak would go on, they came slap up against a barren wall of rock. They much regretted not having sold this to the Guggenheims.

That spring Edward and Hill Barrington became desperately ill from typhoid. Edward died and Hill recovered only after a long illness.

In that same year of 1898 Sydney and Hill Barrington got into the riverboat business. Sydney had master's papers, so the brothers were in a position to found the Side Stream Navigation Company, to operate on the Yukon tributaries. They started with the 110-foot *Willie Irving*. Later on they ran with the *Vedette* and the *Pauline*. They operated successfully for eighteen years and their voyages took them far down the Yukon, to the Tanana, even to the gray waters of the Bering Sea. Fifty years later the memory of one trip across those stormy waters was still fresh and green to Sydney Barrington: a 120-mile voyage across Norton Sound, from the old Russian town of St. Michael to Nome. "The weather was terrible," Sydney said. "I never thought we'd make it." Go west from Nome and the first thing you hit is Siberia, two hundred miles away. Few men would attempt that wide-open sea in a boat that was built for a river.

There would be no end to stories about the Barringtons, but one feat in particular will suffice to paint the picture. In 1900, owing to the completion of the White Pass and Yukon Railroad to Whitehorse, the river steamer, *Clifford Sifton*, was no longer needed on the lakes and waters of the upper Yukon. But she *was* needed for use between Whitehorse and Dawson or below; and barring the way, just above the present site of the town of Whitehorse, lay Miles Canyon, a crooked, mile-long cleft in the basalt, followed by the Whitehorse Rapids. And nobody would take the *Clifford Sifton* through Miles Canyon: they all said it could not be done.

Sydney and Hill Barrington looked the situation over and decided that it could, should and would be done. They made their preparations: they put "bustles" on the *Clifford Sifton*— that is, they slung around her sides bales of hay to take some of the shock in the event of their crashing against the rough basalt cliffs of the canyon. Steam was got up, and then they sent the crew ashore, retaining one man, a volunteer. Sydney went to the pilot house and Hill to the engine room and, with a defiant blast of the whistle, they started downstream with the big stern-wheel thrashing in reverse. The available population of Whitehorse lined the cliff edge to see the smash.

They never once touched the walls, Hill Barrington told me. They came down the canyon in reverse, except at the bends, where Sydney swung the boat and rang for full speed ahead to get out of the eddies and the turmoil of the waters. Then in reverse again to the next bend. They must have worked together to a finely split second: any minute fraction of delay or hesitation would have been fatal. Mutual confidence must have been absolute.[3]

They had their reward. Hill Barrington put it neatly and in few words: "One ship, one mile, three men, three minutes, three thousand dollars." But he said nothing of the tremendous satisfaction and pride of achievement.

That Miles Canyon performance should give the reader a very sound idea of the Barringtons: men of courage and determination, skilled in rivercraft. In general it was Sydney who had the ideas, while it was Hill, with his genius for detail and organization, who made it possible to carry them out. In 1916 they decided to leave the Yukon and move to the Stikine, where river-freighting seemed likely to last longer—where, in other words, there seemed to be less chance of road or railroad interfering with water transport: a sound decision, as events have proved. So they sold out their Yukon company in that year to the White Pass and Yukon outfit and moved down to Wrangell and the Stikine, where they set up the Barrington Transportation Company. They brought with them the *B and B* from Anchorage.

At that time the Hudson's Bay Company had its *Port Simpson* on the Telegraph Creek run "with berth and bathroom accommodation for 36 passengers—round trip $25—berths $1 per day and meals 75¢—electric light throughout." She was a comfortable boat, but her progress upriver was apt to be stately rather than swift. The Barringtons observed her and sized her up and decided to build the *Hazel B 3*. Their boats, incidentally, were named for Mrs. Sydney Barrington, who was one of her husband's most sudden and most successful inspirations: he chanced to set eyes on her as she came aboard his boat at some river landing in Alaska, and his fate was sealed then and there. "That's the girl for me," he said—and later on that same day he asked her to marry him. From then on till the end of their days together they were inseparable.

The *Hazel B 3* was built and finished in the early part of 1917, and she made her maiden run up the Stikine in August. By the time she was ready to leave Wrangell, the Hudson's Bay Company's *Port Simpson* was already on her way to Telegraph Creek. Sydney Barrington was by nature a gambler—by which I mean that he would bet on anything from a mayoralty election in Seattle to the spring break-up of the Yukon and on everything in between. By sailing time he had got $2,300 on in bets that he would not only beat the *Port Simpson* up to Telegraph Creek but also collect the mail there and have it back in Wrangell before the Bay boat ever reached "T.C."

He then proceeded to make the new *Hazel B 3* travel the 165 miles from Wrangell to Telegraph Creek—*and* climb the 555-foot hill of water that lies between—in 26 hours, thus breaking all records. But he was not satisfied: he thought the trip might well be made in 24 hours. However, he unloaded his passengers and freight, took on board the mail, and swept down the Stikine in triumph, passing the struggling *Port Simpson* en route . . . He collected his bets. The *Port Simpson* was soon afterwards withdrawn from the Stikine. The Barringtons remained, lords of their new river kingdom, and we shall hear more of them anon.

The galley on the *Hazel B 3* was right aft of the engine room and over the twin screws—the result being that you literally couldn't hear yourself speak. If you wanted something on the table, you pointed to it; and if somebody bellowed into your ear at about three inches' range, you might get the general drift of what he was trying to tell you provided your hearing was good. I had ample proof of this that morning. I had eaten all the hot cakes and bacon (not forgetting the butter and the maple syrup) that I could hold, and Betty Moore—with that charming Indian smile that was known and remembered from New York to San Francisco by the big game hunters of the Cassiar—was standing over me and indicating, by waving the coffeepot about, that one more cup wouldn't do me any harm. Suddenly a shattering clangour, like that of a giant's alarm-clock, split through the din of the engines. Betty poured the coffee out and I could see her lips moving. George began to shout into my ear, and about the third time round he managed to get it over: that was the signal for a black bear swimming the river. The door faced aft, over the rear deck and the surging wash of the screws, and in that perfect weather it was never closed. We stuck our heads out and, sure enough, there was the black head of the bear thrusting powerfully through the water, dropping astern of us now as we moved upstream. Soon he landed on the west shore, shook himself in a cloud of spray, loped off into the woods, and we saw him no more. They had a code of signals for these various animal events—moose, black bear, grizzly— and that bell was liable to go off at any time during a meal. That morning it sounded for two bears, various seals fishing, and a bald-headed eagle floating downstream, sitting on a log. It was, you might say, quite a bell. What it might have done to a nervous woman with her mouth full of hot coffee I hate to think.

We probably made about seventy-five miles up the Stikine that day. The picture that remains with me is vivid and alive with great splashes of impressionistic colour, yet full of an intricate detail that has blended, with the passage of time, into one all-embracing canvas: rough, snow-capped mountains, rising in places over ten thousand feet above the river; cascades tumbling out of the snowfields; glaciers flowing down from them to lose themselves in the woods of the river flats; strong creeks and rivers rushing into the Stikine through wastes of rounded stones. Only twice did we see signs of human life. On the first occasion it was a snagging crew which had been at work among some sweepers, clearing the low-water, autumn channel. The men came out in their long, light skiff and met us in midstream. A sack of mail and papers and a case or two of grub were handed to them, and away they went, back into the same dangerous water, under the same cut bank and among the thrashing sweepers. Another time a twenty-foot boat with three prospectors in it shot out from a channel in a maze of islands somewhere above the Mud

Glacier. Mail and provisions again and a word or two from the outside world—and then they, too, whined away across the current, outboard going full blast, to disappear once more among the islands. There was never a trace of fire to mar the green, unbroken forest, and over everything was the upstream rush of the summer wind, turning the leaves of the cotton-woods so that their undersides became a glinting shimmer of silver under the sun. From the blue sky and the snows down to the blue-green river, the whole scene was just as I had imagined it might be on that evening in the orchard almost a year ago.

Two places in that day's run stand out clear and sharp, and the first of these is the Great Glacier, better known to the old-timers as Ice Mountain. This comes down on the west side of the Stikine, out of an ice-field nearly seventy square miles in extent, right on to the river flats, and has a front of nearly four miles. When Dawson passed by in 1887 the front was between five and six hundred yards back from the Stikine and receding. Between the glacier and the river were moraines and marshy pools, "the outer tier of moraines, or that nearest to the river, forming wooded hills about one hundred and fifty feet high." Opposite the Great Glacier, on the east side of the Stikine, a much smaller tongue of ice, the Choquette Glacier, flows down almost to the flats from an even larger ice-field. To complete the picture, the valley of the stream that drains this glacier contains, to quote Dawson once again, "a copious hot spring"—the same one that was close to Choquette's old trading post of the sixties.

The Indians have a tradition that, within their folk memory, the Great Glacier bridged the river which, cutting a way for itself, passed beneath a wide-springing arch of ice. There would seem to be no reason why this should not have been so. In the last ice age the whole valley would have been filled with a creaking, groaning mass of ice, grinding its way towards the sea. Then, as the valley glacier receded and the river opened again, the two lateral glaciers, amply supplied from close at hand, would have been left still at river level, still pushing against each other from opposite banks, and still with plenty of ice to keep the bridge intact. Gradually the Choquette Glacier to the eastward, catching the afternoon sun, would have receded from the river, leaving the Great Glacier in sole possession, and with the task of maintaining, the bridge. Nearly four miles now separate the two glacier fronts, and from the age of the trees that follow the retreating ice it is possible to form some idea of the speed of recession.

The existence of this awesome arch of ice across the Stikine is recorded in Tlingit songs and dirges,[4] and of the passage beneath it several accounts survive in Indian legend. The sight must have daunted the bravest heart, for there is no reason to think that the front of the Great Glacier was any less wide in earlier times than it is today. An archway that one could see through: there would be nothing to that. But to venture on a rushing current into a cavern of ice that might be three miles long—that demanded courage. The various bands that came to this obstacle took all reasonable precautions. One lot sent a green tree through, having first dispatched a party over the glacier to watch for the tree's emergence on the downstream side. If it appeared with all its branches intact, then, they argued, one might reasonably suppose the canoes could follow. This would seem to be assuming rather a lot, for branches can bend and a tree can be partly submerged and still travel. However, the undamaged tree proved to be a safe guide and the Indians followed under the arch.

Another party, halted in dismay at the dreadful sight, had a more practical idea. These people were, after all, migrating Asiatics; and from the heart of Asia, from the ancient Kingdom of Jade, there comes a Turki litany which begins:

> "From the thorny branch of the wild apricot,
> From the old of womankind,
> Good Lord, deliver us." [5]

Here and now at the glacier arch was "the time, the place and the loved one all together." Swiftly a surplus wife was escorted to a canoe and sent with the current beneath the ice. She emerged on the downstream side apparently unharmed, though no mention is made of her mental state. The experiment had succeeded: the passage was obviously safe. . . .

In the waning light, too late to take a photograph, we passed through Little Canyon, to tie up for the night a short distance above. Little Canyon, according to Dawson, is about "three-fifths of a mile long and in places not more than fifty yards wide. It is bordered by massive granite cliffs, 200 to 300 feet in height, above which, on the west side, rugged mountain slopes rise." There is a bend in Little Canyon, but otherwise, as an obstacle, it is not in the same class as, for instance, Kitselas Canyon on the Skeena. Dawson says nothing of his passage through it, but he came up in May, before high water. When we went through on the *Hazel B* it was August and the water was well on the drop. But when the whole flood of the Stikine is piling through that narrow gap in the granite, that is the dangerous time, even for a boat with plenty of power.

The best description of a passage by canoe through Little Canyon is by Warburton Pike in his book *Through the Sub-Arctic Forest*.[6] Pike, an adventurous Englishman with a taste for travel and prospecting in the North-west, made his way, with two companions, in his eighteen-foot canoe, up the Stikine in July 1892. They were travelling against the latter end of the flood by the old-time methods of pole, line and "frogging"—that is, wading upstream and lugging the canoe by hand up the riffles. Eventually they fetched up at the mouth of Little Canyon together with "a large salt-water canoe manned by a crew of coast Indians," which, with the aid of the summer wind and a large sail, had overtaken them. These Indians were going up into the drier climate around the Tahltan River to catch salmon and pick berries and to trade with the people of the Interior, and they probably

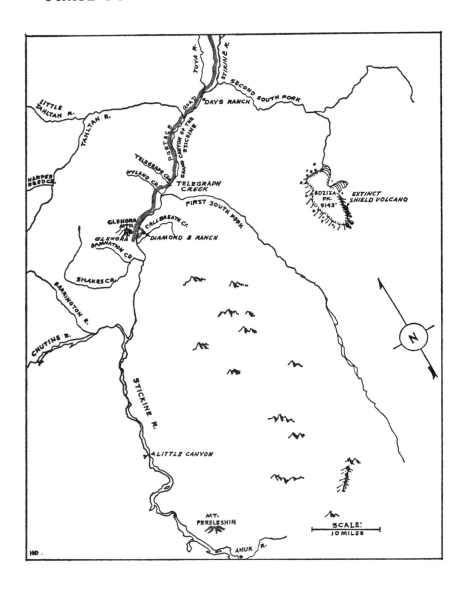

represented almost the end of the great, traditional summer gathering of the Coast and Interior tribes by the Tahltan.

The only thing to do was for white men and Indians to team up together. The river had dropped several feet from its June level, but still the prospect was far from pleasing with the water foaming past the points in overfalls, creating dangerous eddies and whirlpools below. Yet it had to be attempted, and the Indian captain, Tomyot, took charge.

A first-hand account of the large "salt-water" canoes and their crews is given in the late W. J. "Wiggs" O'Neill's *Steamboat Days on the Skeena River,* and a few details from it will give a good idea of the craft and crew with which Tomyot and Pike tackled the Little Canyon.[7]

On the Queen Charlotte Islands grew the giant cedars from which the Haida Indians made their great seagoing, dugout canoes. These canoes were capable of carrying two tons and more of freight up a fast river and were manned by a crew of four or five. They often passed in trade from the Haidas to the coast tribes, who had to be good rivermen as well as seamen since their hunting and fishing grounds lay, at least in part, up such mainland rivers as the Skeena and the Stikine. The big canoes were manned for river travel as follows:

The Captain, who steered from the stern with a sweep, which was secured to the canoe between blocks and with a loop of rope, and which had a vertical peg through the handle to accommodate the left hand.

The Bowman, whose duty it was to pole upstream and to keep the bow out from shore during tracking—also to fend off from obstacles when running downstream.

The Middlemen, usually two or three in number, who had to pole upstream, paddle downstream, and get ashore and track when necessary, attaching themselves to the trackline, each man by means of a "harness"—a loop of hide or fabric that passes over the shoulder furthest away from the river and so round the body like a very loose bandoleer or baldric.

This loop is connected by a short piece of cord with the main trackline. . . . One word of warning from personal experience: *if* the steersman should make a mistake and the canoe, in consequence, should be whirled out from shore into the current and swept downstream, then God send that you extricate yourself from this rigging nimbly and without undue delay, otherwise strange things may happen quickly.

Only a few dedicated fanatics, devotees of the art of canoeing, travel "by hand" nowadays, and so, to show what the old-timers had to contend with, I have roughly tabulated Pike's onslaught on Little Canyon:

Day One: Tomyot decided they could get through with the help of the sail, so they unloaded half the cargo of the big canoe and shot up into the canyon mouth in the eddy. But as soon as they hit the current they were helpless, even with the sail and a good wind and nine men paddling furiously. They were swept back, and, after trying this several times, they called it a day.

Day Two: They went at it again, this time with the line. Three men remained in the canoe while the other six went ahead, climbing the cliffs, clearing the line from rocks and trees, floating the line back to the canoe. In this way they gained a quarter of a mile. It then became necessary to cross the river and to catch the eddy on the far side. If they missed the eddy they were done. They did miss it, being carried down too far by the terrible race in midstream. They whirled the canoe around, avoided with difficulty being smashed to pieces on a jagged point of the canyon wall, and in two minutes were back at camp, thus wiping out the work of three hours.

Days Three and Four: They tried both morning and afternoon (Pike calls it "turning out for canoe drill"), following the same route, but with no luck. They nearly got through once or twice, but always something happened: a pole or a line would break or the steersman would make a mistake, and in no time at all they would find themselves back at camp again.

Day Five: This was The Day. The water had dropped several inches, and furthermore, to make assurance doubly sure, the Indians had painted their faces—the men in scarlet or in stripes of red and black, the women in black. The drill was perfect: by this time they knew every ledge and every crack in the canyon wall by its Christian name and they knew exactly how to pass the line and where to shoot across the river to catch the eddy under the far wall. After six hard and dangerous hours, three white and six miscellaneous faces emerged from the canyon and set thankful eyes on the landing place on the east shore. There they unloaded the stuff—and in eight minutes' gentle paddling they had the canoe in camp again below the canyon.

Day Six: They brought up the big canoe with the rest of the load and the small canoe as well, while the black-faced ladies of the party walked overland across the burnt and log-encumbered portage.

Such was Pike's passage of Little Canyon on his two-year trip to the Pelly and the Yukon and the Bering Sea.

A few years later, in 1897, the only two steamboats on the Stikine met, by an odd chance, midway through this narrow canyon, and a disaster might have ensued had there not been two good men in charge.

At that time the *Alaskan* was running steadily on the Stikine and the *Caledonia,* a boat built by the Hudson's Bay Company for service on the Skeena, was making two side trips a year up the Stikine with passengers and freight. This was the Company's first *Caledonia,* built in 1890 and amply powered. She had been originally a hundred feet long with a twenty-six-foot beam but had proved to be too short and stubby for proper handling on a river. She had, therefore, been hauled out, sawn in two and lengthened to a hundred and thirty feet. Her captain was Captain J. H. Bonser, a man of daring and resource who, like Captain Sydney Barrington, would "tackle anything." On board the *Caledonia* on this Stikine River trip, as a guest of Captain Bonser, was Mr. W. J. O'Neill, then a young boy, in later years well known on the Skeena.

On her way down river from Glenora, this summer of 1897, the *Caledonia* came to Little Canyon, which, you will remember, is fairly straight but has one bend in the middle. She blew her whistle and entered the canyon. Almost immediately —but when it was already too late to turn back—they saw, from the *Caledonia*'s pilot-house, smoke drifting round the bend on the almost permanent upstream wind. It could only be the *Alaskan*—and one can well imagine the remarks and comment that her sudden appearance called forth.

"Presently her bow poked round the bend," writes Mr. O'Neill, "with Captain Takelberry standing at the wheel with his great white beard down in front of him like a pinafore, holding her close to the right wall of the canyon. Captain Bonser was backing at full speed and holding back all he could, until our bows came abreast of each other." Then Captain Bonser rang the stop signal, then full speed ahead, and the ships shot past each other "with barely a foot to spare." Each captain blew three blasts on his whistle—and they were on their way.[8]

Except for those two boats, there was nothing then on the Stikine, neither ship nor habitation, in all the hundred and fifty miles between Glenora and the sea. But the next year would be 1898, when twenty-six river steamers and an army of men would come to break those solitudes.

Little Canyon is the climatic boundary: it marks the transition from the heavy rain and snow of the Coast Range to the more open, less precipitous mountains of a drier country. Devil's club is seen for the last time about ten miles above

Little Canyon, and in springtime this upper country can be a good month ahead of the flats at the mouth of the river. The forest changes: it becomes more open. The Sitka spruce and the hemlock disappear; the birch, pine and white poplar take their places on the gentler hills. . . .

August 4 dawned, fateful date in the world's history. The air was crisp and sharp and, as before, I found my way to the pilot house. Around six a black bear swam the river ahead of us, and during breakfast the din of the giant's alarm clock announced another one, also swimming and in the same direction. But the queer thing was what I saw from the pilot house shortly after sunrise. Ahead of us and towards the western shore lay a low shingle bar, devoid of trees or willows and perhaps forty feet across. Out of the dancing, dazzling water, directly on our course and black against the morning sun, there climbed onto this island a clumsy, disjointed, flapping monster that resembled nothing I had ever seen. What devil's production could this thing be? And I reached for my glass.

It was a very large salmon, terrified out of its native element and fleeing for its life from the seal that was right behind it, so close that in the distance the two had looked like one single beast, some nightmarish hangover from an older world. There they went: two creatures of the sea, yet on dry land, in the Dry Belt, on the east side of the Coast Range and a hundred miles from salt water. On they flopped, straight across the narrow island. Now the seal had got a bite out of the salmon but had evidently missed his backbone. Now the salmon had given a convulsive leap into the water, and the seal likewise, right on his tail—and they were gone. There was hunting for you! And I imagine that that seal got his salmon.

Sixteen years afterwards I had the privilege of meeting Captain Hill Barrington at his home at Oak Harbor. We talked of the Stikine and I told him this tale of the seal and the salmon, which, to me, was a wonderful thing. "But I suppose you must have seen that happen yourself?" I said.

"No," he replied, "I never saw that. But I did see once, on the Stikine, a salmon drown an eagle. The eagle swooped and struck; and he got his salmon all right for he tried to lift him and he couldn't: that salmon was too big. You could see he was a monster: the eagle got him part way out of the water so that we got a sight of him. Then the salmon dived, taking the eagle with him; and that was the end of it."

Why couldn't that eagle have just let go? I wondered about that. I pursued the matter later on, in Victoria, and I was given a story that an eagle's claws have some sort of a locking device, so that he cannot let go of his prey unless he is on something solid—his nest or a rock or firm ground. That, I found, is a widespread belief. It didn't seem reasonable, and I went on with my questions till somebody, probably to get rid of me, introduced me to a man who was making a study of the bald eagle.

Certainly not, I was told: no locking device. Eagles have been seen to let go of salmon that were too big for them. Equally, they have been seen to be pulled under and drowned. It could have been, it was suggested, that there was some malformation in one of the eagle's claws that caught in the tough skin of the big salmon—or that the salmon dived suddenly and the eagle instinctively tightened its grip and was pulled under and then hung on with a death-grip to the only solid thing in a strange, watery world. Or, in a river, the eagle might have let go and been carried downstream waterlogged, to come up unseen under a bank, there to catch, with his beak, some overhanging willow or branch of a sweeper. From there he might have been able gradually to work himself out of the water and dry himself off, to become once more the king of birds, an eagle of the upper air. A fascinating subject, and you can take your choice. But it is nonetheless a fact that an eagle *can* be drowned by a salmon.

"How big was the biggest salmon you have ever seen?" I asked Captain Hill Barrington.

"A hundred and three pounds," he replied. "That was on the Yukon at Dawson."

That was a big salmon, though by no means a record.[9] And, with that much weight to put behind a pull, it was not only eagles that these big fish dragged down but also men. Samuel Black, the first white man to reach the sources of the Stikine, records, in his 1824 journal, his meeting with a downtrodden tribe of upland Indians, the Thloadennis. That was at Metsentan Lake, just on the Stikine side of the divide from the headwaters of the Finlay, up which river he had come. These Thloadennis were kept in subjection by the "Trading Nahannis," who let them have just as much as they thought good for them, and no more, of white-man trade articles and who drove a hard bargain: "a good deal of Powder for a Beaver Skin, but giving nothing for nothing." Black questioned the Thloadennis and they told him that the Trading Nahannis got their trade goods from the Tlingit, and that the Tlingit got them from "white People like us at the Sea where they have a Fort, large Looking Glasses and big Animals." A curious assortment—would they be passing to Black some third-hand account of the Russian establishment at Sitka?

The Tlingit, the Thloadennis said, came up the Stikine (which they called Schadzué) in boats to the annual rendezvous near the Tahltan, "but cannot come farther being all Rapids, that at the foot of these Rapids they . . . spear a large Fish siting on the Rocks and one of them had been drawen into the River and drowned."

I have seen Indians, more cautious than this unfortunate Tlingit, or more experienced, rope themselves to a rock or a tree when spearing salmon. Some such precaution would have been of value to the miner of the 1862-63 gold rush to the Stikine who, having observed the Indians performing successfully and having studied their method, decided to try his hand at gaffing salmon. He cut himself a light, strong pole, and he forged, beat out and sharpened a hook with a long shank which he spliced securely to the tip of his pole. He then went down the river to a suitable spot, stationed himself on a boulder and slid his gaff into the water. The approved method, still in use today, is to wait with the hook turned down till a salmon can be felt, moving upstream and sliding over the pole. The pole is then twisted to bring the hook uppermost and sharply pulled towards the fisherman—and, with any luck, a wriggling salmon is firmly on the gaff.

All this went according to plan, and at the very first attempt the miner got well hooked into a salmon. Elated, he saw, in that fraction of a second before disaster struck, visions of endless variations on the everlasting beans and salt pork; and then, with a plunge and a pull, his salmon had him into the Stikine. He hung on, but he was in up to his armpits, and in no time at all the salmon had towed him a hundred yards downstream into fast deepening water. He had to let go, "Mr. Salmon being in his own element and I out of mine." Away went salmon and gaff, and the miner was lucky to be able to claw his way up the bank and crawl, dripping wet, up to the trail.

He turned towards camp, and there in the trail, still as statues and as unsmiling, stood a group of some twenty Indians. They looked far from friendly; but there was nothing else for it, so, assuming what he hoped might be an expression of confidence and even trying to smile, he squelched towards them. But his smile was of no avail. To the Indians he was an intruder, a poacher in the river that had been always theirs, a thief of their salmon. They seized him and removed his boots and clothes, but before they could complete the job by throwing him into the river after his gaff and his fish he was able to elude them and hit the trail to camp. He did not let the moss grow under his feet on the way there. Loping into camp stark, raving naked, he was pleased to find that his companions were not there. That would be something less to live down in the future—and in short order he was into his spare clothes, had a fire going and the tea-pail on, and was cooking up the regulation beans and pork. Later on he was able to see the funny side of it and wrote an amusing account of the proceedings in a letter that was published in the Victoria *Daily Colonist* of November 18, 1862. . . .

Meanwhile the *Hazel B* had been plugging steadily up the Stikine, and now the old, dilapidated cabins of Glenora were showing ahead. But the boat swung over to the opposite shore and tied up to the trees of the south-east bank. That was the Diamond B Ranch lower landing—a small clearing with a trail winding away from it into the bush—and George and I stepped ashore. A few boxes and cartons followed, and the *Hazel B* departed. I looked at the stuff on the ground, wondering how we were going to get it all up to the ranch, which was over a mile distant; and while I wondered George solved the problem for me by going up to a box that was nailed on to a tree and speaking into a field telephone. We waited, and soon men appeared with saddle-horses and packhorses. The stuff was loaded up and we rode away, up the valley of the stream to the big old beaver meadow, at the lower end of which the barn and corrals were placed. Above and beyond stood the house and a row of guest cabins with the water piped to them.

The weather was perfect and the summer days slid by on the Diamond B, uncounted and unheeded as the ripples on the surface of a quiet river. The outfit was busy down in the corrals, shoeing horses in preparation for the hunting season. They never got started early, but they surely went on late; and around nine P.M., when the sun had dipped behind Glenora Mountain, they would turn the horses out and then, as often as not, set out and fetch in another load of hay. Later yet they would be up for coffee and cakes in the kitchen, and perhaps for a spell of piano and fiddle, for there was music in the Ball family and every member of it could play some instrument. In the evenings, before supper, Agnes would mix, with cunning hand, old-fashioneds that warmed the heart and loosened the tongue; and she and George and I would sit in the wide, screened-in veranda on the shady side of the ranch-house and talk—of that South Nahanni summer twenty years ago, of lining and shoving our canoes up the riffles at the foot of Deadmen's Valley, of the Dease River country, of digging for mastodon ivory in the Yukon Territory, of anything and everything over the whole wide sweep of the North. It was there and then that I heard about the winter evening George had been treed by wolves, quite close to the ranch on his way home from cutting trail. . . . As he worked he had left his rifle hanging in a tree, so he had only his axe with him—and now here were these wolves keeping level with him and herding him between the two arms of a V which seemed to be getting smaller. He didn't like the cold, methodical silence of it at all, and when a nice, commodious tree with the right sort of branches hove in sight he went up it.

"And how long did you have to perch up there? How cold was it?"

"Oh, a nice evening, round about zero, and I was good and warm. What I was really afraid of was that somebody at the ranch would get worried and come looking for me without a gun of any kind. But the wolves just sat there for an hour or so, watching me; and then all at once, as if a signal had gone round, they got up and went away. I waited a bit, and then I came down—and I can tell you I lost no time getting back to where I'd left that rifle!"

George might make light of it now, but Agnes told me that this queer action of the wolves (which, in the West, rarely bother humans) had had him quite worried at the time.

There is no doubt at all that wolves can combine and plan for a purpose, and this is well shown by a story that Harper Reed told me in 1964. Reed was on the Stikine as early as 1902, and for the last twenty years of his time there he was Indian Agent at Telegraph Creek, travelling over the country northward into the Yukon Territory and eastward as far as the Finlay River.

On a certain winter trip Reed and a Tahltan Indian, whose "white-man" name was Larry Martin, had made their night camp on the Klappan River not far from its mouth where it runs into the Stikine. They had fed their two teams of dogs and bedded them down. They had had their own supper and they were contentedly sitting on the spruce mat by the fire. A full moon was sailing across the sky and all was well.

Then the faint, distant howling of wolves broke through the silence of the frost. It was intermittent and it was nothing at first—but it was coming closer. . . . Minutes went by while Reed and the Indian listened, and looked at each other, and again listened—and then Reed picked up his rifle and walked through the trees to the point of the bend, from which spot he could see up the next reach of the Klappan. They had made sure of the dogs before Reed left camp, and the Indian stayed with them by the fire.

There was a high cutbank on the far side of the river. The howling was very close now and it came from above and beyond that cutbank. Reed waited and listened and wondered —but not for long. Down the slope upstream from the cutbank and on to the river ice came moose after moose: Reed counted thirty-three. And after them came the timber wolves. They had rounded up the moose over a great stretch of country and had driven them, as horsemen would drive a herd of cattle, to this place that they knew of on the Klappan where the overflow had seeped over the ice and through the old snow and then had frozen again, so that the Klappan ice just there was bare of snow and like a skating rink with a slope to it, hopeless for hooved animals.

Reed's quiet English voice went on with the story. "It was an awful bloody scene," he said. "I mean literally bloody. A few moose got across, but the wolves got all they wanted—just how many I couldn't see. They had those moose at their mercy on that glare ice. They hamstrung them, they tore at their guts and fetched them down, they tore them apart alive. . . . What did I do? There wasn't a thing I could do; and, besides, I didn't particularly want to attract the wolves' attention. I just watched there till they were gorged and snarling at each other, and then I went back and we made up our fire. We did think, though, that in the morning there'd be a good feed of moose meat for the two dog-teams. But there wasn't even that. Here's the photo I took next morning—not a very good one, but it gives you some idea. You see that heap of stuff in the foreground? *That's all that was left!* Just hoofs and ears and bones and hide that we gathered up—not one scrap of meat. And you see all that blackness on the surface of the river ice beyond the dog-sled?"

"Yes, I do. Black glare ice, I suppose?"

"Not a bit of it. That's blood frozen on the ice: the whole river there was red, but it doesn't show up as it should in black-and-white. What a picture that would have made in colour film!" *

The wolves, of course, had not eaten all the meat they had killed in that night's hunting; that would have been impossible. But they had dragged and carried away all that had remained after the feast and had cached the remnants in the bush for future reference, much as a dog will bury a bone. For the benefit of those who doubt, there exists a moving picture, taken in Mt. McKinley National Park, Alaska, by Mr. Adolph Murie, of a wolf engaged in this operation and making off across a stream with a caribou leg, which he buried, on the far side, in a gravel bank. And in the end, when the feasting and the caching are over, all that remains is a pile of uneatable scraps like that in Reed's photograph of the scene on the Klappan.

It was in the same area, though on a different trip and with

* See Appendix A.

a different Indian, that Reed had a more personal experience of concerted action on the part of the wolves. This time he was on his way from Telegraph Creek and the Klappan River to Caribou Hide, an Indian hutment and rendezvous close to Metsentan Lake and the headwaters of the Finlay. The time was about ten in the morning of a cold winter's day and the two men with their dog-teams were heading south-east down the six-mile length of Cold Fish Lake. Once more it was at the full of the moon and there had been wolves about since dawn. The sound of their howling could be clearly heard.

Reed was in the lead, and he was less than a couple of miles from the outlet of the lake when he saw a moose come down off a wooded point on the north-east shore and head straight across his path towards a big bay or arm that opened off the lake to the south. Down on to the ice, some distance behind the moose, came a big black wolf—and then another and another. Reed's dogs were all for joining in the chase, so he hastily threw his sled over on to its side and that anchored the struggling, excited team. Then he pulled his rifle, a .303 Lee-Enfield, out from under the lashings. What he had in mind was wolves' teeth, out of which buttons and ornaments on winter clothing were made, and a wolf hide or two and paws and tails. There was the bounty to be considered also. . . .

By this time more wolves had come down off the point on the trail of the moose, making about twenty in all visible at the moment on the frozen, snow-covered surface of the lake. The Indian was all against shooting and left his .30-30 where it was, shoved under the lashings of his load. Reed shot and killed two wolves. But there wasn't much in the way of hide or tail to be gained by that, since the uninjured wolves fell on the dead and tore them to pieces.

"And ate them?" I queried.

"No, they didn't eat them—just fought over them and tore them apart."

Soon the moose with his band of pursuers reached the mouth of the south arm. They went on towards the head of the arm, and there they took to the shore and disappeared into a valley between high hills. The dogs, which had been frantic with excitement, snapping savagely and biting at their harness, now calmed down a bit. The men righted their sleds and went ahead slowly—and it was then that it became obvious that the affair was not yet at an end.

Ahead, towards the outlet, more and more wolves were appearing on the lake ice. Reed estimated their number at, perhaps, a hundred and fifty; and they seemed to be gathering into a widespread crescent, with the horns of the crescent advanced as in the attack formation of the Zulu impis—the beginning of a pincer movement. That didn't look so good, and the Indian still refused to take part in any shooting. He was all for letting wolves alone; but it was too late for that now, since this lot was obviously acting with a purpose.

The dark crescent (these wolves were mostly black, or seemed to be black against the snow) was drawing closer, though slowly as yet. The two men overturned their sleds again and Reed began to shoot. The leaders were slightly in advance, rather like captains of companies, "great big black brutes, almost as big as children's ponies." Reed brought down seven of them, and the moment they fell, killed or wounded, the rest were on to them.

Once the leaders were down and disposed of, the pack seemed to lose cohesion and any sense of unity. Seeing this, the Indian took heart and opened up with his .30-30. Chaos supervened: fights broke out between individuals, and very soon, splitting up into families as they went, the wolves, which had been so short a while ago a disciplined horde with a common purpose, scattered in all directions from the surface of Cold Fish Lake.

There wasn't much in the way of trophies to be collected from that battlefield: a few jawbones with the teeth still in them, a few paws, and one large, undamaged strip of mane-like black fur from the backbone of what had been a huge dog wolf. Reed and the Indian moved swiftly over the trodden, bloodstained snow on their light trail shoes, searching, keeping, discarding. The dogs lay quietly in their harness by the overturned sleds, their eyes fixed on the men. They were not struggling and pulling now; they were overawed and uneasy. They lay there watching, sometimes shifting a foot restlessly; it was time their men were getting out of this place that smelt so strongly of wolf—time they were heading on, down the outlet creek to the Spatsizi, and then down the Spatsizi, till, with the dusk of evening, their day's work would be ended and they would know again the familiar, safe-feeling firelight of a winter camp in the clean, untainted snow and the sheltering trees.

"And that was the end of that pack," Reed was saying. "Broken up and scattered."

"You mean, broken up for the winter?"

"Oh, no—not for the winter. But till the next full moon. That was when those big huntings of the wolves always seemed to take place. There's something in that period that has an effect on them, I'm certain—and it has a similar effect on the Indians: if there was ever going to be any trouble with them, that's when you'd get it. As the full moon approaches, the call of the wolf changes: it takes on a deeper, more throaty note—and that's when they're planning something. I can't describe the difference in the call any better than that, but the Indians all recognize the change and take it as a matter of course. They know something's brewing. And of course the wolf, like the rest of us, can see better what he's up to when the full moon's on the snow."

"Do they still sweep the country in packs like that at the full moon?"

"They may in isolated places. But not to the same extent. What I've been telling you happened forty years ago, and since then, what with the bounty and the putting out of poison, and good modern rifles in almost everybody's hands, all the habits of the animals have been changed. Once man steps into the picture, the very delicate balance of nature is upset. And the wolf has always been the enemy. Too late we may find out that he, too, had a part to play."

But timber wolves seemed very far away on those summer evenings at the Diamond B. Always, as we talked, there would drift up to the veranda, through the purple fireweed and the tall delphiniums, the gentle murmur of Fizz Creek (which, on the map, is Callbreath Creek) as it went purling over its gravelly bed at the base of the knoll and flowed away towards the corrals. Once in a while from that direction, and borne on the stillness of the evening, there would come to our ears the sudden slam of a horse's hoofs against timber and then faint, wrathful cries from struggling humans. That would mean trouble in the horseshoeing department; but that, for a change, was somebody else's worry—and if one can't nurse an old-fashioned in the pleasant shade and actually *see* one's fellow creatures hard at work, then undoubtedly the next best thing is to sit and sip and *hear* them at it.

On one evening at this peaceful hour a series of explosions came rolling and echoing down into the home meadow. That was somebody getting a moose up by the lake. Fresh meat at last—and after supper Bobby and Georgiana Ball, two Tahltan ranch hands and the Tahltan cook, Mary, all set off at the gallop for the kill. I caught a glimpse of the ranch wagon departing after them, driven by a fourth Tahltan: it, too, was going at the gallop, all out, just like a gun-team in the Kaiser's war. The party returned at three A.M. with six hundred pounds of moose meat. The following evening the ribs, tended by young Barbara, were spinning slowly, round and round, suspended by wires over a bed of glowing embers just east of the house, glistening and spitting and giving forth a most appetizing smell.

At intervals George and I would take a couple of hay forks and ride or walk to the north end of the big meadow, where there was hay still lying out that had been soaked by a thunderstorm before we came in on the *Hazel B*. We scattered the haycocks into windrows, and we turned and re-turned the windrows till the hay was once more dry; then we roughly cocked it again and waited, seated in the sweet-smelling stuff and talking. Before long a hayrack would appear, creaking and lurching over the meadow like a ship at sea, soon to set sail for the barn again, groaning beneath another load of hay. Slowly the shadows would lengthen, till once more the hour would come when we might, with a clear conscience, head for the veranda and the quiet chuckle of Fizz Creek, and for anything that Agnes might put in our hands. It was a wonderful life for the carefree guest, and it could have gone on forever as far as I was concerned. Actually it would go on till the *Hazel B* came again up the Stikine from Wrangell.

A high ridge, rocky and wooded, separated the big meadow from the valley of the Stikine; the trail to the landing went round the south end of it. I went up there one afternoon, taking with me camera and field-glass and a thing that I was writing for *The Beaver*. Agnes gave me a parting word of warning about bears, which, she said, seemed to be getting crankier and crankier around the Diamond B. But in the places where I had lived, on the Highwood River or the South Nahanni, bears were unsophisticated and usually got out of one's way as quickly as they could. So I did not pay to her words the attention they probably deserved. I just went up to the highest point and settled myself comfortably among the rocks and in the shade.

But what Agnes had said about the bears was no dream. I have a letter here from George, dated the preceding December (1947): "We have been having a very noticeable increase in grizzlies and black bears here during the last few years. Around the end of October Agnes and I went up the mountain to our little cabin for a short hunt. We found that a grizzly had been there just ahead of us—fresh tracks. He had taken a swipe at one of the windows and had broken in the six panes, sash and all. The noise of the glass when it hit the stove on the other side of the cabin had probably scared him away. When we came back down the man who was looking after the ranch was also having some trouble. A big grizzly had torn the side out of our meat-house and had cleaned up all the meat we had there. Bill took a shot at him in the dark —didn't hit him—but scared him away. The next night he came back and tore the screen-door off the porch of the ranch-house, got inside and cleaned up the bacon, shortening, butter, etc., that was in the cooler. Bill took another shot at him and scared him away but he was back again in fifteen minutes. He had a great time that night—cans of butter and shortening. We have saved one of the cans to show anyone what tin looks like after a grizzly has had his teeth in it. We got back to the ranch the next evening about six o'clock. Before I went to bed that night I got my gun ready. We sleep upstairs and about one A.M. Agnes woke me and said she could hear the grizzly down at the door. We then heard him tearing something that sounded like canvas . . . I went down as quietly as I could and picked up my gun. Through the kitchen window I could see he was on the porch and he must have heard the floor creak . . . I got one good shot in at about 15 feet and hit him in the shoulder. I could see he limped as he started off again, and I shot, but it was too dark to get in another good shot. The next morning there was blood on the leaves at the spot where I shot him, but a heavy frost had fallen and covered his tracks . . . I must have killed him as he never came back, but we wanted his hide in payment for all that bacon he took. He must have stood at least four feet high, but he was so thin his legs looked long. I figure he was pretty old and had found it hard to rustle his food till he took a notion to our meat-house. A few days later I found that two other grizzlies (I could see by the size of their tracks) had come in on the trail about fifty yards from the house and then turned off through the woods . . ."

Well, it was looking peaceful enough down below there now. George and Agnes were busy in the veranda with mail and accounts and nobody was stirring around the house; only from the corrals, four or five hundred feet below, did an occasional puff of dust float up, usually followed by whinnyings and human yells. A few horses were grazing on the smooth surface of the meadow: a scene of rural peace.

Yet the outside world had once come, noisily and on wings, even to this quiet spot. That was in August 1920, at the period of the pioneer, long-distance flights of the aeroplane. The New York–Nome flight was in progress and Captain Sydney Barrington had taken a hand in the proceedings: something, therefore, was bound to happen.

It had been decided that, instead of landing near Wrangell, the planes were to make their stop on the big meadow of the Diamond B. It was at this point that Captain Barrington took charge. He dropped down river from Telegraph Creek to Glenora and alerted the Indians of that derelict ghost town under their headman, who was noted for his taste in dress and was known as "the Mayor of Glenora." The whole party then crossed the river in the *Hazel B 3* to the lower ranch landing and went up to the meadow. A spirited harangue by Sydney Barrington on the marvels of human flight had left the Indians rather under the impression that this was another one of his jokes, and they were anxious to see what was going to happen next. So they threw themselves into the proceedings with zest: smudges were lit, any possible obstacles were removed, horses and cattle were driven to the edge of the trees, and linen markers were laid out. All was now in readiness.

Three planes landed, one after the other, and the cattle and horses, making short work of fences, unanimously hit for the timber. The Indians stared unbelievingly—and then, according to the *Wrangell Sentinel,* "the Mayor of Glenora threw his hat on the ground, gave a wild-west yell and followed the stock into the bush," his entourage being just one jump behind him. It took a little time to locate the Mayor, but, when found and retrieved, "he certainly was convinced that the aeroplane is a reality and has come to stay . . ."

They were evidently getting ahead with the shoeing down there in the corrals, for now they were turning out to graze some more of the shod horses. Few of these were the horses that had been brought in two years ago, back in 1946, when the disastrous trip had been made from Hazelton to the Stikine—the time when they turned up with only thirty-nine head out of sixty-two. For that had not been the end of the story—and I turn again to George's letter: "I lost all the horses I put out on the range last winter [1946-47] except one. Altogether, counting the horses I lost on the trail from Hazelton and those on the range, I lost 87 head, and that added up to a $10,000 loss. Besides, I had to hire horses to make up for the ones I didn't have. It was certainly a hell of a winter. That range had been used for seventeen years, and the stock had always come in rolling fat in the spring. Last winter was the first year I put my stock out. It had rained so hard in the summer I couldn't put up all of my hay, and it just seemed the devil was laying for me. Ranger, my only horse that survived, came home to the ranch all by himself this spring. I had kept about 25 head of the thinnest ones at the ranch and fed them all winter and they all pulled through. I am planning on buying another bunch next spring and getting them through from the Alaska Highway."

That worked well. George bought forty head of horses in the Peace River country and had them trucked up the Highway to a point one hundred and ten miles west from Lower Post. "I flew in to Liard and met the packtrain there. They were a fine bunch of horses. I had sent my men in ahead and got them started back on the drive across the head of the Rancheria and the Jennings, and across Level Mountain, and then I flew back here. They brought the horses in here in good shape in fifteen days."

That was a welcome change from the year before—and about time, too, for quite plainly the way of a rancher on the Stikine is hazardous and hard. Just to gild the lily, George himself had rounded off the disastrous year of 1946 by getting George Dalziel to fly him in on a long-projected, marten-trapping expedition to the headwaters of the Whiting River, about sixty miles north-west of the Diamond B, deep in the heart of the Coast Range and the wildest, most hostile type of country imaginable. "You asked how my Whiting River trip turned out. Well, it was a washout. It should be the best marten country on the continent. It has everything that marten require. Here's what has happened, though. The whole place is overrun with wolverine, and they clean up the marten. I caught the only two marten that were there, and they were males. I got them in the first two days. During all the twenty-one days I was in there I saw no more marten tracks, and I went up and down the valley. I never was in such a country in all my life. It's all canyon walls, about 1,400 feet high, glaciers, and a lake ten miles long. Once, when the weather turned soft, I think I heard five hundred snow-slides in two days. They roared day and night. Then, when the weather turned cold and it froze hard again, the rocks would split off and you would hear them roll down and crack into the ice of the lake. I had to almost sign my life away to get Dalziel to fly me in and out of there. He had flown into there some years ago, and he says it's the worst country he ever flew in. The two marten I got were perfect skins, heavily furred and well matched. I had them made into a neckpiece for Agnes' birthday. They had cost me too much to sell them on the fur market."

North-westward from this hollow of the rocks where I was sitting, and in the opposite direction from the ranch-house and the meadow, Glenora Mountain could be seen. One could see it from the cabins, too—and, with the early-morning sun full on the cliffs and the bare uplands, mountain goat were often in plain view, scattered and browsing on the herbage or moving in single file along some trail below the rimrock, slowly, like a string of sliding ivory beads. The summit of the mountain was distant about three miles—and in between, invisible from this point on the ridge, flowed the river. Though it could nowhere be seen, yet one could trace the course of its valley for a long way: downstream into the jagged peaks of the Coast Range, upstream beyond Telegraph Creek till it became lost in a jumble of hills.

There it went, down below but hidden by the cliffs and the trees, the river which had carved this amazing gap in the barrier of the Coast Mountains—and the odd thing about it is that the inquisitive white man left it so long untravelled. Though the Russians were on the Alaska coast as early as 1784, fifty years went by before they took much notice of the Stikine. And from the eastward the explorers of the Hudson's Bay Company felt their way towards it only by slow degrees.

By an odd coincidence the spearheads of this deliberate advance were the two firm friends and former North Westers, Samuel Black and Peter Skene Ogden. By a chance that was, perhaps, fortunate for the peace of the nations, they did not come together. Nor did they come at the same time, or even to the same part of the Stikine—for Black traversed the eastern headwaters on foot in 1824, while it was not till ten years later that Ogden came sailing up to the delta and into Etolin Harbour, where the town of Wrangell was afterwards to be.

The backgrounds of these two men of action had much in common. Each was prominent in the North West Company and also in the war between that company and the Hudson's Bay Company that ended with the union of the companies in 1821. Men were killed in that struggle—Black in those strenuous days favoured gun and pistol, Ogden the dagger—and

Black in particular had got himself into the bad books of Governor Simpson of the Hudson's Bay Company, the man who, after the union, ruled the unruly fur-traders "with a rod of iron." [10]

Simply by existing, simply by his presence at the North West Company's stronghold of Chipewyan on Lake Athabasca in the early months of 1821, Black had succeeded in making Simpson's first winter in Canada "interesting" for him. He had the little man on tenterhooks and in acute discomfort in the Hudson's Bay Company's Fort Wedderburn, close by on an island in the lake, "armed to the Teeth and resolved to sell my Life as dear as possible and never allow a North Wester to come within reach of my Riffle if Flint Steel and bullet can keep him off." Those were valiant words; nevertheless, that winter's anxiety rankled, to the detriment of the career of Samuel Black. Later on, Simpson, who could write as much nonsense as any other man when the occasion demanded it or his dignity was involved, tried to convey the impression that Black at Chipewyan had spent that winter in terror of *him*—a ridiculous claim, as is well shown by the fact that he, Simpson, saw to it that Black and Ogden were, with one other North Wester, specifically excluded from service with the Hudson's Bay Company at the time of the union of the companies in 1821. That, for the moment, satisfied the petty vindictive streak in the future Governor's nature.*

But that state of affairs could not be allowed to continue: there was a danger that the two friends, each one resolute, daring and capable, might enter into opposition—perhaps in association with the American trappers and traders who were already on the move towards the far West, perhaps with the sea captains, the independent traders, English and American, who were venturing into Russian territory. Among the earliest of these was an American, Captain Richard Cleveland,

* See Appendix B.

who, in his ship *Caroline* in 1799, visited "the village of
Steeken." He records days of downpour and the Tlingit war
canoes which lay around his ship, their crews heedless of the
rain, motionless, watching with the quiet patience of their
race for the unguarded moment. . . .

So in 1823 Black and Ogden were graciously admitted into
the fold and began their service in the Hudson's Bay Company, each one with the rank of Chief Trader. Simpson, however, still held the master card: distance. The main thing now
was to get this strong-minded pair as far away from the council table at York Factory as possible. So they were sent "beyond the Mountain," which is to say, west of the Rockies. In
that far country their drive and energy could be put to good
use in the work of exploration and the opening up of new
territory. Simpson wrote of Ogden in his secret *Character
Book:* "His ambition knows no bounds and his conduct and
actions are not influenced by any good or honorable principle.
In fact I consider him one of the most unprincipled men in
the Indian Country . . ." With these outstanding qualifications, Ogden was given the leadership of the expeditions into
the Snake River country. As for Black, Simpson wrote: "The
strangest Man I ever knew . . . Very cool, resolute to desperation and equal to the cutting of a throat with perfect delibera-
tion; yet his word . . . may be depended upon. A Don Quixote,
in appearance ghastly, raw boned and lanthorn jawed, yet
strong vigorous and active . . ." Black was given the task of
exploring the headwaters of the Peace River and the lands
beyond into the unknown country of the Cassiar. His orders
were to lead his little company of *voyageurs* and hunters from
the Company's post at the Rocky Mountain Portage—it lay
just across the Peace from the present township of Hudson's
Hope—"to the Sources of Finlay's Branch and North West
Ward."

North-westward: that was the word that brought Black and
his men into the story of the Stikine, the first of the fur-traders

from the east to reach its waters. They had left their canoe cached at Thutade Lake, the very head of the Finlay and so of the Peace; and on July 14, 1824, they crossed the swampy Finlay-Stikine divide and came to Metsentan Lake, the meeting place of the Sikannis and the Thloadennis. A remote upland, untrodden by the white man—and one might think that there, if anywhere, they would have found the noble savage, the creation of the French eighteenth-century philosophers, in all his primitive glory, at ease and contented in a veritable Garden of Eden, with game and fur for the taking.

Vain imaginings. It was true that "these Wild Inhabitants of the mountains [the Thloadennis] wore no European cloathings," but came into camp "dressed in their best apparel, consisting of white or new dressed skin coverings, Leggings Fringed, painted and garnished with Porcupine quill work, bunches of Feathers stuck wildly into the Hair of their Heads . . ." They still cooked with watap kettles—that is, with kettles made from spruce-roots "woven so tight and compact as to retain water, and in which they boil their Meat by keeping the water boiling with hot stones put into it." But the Stone Age was coming to an end for the Thloadennis, and the Iron Age was close upon them. Their spears, Black noted, were pointed with iron and "they have also rough Iron hooped muskets and two of our trading Guns . . . and one or two Pot metal kettles also bits of Pot Metal formed into Edge Tools. Saw two of our trading Files . . ."

These things were reaching the Thloadennis—but at a price. For their wants they were becoming dependent on the Trading Nahannis, with whom they were, at the moment, in a state of war. They went in dread of these fierce traders who dealt each year with Shakes at the Tahltan rendezvous. They were often starving, for the Nahannis held them back from the salmon reaches of the Stikine—and this band that had come to Metsentan Lake had only reached there by the grace of killing ten caribou a few days before, when they were at the very end of their strength. They were penned into their desolate mountains by their fear of the Nahannis and they had no intention of guiding Black into the more open country that lay to the westward, towards the Spatsizi, where they might meet with these enemies. Yet they told him of the great river, Schadzué,* which flowed to the setting sun and up which the Nahannis came. They and the wandering band of Sikannis that was also at Metsentan Lake sang and danced for Black at his request: the Thloadennis first, and then "the Old Chief and his Sikannis in their turn, dressed and painted for the occasion, the Ladies ornamented with lengths of our Gartering binding the Hair about the ears, Earbobs of the common trading blue and white Beads, Brass Rings on their Fingers, Coat Buttons fixed on stripes of Leather crossing their Breasts, and slips of Red Stroud bordering their Leather Leggings; and leather Belts ornamented with quill work, and this in my opinion is the only handsome part of their dress . . ." Dressed out in all this trade finery, the Sikanni ladies were quite certain they outshone "the Thloadenni Sylvan Nymphs who are realy their superiors in shape and appearance, light and tripping, a soft melodious voice with a timerous kind of under side look that says much without intending it."

Not a man of the Thloadennis would accompany Black on his further progress, even though he tried to reassure them on the score of their enemies. "I told them that I did not like to hear they were in war—but that war amongst Indians did not stop our Business going on and would not in the present case stop me; that we had never done anything to the Nahannies; that if I saw them I would be kind to them and give them some of our Goods if pitiful and in want; but if I found them bad Dogs and wished to quarrel with us, we would kill them; that we had Guns and Pistols, Powder and Ball as well as the

* The Stikine.

Nahannies and never all sleept at one time in the Night; that we had come here to see the Lands and would not turn back . . ."

Nor did they, for Black drove his men on. Somehow, in horrible weather, he got them over the horrible Thloadenni trail. This trail kept to the mountains for two reasons: there the Trading Nahannis never came—and there, just above timberline, the Sikannis who came part way with Black could snare the marmot, the *siffleur*, the "whistling pig," the little haunter of the barren heights. The little beast is easily located by his long, clear whistle; he weighs around twelve pounds and is always good for a meal. And so they struggled on—not indeed north-westward but north-north-westward, for Black had the wrong magnetic deviation on his compass, less than the true by twenty degrees. The Sikannis turned back at the Chukachida Fork of the Stikine, and four of Black's people deserted and hit the homeward trail. But he went on with those that were left to him. They travelled on, powered by the caribou, sheep, goats and marmots that they killed, sometimes climbing like goats themselves, sometimes "slowly sullen striving along" in the swamps and the valleys. Rain fell incessantly, and sometimes snow; and even Simpson, when submitting Black's report to the Governor and Committee, was moved to write: "They pursued their course as near as possible through perhaps as rugged a country as ever was passed." But there was no other word of commendation.

They crossed the three main heads of the Stikine, two by rafting and one with a human chain. In the end they crossed the Stikine-Liard divide without knowing it, and, three days later, they came on a large river flowing to the rising sun. They followed it down till their way was barred by "a lofty majestic mountain" against which the river hurled itself and then swung into the north. Black stared at it, wondering— was this another branch of Schadzué? Or was it water that flowed to the Liard? It is almost a cry of despair that closes

Black's journal for that day: "I wish I had wings to go and see for in such a country our progress is slow." Men have wings now, and the place where Black wrote those words can be plainly seen in photographs taken from the air.

That river the disconsolate leader named the Turnagain, for it was from there that he turned back again towards Thutade Lake, towards the cached canoe, the dangerous cascades of the Finlay, and the river road to Fort St. John. And that was the end of the exploration of Chief Trader Samuel Black.

Ten years later, on June 18, 1834, Lieutenant Zarembo of the Russian Navy was contentedly observing his men as they worked on the new fort at Etolin Harbour. He noted with satisfaction that the stockade and bastions, which were rising on the site of the present town of Wrangell, were rapidly nearing completion. Furthermore, down below and anchored close in, lay the brig *Chichagof* of fourteen guns— a most heartening sight, since, without her, he could well have been caught at half-cock, as it were, by either the Tlingits or the English. But it now seemed as though he would get things finished without interference—and he let his thoughts run on to the great day when the guns would be in position and the flag hoisted to a rousing salute: just let him have another couple of months and he would be there. He would name the new redoubt for his patron saint: it should be called Fort St. Dionysius, and—but at this point in his daydreaming a signal was made from the lookout that a British ship was approaching. That brought him down from the clouds with a run. Trouble was looming.

Not that that was anything new. It had been looming since the previous summer, when the Chief Manager of the Russian American Company, the scientist-explorer Baron Ferdinand von Wrangell, had first got wind of the Hudson's Bay Company's plans for a trading post up the Stikine. Hastily he had sent Zarembo off from Sitka to the delta, to winter there, to choose a site for a fort, to clear the ground, and to start building in the spring. Meanwhile he wrote to St. Petersburg: "Until further instructions I will hinder the British by force from sailing up the Stachin River."

The ship was the brig Dryad from Fort Vancouver on the Columbia, armed and under the command of Peter Skene Ogden, Samuel Black's closest friend and (according to Simpson) fellow ruffian. On board were sixty-four men of the Hudson's Bay Company and eight officers, and the brig carried equipment, supplies and trade goods for the proposed new post up the Stikine.

Ogden was no stranger to the Coast. In 1831 he had sailed north from Fort Vancouver to establish the post at the mouth of the Nass River that was to be known as Fort Simpson. He is said to have slipped into the mouth of the Stikine in the summer of 1833 and to have explored that river upstream for some fifty miles—and it may have been news of this expedition, passed north by the Tlingits, that alerted Baron Wrangell. But the most important factor in that June day's proceedings was Ogden's own character. Meeting with determined opposition—what was he likely to do? Ross Cox, a fellow North Wester who had met Ogden at Lake Ile-à-la-Crosse in 1817, describes him as "the humorous, honest, eccentric, law-defying Peter Ogden, the terror of the Indians and the delight of all gay fellows." Simpson, who disliked Ogden, wrote in his famous Character Book: "Has been very Wild and thoughtless and is still fond of coarse practical jokes, but with all the appearance of thoughtlessness he is a very cool calculating fellow who is capable of doing anything to gain his ends." There you have the man—and meanwhile, in Etolin Harbour, the Dryad was letting go her anchor. The powder keg was wide open. Would some hasty word or rash action provide the spark?

Zarembo, in full uniform, came aboard the Dryad. Ac-

counts of the proceedings differ, but it seems that a heated
discussion took place, complicated by the language barrier, as
to the proper interpretation of the Convention of 1825 between Britain and Russia. Ogden, a well-educated man whose
father was a judge and whose brothers were members of the
legal profession, took his stand on Article Six of that Convention, which, he maintained, gave to British ships the free
navigation of the Coast rivers. Reason was on his side. But
Zarembo refused to see it that way. His orders were to preserve for the Russians the valuable fur-trade of the Stikine, by
bluffing if possible, by force if need be. So, after much wran-
gling, Zarembo presented Ogden with the following docu-
ment: "In the Year 1834, the 18th of June. On the brig of the
Columbia Company of Mr. Ogan at Stakeen—I prohibit to
trade with the inhabitants of Stakeen . . . I neither allow to
enter the river Stakeen in consequence of the instructions
received from Chief Director Baron Wrangel."

That was flat and final: no room for misunderstandings
there. Ogden took time to consider. Having come so far, he
was reluctant to back down without accomplishing his object,
and he was not averse to a fight with the Russians—but then an
unexpected foe appeared: the Tlingits. A party of these grim
tribesmen came aboard. They hated both the Russians and
the "King George men" and would gladly have plundered
both their ships. Unfortunately, that, for the moment, was
impossible; but they were quite clear on one point: if the
Hudson's Bay Company was allowed to go up the river, then
they, the Tlingits, would lose their monopoly in white-man
goods with the Trading Nahannis, and so their position as
middlemen for the trade of the Interior. It would mean the
end of the rich flow of beaver and land otter pelts that came
down the Stikine each year in their canoes from the rendezvous at the Tahltan. This was something not to be contem-
plated, even for a moment; and so, in this quarrel, they were
of one mind with the Russians.

This was too much for Ogden to tackle—the Russian brig *and* Shakes' war canoes—so he was compelled to sail away. He lodged a protest with Etolin at Sitka, and in due course the row was transferred to Europe. High names were involved, as were the governments of Britain and Russia. Finally the claim for compensation for the fruitless voyage was dropped and the Hudson's Bay Company received instead the lease of the Russian Coast Strip for a term of ten years (renewable) at a rental of two thousand land otter skins each year. It was in this way that in 1840 the Company came to Wrangell and Fort St. Dionysius became Fort Stikine.

It is the "ifs" of history that are so fascinating. Had Samuel Black been designated manager of the proposed frontier post in this hostile land—as he well might have been, understanding, as no other man, the involved relationships of the Stikine tribes—then he would have been aboard the *Dryad* with his friend. Here, if one is to believe Simpson,* would have been two men: Black, "very cool, resolute to desperation," and Ogden, equally cool and calculating, a man "whose ambition knows no bounds." To turn back was foreign to their natures. Each one would most certainly have worked on the other— and what would the result have been? A disaster? Or victory? And perhaps, in either case, war in Europe over the Stikine.

Though the English and the Russian companies in North America might combine for some set purpose, such as to deny strong drink to the Tlingits or to oust the "Boston men," as the American traders were called, yet there had never been much love lost between them—and now less than ever after this affair. Comment flew as the news spread, and one warlike Scot, writing in 1835 from the Columbia to James Hargrave at York Factory, expressed a hope that "John Bull will answer these hairy beasts in their own way and see justice done." [11]

From those words it would seem that, even then, the pop-

* See Appendix C.

ular image of the Russian was that of a bearded and be-whiskered barbarian peering through a wild tangle of shaggy hair, very like that of the musk-ox, his fellow denizen of the arctic barrens.

Shadows now were reaching down the face of Glenora Mountain. In the corrals the horseshoeing was finished: the gates were open, the meadow was dotted with grazing horses, and the men were strolling up the slope towards the house. Supper was in the offing and it was time to go. . . .

Late that evening, as we sat in the veranda listening to the music of the fiddlers, Barbara came running in. "The boat," she called out. "I can hear the boat!"

The music stopped and we all went out into the utter still-ness of the evening and listened, heads cocked to one side like so many listening birds. And no sound came.

"I don't think there's any boat," George said. "She must have imagined it."

"Oh no, she hasn't." This from Agnes in defense of her small daughter. "I can't hear it myself, but she's never mis-taken. She can hear it when nobody else can. I'm going in to cut sandwiches and put together the stuff we'll need for Telegraph. You'd better tell them to get the horses in."

Around two o'clock the next morning a bunch of sleepy humans struggled by lamplight with coffee and sandwiches and made last-minute adjustments to boots, moccasins and packs. Then from outside came the thud of horses' hoofs, and we piled out and into the saddle—Agnes, Georgiana and my-self, with Bobby and one of the Tahltans to bring the horses back. Farewells . . . and George a waving figure dimly seen . . . and we were on our way at a fast, raking trot. This was not the trail by which George and I had come to the ranch. We were riding upstream now, towards the upper ranch landing, known as "the Six Mile." There the *Hazel B* would be tied up and expecting us—or so we hoped, for all we had heard was the faint mutter of distant engines—and the pace that Agnes and Bobby were setting indicated that they intended to catch this phantom ship if it was the last thing they ever did. The trail wound through the fleeting trees, dipping now and then into small watercourses. Steadying a loose packsack with two precious cameras in it, dodging the odd overhanging branch, and with my feet in stirrups that were no more than jockey length and which there had been no time to alter, I was having a hell of a ride. But somehow the miles went by; and then came a sudden glimpse of the Stikine and the sweet sound of engines warming up, and we were there. In no time the packs came thudding down off the packhorses. We slung them on board and the three of us climbed after them. The lines were loosed from the trees and we hit the river.

Passing by saddle-horse through the Diamond B and behind the big ridge that made the west wall of the meadow, I had missed seeing some four or five miles of the Stikine. Somewhere in those miles lay Buck's Bar, where Choquette struck gold in 1861. There, too, were the Three Sisters—three fangs of rock that thrust up out of the rushing waters where some sunken reefs cross the river. A spectacular sight they must be, especially when the June flood is piling against them and racing through, as between the piers of a bridge.

The channel, to a boat coming upstream, lay to the left of the Sister nearest the south or right-hand bank—between her and the other two. Here it was the custom for tobacco-chewers to spit ceremoniously over the side and to cut a piece off a quid and throw it into the water. Non-smokers would each be given a piece so that they, too, could share in any good luck that might be going—and so into the river would rain fragments of tobacco of all kinds: small propitiatory offerings to the god of the Stikine.

A couple of miles or so below Telegraph Creek the First

South Fork comes in. Flung out into the Stikine by this tributary there is a great wash of stones that crowds the full force of
the main river up against the north shore. This bar acts as
a partial dam, and in August the rush of the water round
the north end of it has something of a fall. Here the *Hazel B*
hung, engines full out, making not one inch of progress, the
power of the boat exactly balancing that of the river. Twice
we hung there and were swept back. Silence lay on the pilot
house like a wet blanket.

Then Ritchie spoke. "I'll try her once more," he said.
"Then, if we don't make it, I'll have to go back to Glenora
and unload there."

That would not have suited me at all. My canoe was on
board, and to have the outfit at Telegraph Creek and the
canoe at Glenora would mean still more delay and waste of
time. And I could see that we were going to hang again. But
we were brushing against the willows on the north bank: it
would need only a touch. I slipped out of the pilot house and
ran down on to the foredeck. By lying down there and reaching far forward I could just catch, with finger and thumb, a
bendy willow branch that was quivering in the racing water.
I got it—and I pulled. I watched the bank: yes, the *Hazel B*
was moving—and now I could catch a bigger branch with my
right hand. Alone, I was pulling that ship up against the current. Another man joined me, and then a third. Up we came,
inching from twig to twig, till the last obstacle lay behind us
and the trim white houses of the little settlement—famous out
of all proportion to its size—jammed against the big hillside
and clustered around its life-giving creek, were coming
steadily closer.

Telegraph Creek gets its name from the attempt, in the
1860's, by the Western Union Telegraph Company to build
an overland line through the unmapped North-west, across
the Bering Strait and on to Europe through Siberia. The line
was destined by the pathfinder parties to cross the Stikine at

Stevens in his room with the Wrangell raven.

Hazel B 2 and *Hazel B 3* tied up at Telegraph Creek. Harper Reed seated on upper deck on No. 3.

Courtesy, Harper Reed

"A twenty-foot boat with three prospectors in it...."

Lower end of the Diamond B meadow, showing lower end of rock ridge and Glenora Mountain.

The bloodstained ice, the remains of the moose, the dog sled and
team.

Hazel B 3 heading down the Stikine from Telegraph Creek.

Telegraph Creek, looking down the Stikine to the Coast Range.

Canyon of the Stikine from the portage road, looking upstream.

The author at Dease Lake Landing.

Dease Lake, looking south.

The view south from camp on Third Lake.

Dease River and the Horse Ranch Range, looking downstream.

The Fourmile Rapid, looking upstream.

Old H. B. Co. buildings at the Lower Post.

Watson with his water wheel, and Dr. Hildebrand, seated.

Hazel B 1 and scow loaded with wartime freight for Watson Lake.

Wartime freighting on the narrow upper reaches of
Dease River.

Scow running rapid on upper Dease River.

Sternwheeler being assembled at Dease Lake.

Sternwheeler unloading freight at the Lower Post.

Hell Gate on the Liard, looking upstream at low water. At lower right, a twenty-foot canoe rides in the eddy.

George Ball on the *Hazel B 3*. Stikine River.

Courtesy, Provincial Archives, Victoria,
Hazel B 2 heading up the Stikine.

Old Tom the Packer at Dease Lake.

this point; and so, in 1866, the river steamer *Mumford* unloaded a vast quantity of wire at the foot of the little creek
that tumbles down the steep hillside of the northern shore.
This cache of wire remained there for a year or so. Then the
news came that the Atlantic cable, deemed to be impracti-
cable, had been successfully laid; and so all work on the overland project came to an end. Thirty-three thousand pounds
of wire made the trip down the Stikine again, to be re-shipped
to Victoria on the steamer *Otter*. For a time the place was
called Fort Mumford, but this soon yielded to local usage.
Over thirty years went by, and then came the gold rush of
1898 and the need for quick communication with the Klondike. The old scheme came to life again and work on the
Yukon Telegraph Line was started in 1899, following the old
survey. By the fall of 1901 the line was completed from
Ashcroft on the main line of the C.P.R. to Dawson City in the
Yukon. The population of Glenora moved up to Telegraph
Creek, which then became the official head of navigation, thus
adding several strong riffles to the toil of the riverboats. A
wagon road connects the two places.

But Telegraph Creek was more than just the usual northern
frontier agglomeration of police post and Indian agency,
buildings of the Hudson's Bay Company and the independent
traders, gold commissioner's office and the rest. It soon became
known, far and wide, as *the* outfitting point for the big-game
hunting country of the Cassiar. One hesitates to use such
overworked expressions as "sportsmen's paradise" or, worse
yet, "sportsmen's Mecca," since these appellations have been
used to death by every starveling settlement, every squalid
assortment of shacks from the U.S. line to the Yukon that can
muster up a guide's licence among its inmates. Yet "T.C."
was all these things. It really *was* the place where well-heeled
sportsmen from all across the continent—and from Britain,
Norway, Germany and France—hunted even in their dreams,
whimpering with excitement like sleeping hounds as they

lined their sights on some prodigious head of *ovis stonei,* kicking their wives out of bed as in their nightmares they struggled to run, with leaden feet and rifles jammed, from record specimens of *ursus horribilis.* And it was to Telegraph Creek that these men came to put their dreams to the test, pouring out in the process a golden stream of dollars, amply recompensed by the cargoes of wonderful trophies that went downstream with them on the *Hazel B.*

I spent a day and a half in this small outpost, meeting guides and traders, completing my own outfit, helping Agnes and Georgiana, in the cool of George's warehouse, to put up the outfits for the hunting parties that would be upon them with the next trip of the *Hazel B.* I executed a small commission for Fenley Hunter: the arrangement of a credit at "the Bay" for old Nettie, the widow of Albert Dease, Fenley's one-time Indian guide. I wandered around looking at the small, terraced gardens of this sunny hillside, in which, in this dry climate and with unlimited water, it seemed that anything would grow. Some sweet peas were especially gorgeous—and it was of these flowers that Sydney Barrington, having duly celebrated the safe arrival of the *Hazel B* after a tough trip upstream, once decided to take down a bunch to Wrangell. The sweet peas were growing in the garden of Harper Reed, the Indian Agent, who had assisted at the celebration. Together Barrington and Reed walked up the hill, with two of the crew for some reason following.

The reason soon became apparent. Sydney Barrington's definition of the term "bunch" with regard to sweet peas implied the complete works, roots and everything. They dug up a whole row out of Reed's garden—flowers, plants, stakes and wire. This they rolled up with great care, keeping as much soil around the roots as possible. Beneath this burden the crew staggered down to the landing and on board the *Hazel B.* The bundle was gently laid down on the lower deck, in the shade and with provision made for moisture and against the summer wind. . . . The next morning neighbours were amazed to see, in Sydney Barrington's garden in Wrangell, a lovely row of sweet peas where none had been the night be-fore—the sort of miracle that once was wrought by Dumas' Count of Monte Cristo. Those sweet peas were away ahead of anything that Wrangell had to show; and, after stoutly main-taining, for a while, that they actually *had* sprung up over-night, Sydney Barrington abandoned that line and let the neighbours draw their own conclusions as to climatic differ-ences between the land beyond the mountains and the humid Coast. . . .

I hunted up Steele Hyland and arranged with him to freight me and my outfit over the portage road to Dease Lake the following afternoon. Then I climbed up on to the bluff above the village, to the Indian cemetery from which the queerly carved, totemic symbols of the dead look down on the house roofs and on a splendid view of the Stikine. Forty miles away into the south-west the snows of the Coast Mountains glinted in the heat haze. Down below, the *Hazel B* had cast off from her moorings and was making out into midstream, headed down the river.

The first of the long line of Stikine River steamers was the *Flying Dutchman,* commanded by Captain William Moore. That was in 1862, when the rush came to get in on whatever it was that Choquette had found. The *Flying Dutch-man* was a stern-wheeler, and she came churning into Wran-gell Harbour one summer's day, pushing a barge loaded with freight for the diggings and with a hundred and twenty-five prospectors on board. From Stikine Village, as the miners called Fort Stikine, Moore headed up the river, cutting wood as he went, the pioneer voyage of all the steam and power boats to come. In the very good time, for an exploratory trip, of three days Moore made his way up to Buck's Bar, where Choquette and the first comers were at work. There he un-loaded his would-be miners. Then he returned to Fort Stikine to find, awaiting him, an assemblage of angry and riotous Tlingits, outraged because this monstrosity of a fire-canoe had violated the peace of their river. With her churning paddles and the wolf-like howls of her whistle, the *Flying Dutchman,* the Tlingits were convinced, would drive away their salmon and their moose. They regarded the whole thing, with its hissing steam and clatter of machinery, as a magic of the worst kind.

A big meeting was held, and floods of eloquence poured forth on both sides. More potent, however, than mere words was the purchase by Moore of two hundred dollars' worth of the famous Hudson's Bay blankets, which he distributed among the Tlingits. This brought about peace. The Indians allowed their fears to be quieted and their feelings soothed, and Moore obtained their permission to navigate, unmolested, on the Stikine. He made several more trips up the river that season and then, when winter was drawing near, he brought downstream a last load of disappointed miners and headed south for Victoria.

That excitement soon died down; but it had lasted long enough and caused enough stir for an Order in Council to be made, establishing the new Colony of Stiken, a tremendous territory that ran north to Latitude 62° and south to the boundary of British Columbia—wherever that may have been. In the west the new colony lapped over into what is now Alaska, while in the north-east it included the headwaters of the South Nahanni River, biting deep into the North-west Territories. But it was a short-lived colony: within a year it was gone and the Stikine country became a part of British Columbia.

Rather a pity, in a way; for, with those boundaries, it would have been a most exciting place to live in. . . .

All this fuss about Choquette's gold and the new colony not unnaturally aroused the interest of the Russians, and in the spring of that same year of 1862 the corvette *Rynda* was sent across the Pacific from Hakodate to Fort Stikine with orders to make a survey of the river and to find out whether Russian territory was involved. A party under the command of Lieutenant Pereleshin ascended the Stikine in one of the ship's boats as far as Little Canyon, producing the first map of the river up to that point. Near there a seaman by the name of Sergiev was swept off his feet and drowned while lining up a rapid. Rynda Island and Sergiev Island in the delta commemorate that expedition, and for long afterwards the scene of the drowning was known as Sergiev's Rapid.

In the end nothing much came of it all and peace settled once more on Wrangell and on the Stikine. The Russians departed and the Americans came. Then in the fall of 1872 a canoe slipped silently into Wrangell Harbour. It carried Henry Thibert and his partner, McCulloch, and a poke of gold from the Liard and from Dease Lake in the Cassiar country. That was all that was needed to start the Cassiar rush, and for the next five or six years Wrangell was a madman's town and the Stikine a much-travelled highway. According to Dawson, some five million dollars was taken from the creeks of the Cassiar up to the time he passed by in 1887; but long before that the richer placers were becoming worked out. Once more the miners moved on, the Wrangell dance halls closed and the gambling joints shut down. Wrangell slept, and the river was quiet. The great days had gone, men said, never to return, and the bush crept quietly over trail and camp site, taking back its own. For almost twenty years nothing of any moment happened: the salmon came as they had always done, the river froze and broke, the odd load of freight was taken up to Glenora by the *Alaskan* or the *Caledonia,* and that was all.

Then, in 1897, news of the Klondike filtered south and the greatest rush of all began. The crest of that flood came in '98, and much of it turned aside up the Stikine, bound for Glenora and the Teslin Trail, the All-Canadian route to the

Yukon. This was no ordinary gold rush. Reports from the Klondike went beyond any man's wildest dreams. There was a sort of magnificence, and almost a feeling of permanence, to this affair that had never before been known. And so up the Stikine came an army of men that was in proportion to the magnitude of the strike. They came as did the men of '62 and the men of '73, battling the summer flood, poling and tracking against the slowly drifting mush ice of the fall, breaking trail and hauling their sleds over the winter snows. And, since we have already seen something of the Stikine in summertime from the pilot house of the *Hazel B,* it is of this last that I want to write—and in particular of the winter trail as one young man of all that multitude saw it in the early months of 1898.

George Kirkendale * was twenty-six when the news of the Klondike broke. Unlike many, he was not swept off his feet by the excitement; he was fishing on the Fraser River that summer of 1897 and he saw the season through there before moving over to Victoria, still fishing but now also on the lookout for some party to go north with. Eventually a group of fourteen banded together, the nucleus being two men who had secured a cordwood cutting contract from the Hudson's Bay Company with a view to fuelling the stern-wheelers which the Bay proposed to put on the Stikine in the following spring. The party made its preparations, and then all fourteen, with their outfits, embarked on the steamer *Danube* in the early days of January 1898. Kirkendale describes some of the ships that carried the stampeders up the Coast as "floating coffins that went north with their gunwales awash with passengers and freight." The *Danube* seems to have been no exception: "Men and women with their outfits, dogs, horses, cattle, lumber, all packed in till there was hardly room to breathe."

* See Appendix D.

Still not satisfied, the owners then sent the *Danube* over to Vancouver, where, for a whole day, more cargo and outfits were loaded. Then, when there was not another inch of space, the overloaded steamer put to sea, headed north into the rain and snow squalls of a dirty Coast winter. . . .

Wrangell, that January, seems not to have been the roaring hell of a town that it became later in the year, with all its own traditional trappings of 1873-78, only on a larger scale this time, and with hangers-on of the Soapy Smith gang operating there—a subsidiary, as one might put it, of the parent enterprise at Skagway. Yet there was no lack of discomfort. The *Danube* came in at two A.M. and the Stikine outfits were unloaded, in pitch darkness, into six inches of snow with the rain pouring into it. By four A.M. Kirkendale and his friends had their stuff under cover in a shed on the dock, and then they went uptown, looking for something in the way of accommodation or even for room to pitch a tent. They found neither: even the barrooms were floored solid with sleeping men. Eventually three of the party got some sleep on a billiard table.

When daylight came they prospected around some more and found a deserted church with the doors and windows out. They were considering that when a friendly storekeeper came to the rescue. "Why don't you go and see old Brick Lewis up at the jail?" he said. "He might find room for you."

So off they went and called on Mr. Lewis, meeting with a ready welcome. "Sure, boys. Come on in; there's lots of room. Make yourselves at home."

They took him at his word, and the fourteen of them went happily to jail. They lived there for three days, warm and dry, while they hunted up a boat to put them over to the delta and on to the ice of the Stikine. They could not have been better housed, for there was a huge cooking range that they could use and a Tlingit prisoner to cut the wood. The building was large and of massive squared logs, cut and shaped by

Zarembo's sailors more than sixty years before, part of the old Russian fort that had greeted Ogden's eyes that June day of '34.

As to getting freighted over to the Stikine ice—that was not so easy. The Tlingits displayed, as ever, a well-developed business sense: they wanted $25 per man of the stampeders and $100 for the outfit before they would undertake to carry them by canoe—and, at fourteen men, this came to $450. Finally the party found "a white man who had a little stern-wheel boat, called the *Alaskan*, that had formerly run on the Stikine. The boat had been laid up for a couple of years,[12] but he said he thought he could make it go; and sure enough, after a couple of days work parcelling steampipes, plugging up boiler tubes and pounding with a sledge hammer, he finally got the engines to turn over." The price agreed upon was $100.

The *Alaskan* was not large and the outfit was far from small. "We had seven Klondike sleighs with us on which to transport our outfit. These sleighs are about seven feet long by eighteen inches wide and eight inches high, the runners being of wood about four inches wide. Our outfit consisted of our camp stoves, kettles, frying pans, dishes, etc., about two tons of flour, a ton of beans, sacks of rolled oats, sugar, bacon, cases of dried apples, and apricots and potatoes, coffee, tea, canned milk etc." With all that stuff and the fourteen of them and all the untidy gear of a laid-up ship, the decrepit *Alaskan* had about all she could safely carry. However, the luck was in and they got across the eight miles of sea, to be landed on the ice at Cottonwood Island, right in the mouth of the Stikine. The *Alaskan* then departed on what proved to be her last run: her engine broke down before she reached Wrangell, she drifted ashore, and that was the end of her.

Kirkendale's party was the first on to the ice of the Stikine; nobody else was travelling. So ahead of them lay the heart-breaking task, not only of hauling some four to five tons of stuff up the frozen river, but also of breaking trail. They were in the deep-snow country of the Coast Range and they were starting too soon, in the shortest days and the worst weather of the year: in short, they were tackling an impossibility. Very likely nobody warned them of this, in the hope that they would get ahead and break a river trail. That has happened again and again at northern posts: everybody keeping silent, hoping that some unsuspecting party will get out and do the hardest work, leaving a packed and pounded trail for those that follow.

"The snow was so deep and soft," Kirkendale writes, "that we could never travel without snowshoes, and the first man breaking trail would sink eight inches in the snow, even with his snowshoes. It never seemed to let up snowing on the Stikine, sometimes more and sometimes less, and when I tell you that the average fall of snow there for the winter is thirty-five feet, you can form some idea of the difficulty of travel. I have seen it fall three feet on the level in one night, and that was nothing unusual. One day I pushed an eight foot pole down through the snow right out on the open windswept river where there were no drifts, and I could not touch the ice underneath. When we were cutting wood for our fires we would drop one tree and that would go out of sight in the snow. Then we would drop another across that, and finally drop the dry tree we wanted across the first two, so that we could find it in the snow. To make travelling worse there was always a strong breeze blowing down the river in our faces, and sometimes this would amount to a perfect gale."

That was the heavy, cold air from the far-away plateau flowing downhill through the gap in the Coast Range to the sea, the everlasting winter wind. Yet, even with all this, there was something to be thankful for, had they only known of it. Here, almost at sea-level, it rarely went below zero and the snow was thick and heavy. But in the greater cold of the Interior, and after one of its rare deep snowfalls of finely powdered snow, it would have been not eight inches that the first man sank but a couple of feet, even with sixty-inch snowshoes. And the sleds, instead of slipping over the warmer snow, would have scratched along as if hauled over drifted sand.

They slugged away at it under these horrible conditions with a stubborn persistence, leaving, of course, the solid foundation of a trail that would be used by those who would come after them and who would, therefore, make double the time with far less effort. They had to relay the outfit, and they got that down to a system. They would establish a sort of base camp and set two men to cutting wood and cooking there. Meanwhile the rest would haul the outfit up to and as far beyond the tent as possible, caching it in a dump on the river ice and coming back at night to camp and a hot meal ready. They could move the whole outfit in three relays, two men to a sled; so, with the last relay, they would pick up the tent and camp outfit, go on as far as possible beyond the dump of stuff on the river, and establish a new base camp. And then they would do it all over again. By the middle of February they reached the British Columbia boundary, thirty miles up the Stikine. "We just averaged a mile a day for that first month, and we travelled every day but one. On that day it was blowing such a blizzard that we couldn't face it."

At this rate, with a hundred and twenty miles still to go to Telegraph Creek and then a further hundred and fifty miles of the Teslin Trail to reach the headwaters of the Yukon, it almost seemed that the Klondike for Kirkendale and his companions, as for so many others, was receding instead of coming closer. Still they struggled on, for there was nothing else to do.

They had been told of a cabin in that boundary country that belonged to Shakes, and they decided to make it, if possible, for a night camp. Darkness caught them still on the trail, and still there was no sign of any cabin. They went on, hugging the bank of the river, watching in the faint light off the snow for the creek mouth that was their landmark. They came to it, and they could just discern the loom of an extra big mound of snow up on the bank among the trees. They scrambled up on to this, dug down with their shovels, and found they were on the roof of a cabin. "We then went to the bottom of the mound, dug a tunnel through the snow, found the door and got in. The shack was about sixteen by twenty feet in size, with a wall about ten feet high. The peak of the roof was around eighteen feet from the ground, and when I tell you we had to dig down through six feet of snow to find the roof, you can form some idea of the depth of snow on the river bank. It was after seven o'clock when we got into the cabin, and as we had not had anything to eat since noon you can imagine we were all ready for a meal."

They soon had a couple of stoves rigged, and in short order they were hard at it after their long day: hotcakes and bacon, beans and rice. The last two items they always carried on the sleds, cooked overnight and ready to warm up as soon as camp was made. They ate for two hours—and then, well stuffed and content, they began to wonder what had happened to three boys who were following on their trail, relaying an outfit with two sleds. These boys had no snowshoes—and it is difficult to imagine anything more insane than that—so they had to follow in every track the Kirkendale party made; and now there was no sign of them. Eventually Kirkendale and his partner, George Murton, put on their snowshoes, took a lantern and went back on the day's trail, now just a dimly seen furrow in the snow, for it was storming hard. They found the boys about a mile and a half back, played out and sitting huddled on a sled with a tarpaulin over them as shelter from the wind, and with the snow drifting in around them. They had no wood and no fire, and they were right out on the river: it had been dark about six hours by this time, and already they were well on the road to freezing. Somehow the men got some life into them and towed them and their blankets up-river and into the warmth of Shakes' cabin.

Very soon the Stikine would be cluttered with misfits and incompetents who had no business to be in the North at all; these boys were only the forerunners. Near the Alaska-B.C. boundary, for instance, Kirkendale's party came on three men denned up in a small log cabin that one of them, the only axeman in the party, had built. The other two were office men from California. These people "had started up the river in the fall with some horses and a big outfit on a scow, intending to take it up the river to Telegraph Creek, and then pack over to Teslin Lake. How they ever expected to get that scow up the river I could never make out, when even the stern-wheelers had to line up the canyon." However, poling and tracking, and helped, perhaps, by a sail, they had managed to get this far—and here winter had caught them. For lack of feed they had been forced to kill the horses, and now here they were, stuck with a useless outfit; the axeman, McGinty, cutting steamer cordwood in a good stand of timber on a nearby island, and the two Californians with their feet rotten with gangrene and in danger of death. . . . It seemed that, around New Year, they had quit and tried to walk down to the delta in a warm spell when it was actually raining into the snow. They started out in leaky gum-boots—of all the useless footwear—and that night the sky cleared and the wind switched and blew again from the plateau. While making camp they smashed their only axe and so were unable to keep a fire burning. All through that night they tramped around in a vain effort to keep their wet feet from freezing. Next day they made it back to the cabin—seventeen hours on feet they couldn't feel—and when Kirkendale found them, six weeks later, their feet were in a ghastly condition and the gangrene was spreading.

I have a feeling that at this point the Kirkendale party had become thoroughly fed up with its one-mile-a-day progress and was inclined to wait awhile and let somebody else get ahead and do some trail breaking. Also—and as usually happens—there was a tendency for the large party to split up, congenial spirits having sought each other out and dislikes having set and hardened. Anyway, seven out of the fourteen decided to get the Californians down the river to the delta while there was still a chance of saving their lives.

"So the next morning we bound up their feet as well as we could, rolled each man up in blankets and lashed him to a sleigh, took another sleigh with our blankets and grub, and started down the river. Almost from the start we began to meet parties coming up over our old trail, and before we had gone many miles we found the trail well beaten. We made the mouth of the river in thirty hours, the distance it had taken us thirty days to relay our outfit over. We found about 800 people camped on Cottonwood Island or starting up the river. There happened to be two young doctors in a tent on the Island, so we got our invalids into the tent, made a hot fire, heated plenty of water, and the Doctors took off enough of the frozen feet to stop the gangrene. We stayed with them a week to nurse them and then a friend of theirs came along and took them back to California.

"On Cottonwood Island there was the greatest assortment of people you can imagine. Old men, young men, women and children, all starting up the Stikine trail with every kind of conveyance, and with horses, mules, dogs, goats, sheep, cattle, anything that could pull a sleigh. None of the animals except dogs were any use in the deep snow until the trail was well packed, but everyone was full of excitement and confidence."

Things had been happening in the outside world since that day the *Danube* sailed from Vancouver. Men everywhere were talking of the Klondike gold, and now the brilliant idea had taken root in Ottawa of a railroad from Glenora to Teslin

Lake—a railroad with one end based on a swift and hazardous river that was frozen for five months of the year, and the other end on a lake that was frozen for even longer.

Clifford Sifton, the Canadian Minister for the Interior, was behind this; and behind the whole thing was London money, attracted by a large land grant, confidently asserted to be mineralized. Mackenzie and Mann, the famous railroad contractors, were to build the line. Its name was to be the Cassiar Central and, together with the Stikine, it would provide the All-Canadian route to the Yukon, bypassing Skagway, the U.S. Customs and the Chilkoot Pass. But whose brainchild was it? Somewhere there must have been an original suggestion, some casual remark. Could it have come from Warburton Pike?

For he was here in this milling mob of stampeders on Cottonwood Island. Kirkendale ran into him (the two men knew each other) and Pike told him that he was headed for Glenora as agent for the syndicate that had secured the charter for the Cassiar Central. He had already sent ahead a small crew to start work on the warehouses. Now he wanted Kirkendale and Murton to go up to Glenora and join the building crew there. And there was work, also, that they could do on the way: "Here's half a ton of grub," Pike said. "I'll give you four hundred dollars if you'll take it to Glenora."

The seven held a conference. They were hard as nails now and this would be jam after what they'd been through. "They agreed like a shot," Kirkendale says.

They started off the next day. By this time it was late February: the days were longer and sometimes a little warmer; the trail was packed and hard as a paved highway; sometimes they didn't even have to use snowshoes, and they had no relays to make. The early days of March saw them at Glenora, "and no party had passed us on the trail."

Just before reaching Glenora they passed a party of four, all British Columbians: Jerry Payne of Saturna Island, Fred Robson of Mayne Island, and two other men. The other five of Kirkendale's party of seven made a deal with Payne and his friends to relay a ton of supplies to Teslin Lake. They went straight ahead with the new job while the going was good. There was no time to lose, for the March sunshine would soon be at work on the winter trails. Soon the best travelling would be in the small hours and up to midday, while the warm afternoons and the evenings would be the time to camp and eat and sleep, rising and breaking camp around two A.M., when the frost had once more tightened up the trail. . . . The travel-hardened five got that ton of stuff to Teslin Lake. They got back to Glenora in May—and the feat is worth recording because, out of all that struggling multitude, the Payne party was the only one to get over that hundred and fifty miles to Yukon water—the "short portage" of the *Daily British Colonist*—before the frost went out of the winter trail.

Kirkendale and Murton stayed at Glenora till the end of June. In those three months they built, with Pike's gang, four log warehouses for the Cassiar Central: two twenty by forty feet and two twenty by thirty. They hauled the jack-pine logs from across the frozen river with a team of mules; then Murton, a good axeman, got at the building while Kirkendale split and dressed jack-pine shakes: "940 shakes was my record day." How many men, employed on a job today, take that same sort of pride in the amount of work they get through?

But the best thing was that, working through these months on the flat above the river, right by the landing at Glenora, and then up on the walls and roofs of the warehouses, they had grandstand seats for what, just then, was "The Greatest Show on Earth"—the Klondike rush.

"And of all the mad, senseless, unreasoning and hopeless rushes I doubt if the world has ever seen the equal. Day after day crowds of men of all classes and conditions, hauling their sleighs, struggling, cursing, and sweating, thrashing their horses, mules and dogs, all filled with the mad, hopeless idea that if they could get as far as Telegraph Creek they would

be in good shape for the Klondike . . . Some gave up on the
river, sold their outfits, and went back. Many threw away
parts of their outfits to lighten their loads. Thousands arrived
at Glenora and Telegraph Creek and started over the Teslin
trail, but by this time it was April or May, and the snow was
beginning to go off the trail leaving pools of water and swamps
through which it was almost impossible to transport their
outfits. You could buy food and outfits at Telegraph for less
than half what they would cost in Victoria. Hundreds stopped
at Glenora until the river steamers started to run in the
spring, and then went home poorer and wiser.

"There was very little disorder or lawlessness in Glenora
or Telegraph. Sergeant Morton of the Provincial Police was
in charge in Glenora, living in a shack next to us, and he kept
a firm hand over the crowd. When any would-be bad men
came along packing guns in their belts Morton would just
step up to them and say, 'Here, I'll take that. I'll give you a
receipt for it and you can have it when you go out.' Sometimes
there was a little bluster and cussing, but most of them
handed over like little lambs. It was amusing, the idea people
had that they had to go armed for safety. I remember two
young Englishmen coming up, each with a rifle and shotgun,
and a belt around them with an axe and a revolver on one
side and a sheath knife and a revolver on the other. Morton
relieved them of their revolvers, but he always allowed the
men to keep their rifles."

As parties pulled up from the river trail on to the Glenora
flat they would naturally halt by the Cassiar Central warehouses while they figured out what to do next: go straight on,
camp and re-organize—or, as many did, call it a day and wait
for the ice to break and the first boat to come up the river.
And then, downstream to Wrangell and "the outside," poorer
but wiser men.

Not all were so fortunate as to have that choice. There were
men who hanged or shot themselves on the banks of the

Stikine—men who had come, perhaps, overland from the south, from the Cariboo or from Ashcroft on the main line of the C.P.R.—men who were worn out and disheartened by the wilderness that lay behind them and who were appalled at the thought of that which lay before.

The American author, Hamlin Garland,[13] came with his party to Glenora by the overland trail, and he describes meeting with a German who had made the same trip, all the way from Ashcroft and then through all the desperate miles of howling wilderness from Hazelton northwards. The German was camped on the Glenora flat, worn out and utterly discouraged. "A week later," writes Garland, "this poor fellow was discovered by one of our company swinging from the crosstree of his tent, a ghastly corpse." In the dead man's pocket, along with a letter to his wife in the States, was found a note: "Burry me right here where I failed, here on the bank of the river."

There was the man who was standing on the shore at the foot of a cliff across the river from the camp: a rock, loosened by the frost, crashed down on his head, killing him instantly. Then it would seem that many of the stampeders, sweated out and dry, had formed the dangerous habit of getting down to the open patches of water, kept free of ice by some hidden spring or some peculiar motion of the Stikine current, and kneeling there to drink. But of all the places on a river, these waterholes are the ones to keep away from, especially if there is any depth of snow. One incautious movement, or a flaw in the treacherous rim ice—and one more man would go sliding down into the dark swirling water, never to be seen again. . . . Yet there passed by Kirkendale, at the Cassiar Central camp, one party that swore blind that one of its number "in kneeling down to drink, accidentally slipped into the water. The strong current immediately whipped him under the ice, but he popped up in another hole about fifty feet further down, and they dragged him out alive. They all declared the story to be true, so we had to believe them."

Men vanish beneath the ice . . . but not always, for a waterhole can work in reverse. Kirkendale and Murton saw one day a man speeding up the river trail on a sled drawn by a buckskin pony. Next morning Sergeant Morton came looking for them. It seemed that there had been trouble down the river —and the three men set off together to investigate. About four miles below Glenora they found a tent on the bank, slit and bloodstained; and there was blood on the snow between the tent and an open waterhole. And in the waterhole were two shattered bodies drifting slowly round and round, all that remained of two Vancouver men, Hendricks and Burns. The third man of this party was Belgian Joe, the man behind the buckskin pony, a miner from Nanaimo. These three had quarrelled all the way up the Stikine from Wrangell, and this was the upshot of it: Belgian Joe had smashed Hendricks' head in as he slept, driving his axe through the tent wall from outside; then he had shot Burns as the latter woke up. He had then dragged the bodies down to the waterhole and shoved them under the ice for the river to take away. But this waterhole was less obliging than most: it happened to be in an eddy, and, as soon as Belgian Joe had gone, the bodies came back upstream again to float around and show their wounds to the first men who came behind them on the trail.

The policeman from Telegraph Creek took after Belgian Joe and caught him on the Teslin trail; but he cheated the gallows in the end, for his wife smuggled poison to him when he was awaiting execution in Nanaimo prison. . . .

Into the midst of all this turmoil and tragedy there burst a party that was far from tragic—that was, if anything, a bit too full of life. This was the Mackenzie and Mann outfit, two hundred and fifty men, "all big and husky and ready for any devilment, with dozens of teams of horses hauling big bobsleighs loaded with the outfits." Their tents went up, "some of them as big as circus tents," and a wild time was had at Glenora on that night of their arrival. . . . By the time they were landed on Cottonwood Island, they told the building crew, the trail was well packed and they had never allowed their horses to get off it into the deep snow. "When they had to pass any other party," Kirkendale writes, "they made them pull out and give way to the railway outfit. They had one man with them called Big Joe, a man about seven feet tall and built in proportion. They said that Big Joe took the lead, and, when they met or tried to pass other outfits, Big Joe would order them off the trail. If they refused he would pick up sleighs and horses or dogs and throw them off. He looked big enough to do it, too."

That would have been a sweet bunch to meet with on the trail; and some first-class rows must have started up between the railroad gang and furious dog-drivers with their sleds and loads sunk deep into the soft snow, and the job ahead of them of getting their outfits back on to the packed wall of the winter trail again. But what could one or two men do against so many?

No snorting engine, no long line of freight cars, ever rolled over the tracks of the Cassiar Central towards the Yukon, for never a rail was laid. The scheme fell through due to opposition in the Canadian Senate to the land grant, and also due to the threat of the White Pass and Yukon Railway. A consignment of rails and a steam tractor, however, did actually reach the Stikine in the late fall of '98. The boat and scows were able to ascend a few miles above the tongue of the Great Glacier, but then the river fanned out between the bars and islands that continue as far as the Mud Glacier, and the water became too shallow for this heavy load to proceed. The season was over; there was no hope of a freshet and it was time to be getting out. So they ran the scows up against the first big bar and unloaded the rails and the tractor there, hoping to pick them up again before high water in the spring. Then they backed off and ran for the delta and the channels of the inland sea.

Spring came round according to schedule—but by that time the Cassiar Central was dead. The rails and the engine lay there on Mackenzie and Mann's Bar, and nobody came for them. Flood followed flood, and the Stikine got busy and buried the Cassiar Central cache in shingle and in sand. The bar grew in size, and willows and young cottonwoods seeded upon it—and forty years went by. . . . Then Hitler's war came, and the government, hungry for scrap metal, circularized even far distant posts like Telegraph Creek in its quest. Big old anchors were remembered and fetched from remote Dease Lake, to be shipped down the river; and the Stikine, in a fit of patriotism, changed its course and began to excavate the old dump of rails, cutting deep into the island it had so carefully built up. Then men bethought them again of the stuff on Mackenzie and Mann's Bar. But that was just one too many for them, war or no war. Red iron oxide oozed from the gravels, and here and there rusted and pitted rails protruded from the new-formed cutbank, just as long-buried tree trunks will often do. To get that dump out would have been a tremendous job—and no vast amount to show for it in the end. So there it is likely to remain till the last flake of rotten iron is carried away on some June flood to enrich the sands of the delta—a memorial to a gaily optimistic age. . . .

May 21, 1898, at Glenora was just another working day for the Cassiar Central crew. But around midday the beat of engines made itself heard on the upstream wind and men who were busy up aloft, tying the rafters together on the new warehouses, could see a steamer approaching. That was the *Stikine Chief,* and aboard her was the advance party of the Yukon Field Force.[14] Not far behind came another stern-wheeler, the *Strathcona,* and the two steamers between them unloaded 203 men of all ranks, four nurses, and Miss Faith Fenton, correspondent for the Toronto *Globe.* They also unloaded 100 tons of supplies, 300 rounds per rifle, two maxims, two seven-pounder field guns, and further ammunition for these weapons. In view of what was there already, one wonders where they found room for all those people and things on the Glenora flat.

This detachment had left Ottawa on May 6. It was composed of picked men from various regiments and represented about a quarter of the Canadian regular army as it then existed. Its presence at Dawson City (when it should get there) would also represent effective occupation of the Yukon Territory. American newspapers never referred to the Klondike except as being in Alaska, and, with the tremendous influx of foreigners to the gold-fields, it was felt that a demonstration in force was necessary—and also that the Mounted Police could do with a helping hand.

Military discipline was maintained and certain parades were held—and then this party, like all others, faded into the mountains and muskegs of the Teslin trail. Legend, of course, has it that they endeavoured to march through the wilderness in fours, floundering in step over fallen trees, between rocks and over beds of lava, sloshing in formation through the swamps, knee-deep in the peat water. It makes a good story, but we need hardly put too much faith in it. All the same, it was *a hell of a trail:* there are no two opinions on that. Nurse Georgia Powell has left a record of it. "Only the strongest and most sinewy women," she says, "could have tackled it at all." They went over the few miles of railroad grade that the C.C.R. had so far built, up Telegraph Creek and to the heads of the Tahltan . . . then over the four-thousand-foot pass north of where the Sheslay line cabin was to be and north to Nahlin . . . and then down into the dreary muskeg country, leaping from log to log, bending the willows flat to make some kind of footing, wading up to the knees in the muskegs, with the frost as the only solid thing to walk on. How they did it passes the imagination. It would have been bad enough for one or two men alone with a mule or two. But with a mob like that churning the trail to sludge, and with millions of mosquitoes on the war path . . . the mind reels at the thought alone!

Major D. C. F. Bliss was in charge of the transport. He endeared himself (and so also the Force) to all who were headed north towards Teslin Lake by corralling for army use, and with government funds at his disposal, one hundred and seventy mules and horses. This sent prices sky-high, and people coming in to Glenora at that time, and banking on buying horses, were not only unable to find a single one but were offered two hundred and fifty dollars a head for those they had—eight hundred dollars at least, as money goes to-day.[15]

The Y.F.F. averaged about twelve miles a day when on the move. By about mid-July they were pretty well assembled at Camp Victoria at the south end of Teslin Lake, with a four-hundred-mile water voyage still ahead of them and no boats to make it with. A few graves remained along the trail to mark their passing. . . . The last man to leave Glenora was Major Bliss, who had remained there till the last load of supplies was on its way. He had had his troubles, soothing temperamental packers, coaxing men who were subject to no army discipline. One of the mule trains he had hired belonged to a French Canadian named Durand and had French Canadian packers and foreman. This pack train arrived back at Glenora from Teslin Lake after some considerable time on the trail, and the foreman rushed straight to Bliss' office tent and burst in upon him in a fury.

There had often been, it seemed, mules bogged down in the muskeg in the swamp country. When this happened a bugle was blown to summon up help from the walking soldiers. The mule would be unpacked, if that were possible, and then pulled or prized out of the muskeg onto firm ground and re-packed again. The other mules, being intelligent an-

imals, soon learned to stop at the sound of the bugle. As soon
as the bogged mule was ready to go another soldier would ring
a bell and then the whole outfit—animals, men and women—
would move on again. Everybody on the way out had been
delighted at the sagacity of their four-footed companions:
rather less so, however, on the way back. All this the foreman
carefully explained to Major Bliss.

"You spoil my damn pack train," he shouted, banging on
the table. "My mule 'e go down, your soldier 'e go 'toot-toot'
on bugle—soldiers come, get my mule up. Soldier 'e ring a
bell 'ting-a-ling-a-ling,' my train go ahead. That all right. But
come back, no soldiers. My mule 'e go down, 'e wait for
'toot-toot,' 'e wait for 'ting-a-ling'—no hear, no get up, no go!
Your damn soldiers spoil my pack train!" [16]

At the time when the Yukon Field Force passed through,
Glenora was described as being "a wretched place of six or
eight houses." Yet it is estimated that some ten thousand
people landed there in 1898 and that its population rose to a
peak of five thousand. . . . All this vanished, and when I passed
by, fifty years later, the place was deserted: just a few old,
grey log buildings and a few old graves.

Part Three

The Portage Road

$\mathbf{T}$HE road from Telegraph Creek to Dease Lake has a history far older than that of man on this arctic watershed. Fifteen thousand years ago the land lay hidden beneath the Pleistocene ice. The game trails of former ages were gone, smoothed away by the grinding glaciers. But already the climate was changing: soon there would be a new beginning. . . . Slowly the last of the icecaps vanished and the roaring torrents of their melting sank to the streams that we know today. There remained a morainal desert of boulders and gravel, polished and eroded by tremendous winds laden with driven sand.

In the wake of the retreating ice life would creep back to the bleak landscape—first the lichens and the mosses, then the grass, then small bushes such as could stand the fierce post-glacial winds. And then, when all had been made ready for them, there would come, venturing from the crowded south, the first of the grazing animals—who were also the world's first road engineers—making their trails along the valley flats, round the projecting spurs and over the low places in the barrier ranges—moving always northwards into ungrazed valleys, since, to animals as to men, "far pastures look green." A few of our animals, such as the wolverine, have survived almost unchanged from earlier ages. Others, beasts that were new to North America, had crossed from Asia by the intermittently emergent land bridge of the Bering Strait, and had then taken refuge in the unglaciated parts of the Yukon or been driven south by increasingly severe glaciation. And now, perhaps nine thousand years ago, these last were returning.

As time rolled on, the first pioneering trees would take a hold in the sheltered places and a little of the grazing would be lost to them; but, apart from the advancing forest, the world belonged to the wild game and to the animals that preyed upon them. And so this way, northward from the Stikine, there would come the bison and the bears, the caribou and the great wolves, the sheep of the windswept heights, the goat whose home is the ledge of some dizzy precipice, the lordly moose of the swamps and the willow meadows. And the game trails would be trodden more deeply into the soft ground of the flats, while round the gravelly spurs they would appear as carefully graded ledges, becoming ever wider and safer with the trampling of millions of hoofs. So the millenniums passed by—good seasons and poor seasons, and always with a lacing of catastrophe: drought and flood, lava flows and pestilence, lightning fires and showers of volcanic ash. On top of all these natural disasters there came that which was to be, from the point of view of the beasts, the greatest disaster of them all—a two-legged, feeble-looking creature that, for lack of strength, used its brain and the queerly shaped paws that we call hands.

Heading southward from the land bridge across the Bering Strait, the first human beings to pass over the Dease Lake–Stikine divide would find a network of game trails awaiting them, each one following the line of least resistance. The Indian had no more use for unnecessary effort than had the animals: soon, by combining the most suitable of the game trails and by throwing a tree or two out of the way, he had a beaten track that led by the easiest grades from Dease Lake and arctic-flowing waters to the lower, more sheltered valley of the Tahltan, where the salmon came each year up the Stikine in countless thousands, a new and unfailing source of food, one well worth camping by and fighting for.

This trail that united two separate worlds—that of the nomad hunter and that of the settled fisherman—might well be worth improving. The Indian gave that proposition some thought; and, as time went by, he built bridges, using the materials that lay to hand. These crossed the mountain torrents and eliminated at least part of the giddy, zigzag descents that the animals had made down into the deep canyons and out again. One such bridge, over the Tuya River and of particularly hair-raising design, was encountered in 1834 by John McLeod, the first white man to reach Stikine waters from the Liard. He called it Terror Bridge.

This trail, developed by the wild animals and the Indian, served the first white explorers of the Cassiar, the Hudson's Bay Company's traders and *voyageurs*. The first miners used it: Henry Thibert, a French Canadian from Montreal, and his partner, McCulloch, came and went that way. They came from the Mackenzie, finding en route gold on McCulloch's Bar, on the Liard near Fort Halkett. In 1873 they found gold on Thibert Creek, which flows into Dease Lake from the west near the outlet. Dease Creek was discovered that same year; the news spread like a prairie fire and the Cassiar rush, till then a trickle, became a flood. It was then that the age-old trail entered upon its second incarnation: it was made suitable for packhorses.

The year 1874 was the peak year for the Cassiar creeks: the population rose to fifteen hundred and the output of gold for that year to $1,000,000. Some of the claims were very rich— that is, by pre-Klondike standards—but many were only marginal and rendered practically worthless by the cost of provisions. Men staggered in to Dease Lake over the seventy-four

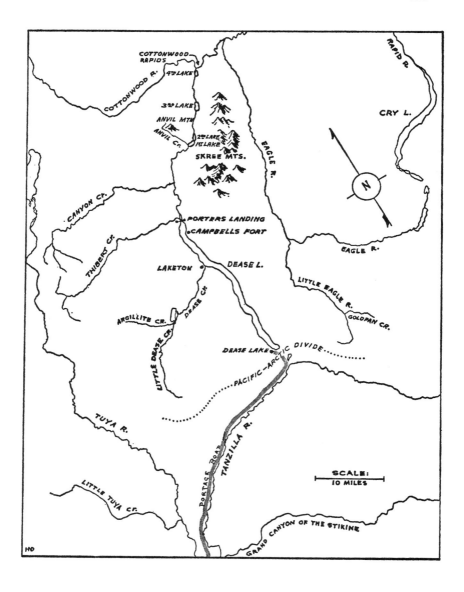

miles of trail "under packs more suited for mules than for
men." Indians demanded "$50 per 100 lbs. and eat out of the
pack, which would leave us about 70 lbs. at Dease Lake—so
we shouldered our own packs." Even the roast beef had to do
its share: "The oxen that went up on the *California* from
Victoria were each packed with 400 lbs. at 50¢ a lb. freight,
and so went into the diggings where they will fall beneath the
butcher's knife." What sort of shape they were in when they
hit the head of the lake is not recorded. In 1875 three hundred
head of cattle were brought from the Fraser overland—a long,
hard drive.

Captain William Moore (he of the *Flying Dutchman*) and
his three sons were among the first to locate on Dease Creek.
Between them they are said to have taken out from their
claims about $100,000. As a man of substance, therefore,
Moore was able to convince the British Columbia government
that a good pack trail from Telegraph Creek to the diggings
was a necessity. He also convinced the government that he
was the man to handle the contract, and in 1874 he set to
work. The main thing to do was to improve the deep and
precipitous crossings of the Tahltan and the Tuya, and Moore
put men and horses on the job. Judging by the letters to the
Colonist, he satisfied few, the following being a fair sample:
"What we want is cheap grub, and there is no reason why we
should not have it. But the present trail company is a humbug
and a fraud. When I came through there were four graders
at work, hired for $50 a mile. I sat and watched them for long
enough to satisfy myself that four active chipmunks would
get through the same amount of work in a day." [1]

Eventually, however, the pack trail was "finished"; or else,
if it was not, government funds were exhausted and Moore
had called it a day. At least it was passable, though it came
a bit late, since gold production was dropping and many were
leaving in search of "fresh fields and pastures new." It was not
long before the new trail was suitably inaugurated in true

western fashion. In August 1874 a Mr. McLeod, a well-known packer, arrived in Victoria "from the diggings with a good deal of gold dust." Riding alone over Moore's trail towards Telegraph Creek with his treasure, he had been ambushed and shot at by two men, with blackened faces, using pistols. Fortunately he had been riding a slow, poking type of a horse—the sort of animal that everlastingly wants to stop and graze. For the hundredth time he had fetched the unwilling brute a crack with the lines. The horse had leapt forward; and at that very moment McLeod heard the whistle of two bullets behind his back and two sharp, barking reports. That horse then found himself doing the gallop of a lifetime, and McLeod and his gold were soon out of range. . . . This was the same McLeod who had been on the Bentinck Arm Trail in 1864 with a party of eight men, of whom three were killed in an affray with Chilcotin Indians.[2]

Over Moore's trail in the early months of 1876 there passed a notable character. This was Nellie Cashman, originally from Arizona, a woman with no nonsense about her and the first white woman to reach the Cassiar. She passed through Wrangell without any fanfare of trumpets and quietly started up the winter trail on the Stikine. Word of this got around to the commander of U.S. troops: he was advised that a lone woman was proceeding on some mad adventure into the frozen wastes, and he gallantly sent a party of his men to rescue her from the consequences of her folly. That was easier said than done: Nellie must have been a dog-driver of the calibre of Jack London's "Joy Molineau,"[3] for the detachment had quite a job catching up with her. And when they did they found all the comforts of home waiting for them at her camp: "She served them a warm meal, thanked them for their kindness, sent them back and then went on," leaving her would-be rescuers to return to Wrangell. She was to become a well-known figure in the mining camps of the North in the years that followed.[4]

The Dease Lake trail was still a pack trail when Dawson and McConnell went over it in 1887, and it had not changed when Kirkendale went by in 1898. He and his partner had finished work on the warehouses towards the end of June, and then, while they were wondering what to do next, they discovered that the cook of the outfit had a cabin and a claim on McDame Creek, eighty reputed river miles below the outlet of Dease Lake. The old cook, Darkey Smith, wanted Kirkendale and Murton to come in with him for the summer and work the claim on shares. Since the season was getting on and packers' rates on the Teslin trail were $500 a ton and over, that seemed to be the sensible thing to do. So they back-packed in to Telegraph Creek, and there they fell in with another member of the original fourteen, George Fenn. They promptly co-opted him as supernumerary gold-miner, and the four of them hit the trail for Dease Lake. Darkey Smith carried a light pack and the cooking outfit. His dog followed with a twenty-pound pack and the other three carried seventy-five pounds apiece. With those loads, and in blazing heat and clouds of mosquitoes, they made the seventy-four miles to the head of the lake in three days. They found the trail "well worn and in good shape, and fairly level except at the crossings of the rivers Tahltan and Tuya. At both of these rivers we had to descend into a canyon about 1,200 feet deep with the trail zigzagged and cribbed into the steep banks." The strain of bracing oneself with a heavy pack down a steep slope in the summer heat must have made those canyons *feel* that deep, for Dawson, a trained observer, set them down as around six hundred feet. But then he had horses while Kirkendale had only his own feet: two entirely different points of view.

By degrees the old trail of the game and the Indians and the Cassiar miners became a wagon trail. The Hudson's Bay Company used it to freight the Company's outfits up to their post at Dease Lake, but they made little use of wagons and horses, finding it easier to get supplies through by pack train.

Pick and shovel were standard equipment on the wagons and, more often than not, the teamsters had to get down and use them. Then Agnes Ball's brother, Jack McDonald, brought in the first truck, and in 1924 Clarence Wrigglesworth took the first car, a Model T Ford, over the trail. That meant that a few more corners had to be rounded off and a few more steep grades eased and bridges strengthened. This went on from year to year, a little here and a little there, till a man could at least say it was a fairish truck trail without being called a liar. There was something of a stampede to Goldpan Creek, east of Dease Lake, in 1924 and the road was then further improved. What with one thing and another, the miners of that last flurry had it on a plate compared with those of earlier times.

It was not till about 1928, however, that the road was considered to be really fit for cars—that is, when it was in good shape. By that time it was possible to haul, mechanically, heavy loads over the trail, for it was in 1928 that Joe Morrison, a relative of Mrs. Sydney Barrington, put the first power boat to freighting on the Dease. But there was not enough stuff moving to make that a paying proposition, and Morrison only stuck it for two summers before moving to Alaska.

It was in 1925 that the Hudson's Bay Company got the tractor idea, inspired by successful operations back east. They brought in one tractor to start with but found that was not enough to handle their freight, and so, for that first year, they continued to run their pack train. Then they brought in another tractor and got rid of the pack train. Passengers, loading their outfits onto the trailing wagons, were charged $5 to Dease Lake. As a matter of course they were issued with pick and shovel, and Harper Reed tells me that he, as a passenger, spent one whole week of 1925 digging the one and only tractor and its train out of (or should one say "through"?) Beaver Swamp. The road may have "been fit for cars" by 1928, but Mr. Dan McPhee of Telegraph Creek writes that he can remember taking three days over that seventy-four miles in 1930—"and not too *damn* good even now [November 1964], though they do make it through in three hours."

To take charge of the freighting, the Hudson's Bay Company brought in to Telegraph Creek an experienced tractor driver from down east, Art Leverett. Art, as he was known, made a big success of the Bay's tractor outfit until, after two or three years, he and the Company ceased to see eye to eye and they parted. It was Art who staged the most spectacular crash to date on the portage road. Making an early spring trip for a mining outfit, and driving a tractor hauling two wagons fully loaded with camp supplies, he turned the whole lot over on six-mile Gumbo Hill and rolled—wagons, tractors and all— two hundred feet down into the valley. Somebody must have made a real job of packing that load, because the remarkable thing was that, after going to all that trouble, Art only succeeded in smashing six eggs. He himself came off decidedly less well, and he spent the next three months in hospital.

By the time I came along things had improved some more, and the wagon trail of the Kaiser's War years and the truck trail of the twenties and thirties had blossomed into a very passable road. This development had been brought about by the war against Japan; and the reasons for it and the queer freight that went that way will be dealt with later in this story. In the meantime there it was: a good enough road and stout enough bridges so that Steele Hyland could get his truck over it with a large and varied load of freight and two passengers. The seat in the cab of the truck had been pre-empted by an old prospector who was "on to something" in the mountains east of Dease Lake and who was going back in to run his prospect down, once and for all. He was a silent man and he looked as old as the hills—though, in reality, he was probably not yet seventy. He spoke hardly at all, and you could tell that his thoughts were far away in his mountains, in the quiet places where silence, if nothing else, was golden, and where a man didn't have to wear himself out, eternally jabbering and arguing. And there's a good deal to be said for that point of view.

In the back of the truck were the old man's outfit, my outfit, a bunch of stuff that Hyland was taking over to his warehouse at Dease Lake, drums of gas for the radio and weather station on the divide, and, crowning the lot, my canoe. A fairish load—and I was wondering where I was going to sit when Hyland said: "The old man bespoke that seat quite a while ago, but I think I can fix up something comfortable for you on the load." Anything was all right with me so long as I got to Dease Lake; and so we parted, I to buy some moccasin rubbers at Thorman's Taku Trading Post and to gossip and have midday dinner with Marrion, at whose stopping place I had slept and eaten. The day was getting steadily hotter. . . .

When I got back to Hyland's place the arrangements for my accommodation had been made: the load had been shifted around a bit and, right on top of it and just behind the cab, was lashed securely the seat of an armchair. It was high up, so that one's feet would rest comfortably on the roof of the cab as one sat there. I don't remember that the thing had any legs, so that would mean that the load was stacked a bit above the roof, blocking the back window. That didn't matter a bit; this truck would probably be the only moving thing on the seventy-four miles of road: we were going to be the traffic problem and the rush hour, all in one.

"I'll have to go slowly on the turns and the hills," Hyland was saying, "and I'll go easy through the trees. I don't think there's any that'll wipe you off, anyway. And if you want to stop and take a picture, just stamp on the roof with your feet. No use shouting; I wouldn't hear. Will that be all right for you?"

Would it be all right? That, when I thought of the magnificent view I was going to have, was putting it mildly. So off we went, climbing out of Telegraph Creek, running along close to the rim of the Canyon of the Stikine. The afternoon was perfect and I sat up there, enthroned on top of the whole works like an archbishop, the warm, dry wind rushing through a thin shirt thrown wide open. How free it felt, and never a mosquito! Once or twice I stamped on the roof and we rolled gently to a halt: to look down three hundred feet or more into the canyon; at the crossing of the Tahltan (but the village was deserted and the Indians were all away hunting or making ready for the guiding season) and on the lava beds. We passed by Ira Day's Ranch and we stopped on the high land above the Tuya crossing. Some thirty miles away to the south-east a symmetrical, shining mountain had attracted my attention. It stood alone, and it rose like a distant cloud out of the quivering heat haze that danced on the plateau. In form it was perfect, and it seemed almost to hang in the sky, shimmering with an unearthly beauty. "What's that mountain down there?" I asked Hyland.

"That's Ice Mountain," he replied.[5]

"You mean, there's snow on it all the year round?"

"Not snow—ice. It's an old volcano. It's over nine thousand feet and it stands out alone, away from the Coast Range. What snow doesn't melt there packs into ice. There's lava flows and craters all around it and creeks going every way out of the ice . . ."

We dropped down into the deep valley of the Tuya, down the hill that Dawson said was six hundred feet but which, to Kirkendale, burdened with his heavy pack, had felt more like twelve. It was down there, in that sun-baked valley and many years ago, that a strange thing befell Harper Reed. In fact, it was one of the very strangest things that ever happened to him in the course of a long lifetime spent in the North, ranging from the Stikine to the arctic coast and from the Finlay River westward to the Pacific Ocean. In the far North he had watched the polar bears manoeuvre the Dall sheep out onto the sea ice—and that was a wonderful thing to see. But the night he spent at the Tuya crossing—that was the queerest experience of them all. "It was the sort of thing," he said, "that might happen to one man once in a hundred years—if he chanced to be in the right place at the right time."

The Tuya valley was far from being sun-baked on that memorable night. Both the Tuya River and the Stikine were frozen, and the portage trail lay under a light covering of snow. Once again the moon was almost at the full, and as Reed drove his dogs south-westward from Dease Lake towards Day's Ranch and the Stikine he could clearly hear the deeper note in the calling of the wolves—the sure token that something was afoot. Wolves were around and about, scattered or in twos and threes, and as Reed approached the Tuya it seemed that he was passing through a cordon of them. Later on he realized that that was exactly what it had been: a siege line tightening around its prey.

Reed's outfit dipped down into the ravine of the Tuya, down the winding trail towards the bridge at the bottom. And it was round a left-hand bend in the old trail that he met with the first of the moose. The dogs shot forward before he could check them—but then they hesitated; and then they came to a stop. These moose were not acting like the moose of the open lakes and meadows that they had tried to chase on so many winter trips: these moose were not running. In fact they were not even making much effort to get out of the way. This was something new and also unnatural, and the dogs' tails sank between their legs. The team refused to move to Reed's word of command.

It was as always at a time of disaster: the greater fear had taken charge *—in this case the fear of the wolves. Men and dogs on this night meant nothing to the moose—and only by going ahead and cracking his whip could Reed clear a way for

* See Appendix E.

himself and the team. He got the dogs over the bridge—but then the trail up the far side was seen to be dotted with moose and Reed was afraid that something might happen to stampede them. And if he and his dogs should happen to be caught on the narrow trail in the way of that mob, there would be nothing left of them but a bloody pulp. So he decided to stop where he was and make a fire. There was some old dead cottonwood lying around and a broken-down old Indian cabin. . . .

What had happened was that the wolves had made a sweep—probably taking the whole of the Tuya country from forty or sixty miles back—and had corralled these moose in the Tuya ravine near the mouth. The horns of the hunting crescent had evidently reached the Stikine on either side, and the Stikine here was in its sheer-walled canyon. It had frozen early in the winter, then broken up—and finally piled up and frozen again in blocks and hummocks, hopeless for a moose to attempt. So there was no escape that way. But now Harper Reed had come along, blundering into the wolves' plans and sending up a blaze of fire in the dark valley that was to have been the place of the killing: man's interference once again.

Reed spent an anxious night down there by the Tuya. He made a little rope corral around the fire—for what that was worth—and he said the worst part of it was after the moon had set: the long hours of darkness when all that could be seen was the dimly outlined circle of great Roman-nosed faces peering at him from out of the shadows. When they came too close to the rope he would crack his whip and they would withdraw a little way, but not for long. The tension was always there, and he felt that any small thing could easily have started a stampede. It was a weird and nerve-racking night, surrounded by the biggest deer in the world, and in a dead silence except for an occasional snort and the squeaking of hoofs on packed snow. Now and then a burnt-out log would collapse with a woof of sudden flame and a shower of sparks—and the great prehistoric faces would draw back for a while into the darkness. But from the wolves there came no sound or sign.

By the time daylight came, Reed said, the pressure seemed to have eased. What had happened he didn't know: possibly something had caused the wolves to withdraw their cordon on the Tahltan side of the Tuya and some of the moose had then escaped that way. Whatever it was, things were easier and some of the dogs' courage had returned. Quietly and carefully Reed hitched up the team. Then, slowly and with much whip-cracking, he led the way out of the mob of bewildered beasts—up the trail out of that hole and on to the open bench where the early-morning sunlight sparkled on the snow. It was with a feeling of tremendous relief that he saw the empty winter trail running on into the south-west towards Day's Ranch and Telegraph Creek.

As he travelled on he alerted Day's Ranch, and he passed the word to the Indians in Telegraph Creek that there was moose meat to be had for the taking. And no doubt, in the end, the wolves also got their share.

Hyland and the old man and I went on. A few miles beyond the Tuya crossing, the road, without deviating, runs straight into and up the valley of the Tanzilla, leaving the Stikine to turn off eastward through its Grand Canyon, to split up eventually into those far-off headwaters that Samuel Black and his men waded and rafted a hundred and forty years ago. This valley of the Tanzilla is the continuation of the main valley that the Stikine has followed in an almost direct line all the way from Little Canyon, and the road for about ten miles just here is dead on that pencil line that we drew on the map connecting Rothsay Point with the Lower Post on the Liard.*

In past ages some vast river flowed in the valley of the Tanzilla; and, even in post-glacial times, Dease Lake drained

* Pages 29-30.

this way, to the Stikine. Then something happened and the southern outflow of the lake was blocked. Now a gentle gravel ridge, three miles across, separates the head of the lake from the Tanzilla stream, while the height of land is no more than seventy feet above the lake waters and a few feet more above those of the Tanzilla. Yet this insignificant gravel ridge, with its poplars and its sparse alpine herbage, *because it is a pass, and because it is an easy one,* is a link in the Arctic-Pacific Divide that is far more important than the highest mountain range in that long and intricately-winding barrier.

A short spur road runs up to the radio station, which is sited on a high point of the ridge. There we unloaded our gas drums, trundling them down a plank from the truck to the ground. Seeing that one of the drums was going to fall off the plank, I reached out and caught it with my left hand, cutting it back into the straight. It was an awkward grab at an awkward angle and some muscle in my wrist objected strongly, but I thought nothing of it at the time. Then we ran on down to the head of the lake and pulled up at Hyland's house, an old building of the Hudson's Bay Company which stood at the west end of the beach and slightly above it.

There we unloaded and spent the night. Around supper-time two cheerful-looking children came over from a large and well-built log house down on the flat. That was George Dalziel's base of operations and the children were Bonnie and Robin Dalziel. With them and Mrs. Dalziel and Farrell, the storekeeper, the population of Dease Lake was complete. Some Indian houses could be seen to the eastward, across the lake on a small reserve, but no wood smoke rose from them and they appeared to be deserted.

Hyland and I talked late—and then, when it was getting dark, I took a stroll down to the shore. Not even the smallest ripple lapped against the pebbles and the lake was utterly still. It lay there like a dark mirror, long and narrow, pointing straight at the North Star whose reflection gleamed unwinking from the quiet waters. There was a sense of freedom to it and of vast distances: one could almost *feel* the water flowing away into the North—down the Dease to the Liard, and so to the Mackenzie and the frozen Beaufort Sea. Five years had gone by since I had last stood by arctic-flowing water, yet for me nothing had changed. Behind my back, southward over the divide, lay the humdrum, workaday world of men and cities. Ahead, beneath that shining star, where the last faint light of the summer evening still lingered in the northern sky, lay the clean, unfenced, unparcelled land where a man is on his own and anything can happen. And all the room in the world for it to happen in.

Part Four
The Arctic Slope

THE rising sun found us at breakfast; and then Hyland departed and I set to work to pack the outfit down to where we had left the canoe. I laid the canoe half in the water, alongside an old, stranded raft that I used as a landing stage. I found and trimmed three driftwood poles and laid them lengthways on the canoe floor; then I slid my big tarpaulin under the thwarts and spread it out over the poles, pulling one edge of it up level with the gunwale. Next I laid the load in the bight of the tarpaulin so that, when it should be all packed, I could pull the loose roll of proofed canvas across, under the thwarts and over the load, and then tuck it down *outside* the opposite edge—the one that had been pulled up to the gunwale. In this way, provided the two ends, fore and aft, are folded and tucked in properly, it can rain cats and dogs or the spray can come splashing in and the outfit will remain perfectly dry. The tarpaulin will shed rain in every direction and, with the poles laid under the canvas, the water will all drain to the rear end, whence it can then be bailed.

Getting all this fixed up, together with sorting out small quantities of stuff for the grub box—tea, sugar, raisins, cheese, bacon, a few cartridges and so forth—takes time. Meanwhile the sun climbed up the sky, and towards the end of the opera-

tion I was joined by Bonnie and Robin. They were anxious
to lend a hand, and while they carried and shoved and stowed
they discussed each item in detail. What was this? Where did
that come from? Why did I have two axes in the outfit, one
of them so very small?

I carried stuff down from the house and shoved and stowed,
too, getting hotter and hotter; and while I worked I had to
answer more questions per cubic inch of outfit than any man
has ever answered since the first Indian loaded the first canoe.
I began to laugh, and finally I said: "Look here, you two!
I'm getting dizzy with all these questions. We're going to have
five whole minutes without one single question. Five minutes
from now you can start again. Go!"

Silence fell on the party with a thud. It lasted a good thirty
seconds, and then:

"Is it five minutes yet?"

"Well then, how long *is* five minutes?"

"When will five minutes *be?*"

Obviously this silence idea was not going to work. It would
be easier to swim with the tide.

I swam. "Five minutes is now," I lied brazenly—and away
we went again. The sudden flood of pent-up chatter reminded
one of an ice-jam giving way in the break-up of a river.

The axes and the rifle were slipped into their places, the
spare paddle was shoved under the thwarts, and that was that.
Mrs. Dalziel came to the rescue and up we went to the big
log house for coffee and a lunch. Dalziel was away on a flight;
I was sorry to miss him, I had heard so much about him
for so long that I almost felt I knew him. I left a message for
him about Frances Lake—and then we all went back to the
canoe and I shoved off for Dease River and the Liard and
whatever might lie beyond.

I paddled seventeen miles down Dease Lake that day and
never a breath of wind came strong enough to raise a ripple
on the water. It was very hot, and long ramparts of piled-up

thunderheads lay all around, north and south, east and west. They were far distant when I started, but all through the day they climbed slowly, coming closer; from them faint wisps of mare's-tail cloud reached out like ghostly hands into the blue above the lake. I was experimenting with the first colour film that I had ever used, and periodically I stopped paddling and lay dead still, hardly daring to breathe for fear of breaking the perfect reflection. The resulting pictures are before me as I write—a perfect souvenir of that perfect day.

Dease Lake is twenty-five miles long as the crow flies and averages just over a mile in width. I set a course from point to point, keeping always a wary eye on the mounting thunderheads. This took me almost dead straight and due north down the lake for sixteen miles and brought me to the east shore on its short north-west bend. A mile's further paddle along that shore closed the long view to the southward and revealed a wooded point that guarded a small natural harbour with a good sandy beach. I was glad to see it, for the little canoe, only a fourteen-footer, was, if anything, overloaded. It carried supplies for a longish trip, and it carried extras, such as fall clothing for the early snows. With this load it was deep in the water and, being short, it had little momentum. This meant that every two or three yards of distance travelled represented a thrust of the paddle under that blazing sun, with never once the shelter of a cloud shadow. And now there lay ahead a long stretch of sheer cliff with no landing place, and I could not tell how far that continued. This bay was the safest spot in sight for a night's camp and I stepped ashore thankfully. I cruised around among the trees: here was a good, sheltered spot for a man to sleep; and there, on the beach, was good driftwood for a fire. Soon blue coils of smoke were wreathing out over the lake: soon the tea was made and the bacon and eggs were sizzling in the pan.

As I was having supper the noise of a distant engine came to me. It grew louder—and then a boat with a single man in it shot round the point. The man cut the engine and the boat slid up on to the beach alongside my canoe. The small wash rippled amongst the gravel and then died down again. The man stepped ashore and introduced himself: he was Barney McHugh, the sole inhabitant of Laketon, the ghost town of the Cassiar rush of 1874.

The town—what remained of it—I had already examined through the glass. It lay directly across the lake at the mouth of Dease Creek and, at the moment, straight into the evening sun. Against that dazzle of light all I had been able to make out was the grey of old, abandoned houses, seemingly arranged in some sort of order but now buried in the bright green of the encroaching trees. Poplar, cottownwood and willow—they seemed to be growing *in* the houses, some of them, and soon, by the look of it, they would be taking the old place apart. Yet there was one house down near the lake shore, on the south end of this township of ghosts, from which smoke seemed to be coming. The bank nearby was revetted with logs as a protection against the waves, and above the revetment there was a garden sloping to the morning sun. Long rows of vegetables, neatly sown and running east and west, caught the evening light. Some lonely Chinese miner, I had decided, working over some old placer. . . .

But it was Barney McHugh. Barney had been at Laketon for twenty years. He had made his home there and done a bit of trapping and a bit of prospecting—but now, he told me, the trapping was all shot to hell because "they" had been putting out poison against the tremendous upsurge of wolves that had taken place during the forties. The crazy fools had probably fixed up a few wolves all right, but they had also managed to wipe out about every other damn thing in the country that ate meat, from weasels to wolverine and from ravens to eagles.

That reminded him: was it Friday, August the twentieth? He had forgotten to ask at Dease Lake.

No, I told him, it was Wednesday, the eighteenth.

Ah, well—that was just as good, and a couple of days longer for a man to live. . . . No, he went on, trapping was played out. But a man could get a moose easy enough, and there was always beaver—thanks be to God, they didn't eat meat.

Silence fell between us for a minute or two, broken only by the crackle of the fire and the mad laugh of a loon from somewhere out on the lake. I had my eye on an appalling thunderhead that was building up into the eastern sky. In the distant north lightning was flickering beyond low mountains: it was camp that I should have been making at this moment —not sitting on my eiderdown and yarning, with the outfit scattered all over the place from hell to breakfast time.

Suddenly Barney spoke. "I was in town, early on this year," he said.

"Wrangell?" I asked, wondering whether I ought to have said Vancouver.

"God, no! Telegraph Creek. Telegraph is town enough and people enough for me. I slept in Marrion's attic, same as you did, and a thing happened to me there. There came an afternoon when I felt the sleep comin' over me after Marrion's good dinner. So I went up to the loft, as you call it, and I took with me a book—a reading book, as it might be—and I laid me down there to rest awhile and read, but I soon fell sound asleep. And I was a long time sleeping . . . Then I heard the noise. There was lots of children in me dreams—little ones, you see, all kickin' up a row and far too many of them. And all the while, in the roadway outside Marrion's, there was a callin' and a cryin' of children—and slowly I knew I was awake. But I kept me eyes tight shut, for I was leery, you see: I feared I was crazed at last and hearing Things at Laketon— for why would a man not hear Them once in a while in a queer old place like that? Then I opens me eyes, slowly, and I see I'm in Marrion's loft and not at home. 'Thank the good God,' I says, 'and I'm gettin' out of here while me soul is still me own.' No—there's people enough and to spare in Telegraph, and it's quieter here at home."

Then we somehow got on to the Boer War, and Barney went back in time almost fifty years. He still sat there, gazing at my fire; but he was thousands of miles away from Dease Lake. What he was seeing was the flicker of other fires, long since dead and cold—long lines of camp fires dwindling away into the hostile darkness of the Transvaal high veldt. He spoke of raids and ambushes, and of freezing nights beneath strange, alien stars; of tense, nervous hours of outpost duty when the pounding hoofs of a cunningly stampeded herd of cattle could rouse an army into sudden, furious action— Maxims, pom-poms and Lee-Metfords all blazing away—and all the while the Boer commandos would be slipping past in the darkness, listening with quiet smiles to the distant din of futile battle against the mob of scared, bewildered beasts. . . .

Lightning flashed suddenly in the hills to the eastward and a rumble of thunder came. A cold wind rustled the poplar leaves and the water of the little bay. Then all was still again —but the warning had been sufficient. Galvanized into sudden life, the only inhabitant of Laketon made for his boat and departed at speed, calling on me to be sure and visit him in the morning. I hurtled around camp, piling the scattered stuff, tarping it up and setting rocks on the corners of the tarpaulins, putting up a lean-to shelter of green proofed canvas between two trees. Beneath that, on the dry, warm sand I arranged my bed and mosquito net. Then I slung the camera sack and rifle under the lean-to and followed these with a bundle of dry kindling and split beach-wood. I pulled the canoe a bit further up the beach and re-tied it; the wind was in the north-west now and the little harbour was calm and still—but one never knew: the wind might switch in the night. One last look around: nothing seemed to be out of place and all was well. Thankfully I went to bed. For some reason I was feeling rotten, and on top of that my left wrist

had swollen badly. As I loosened the wrist-watch strap to ease
the pain a bit the first heavy raindrops came pattering down.
The wind was rising, and soon the crash of the waves on the
outer beach mounted to a steady roar, like the pounding of
the sea. The thunder was close—it sounded like the splitting
crack of field-guns—and the lightning became a steady blaze.
The rain drummed on the canvas of the lean-to.

Well, let it drum, I thought—there was nothing it could do
to me. Wondering vaguely what Barney did with his boat in
storms like this, I fell asleep—and in almost no time, it
seemed, the first rays of the sun were streaming down the hills
to the eastward and it was day.

Great white summer clouds swept out of the north-west,
spinning across a sky of royal blue. The lake was a dark,
stormy blue up which the white-crested rollers surged like
lines of white-plumed horsemen coming into action over a
level plain. The waves came crashing on to the outer beach
of the little point, throwing a small drift of spray, and the
line of cliffs to the northward seemed to be dancing in the
water, suspended above the mirage. For a fourteen-foot canoe
there would be no moving till this wind went down.

I baked a bannock and did the camp chores. Then I cut a
spruce and whittled it down with axe and drawknife into a
canoe pole that might take me up the Frances River. It wasn't
a good spruce to make a canoe pole from, but Dease Lake is
2,500 feet above the sea and in the year that Dawson passed
that way the ice lingered on in the lake till June 16—almost
till midsummer. A June or late May opening of the lake is
quite normal. So the spruce had grown under alpine conditions, slowly and with difficulty. It tapered and was knotty,
and there was a lot of fining-down to be done at the butt end
with drawknife and wood-rasp. I did it, doing my best to ease
my half-useless wrist, which, I could see, was going to hamper
every movement. Finally I drove an iron shoe that I had

brought with me on to the butt end of the pole, and the job was complete.

I couldn't raise much enthusiasm for anything and I coudn't seem to keep warm. So I took my eiderdown and the field glass and Dawson's *Report* and walked across the little point to the open lake shore. There I made myself comfortable, propped against a tree, wrapped in the eiderdown, in the full sunlight and beyond the reach of the spray.

Across the half mile or more of stormy water I could see Barney McHugh hoeing in his garden, surely one of the loneliest gardeners in British Columbia, but, for that very reason, one of the freest from garden pests. With the sun swinging into the south one could plainly see, now, how Laketon was built on the delta that Dease Creek had flung out into the lake, making almost a narrows at this point. About eight miles further north down the lake Thibert Creek comes in, also from the west, making with its delta the natural dam that holds Dease Lake in place. There, at the outlet, is the little settlement of Porter's Landing with its monument to the memory of Warburton Pike, erected by the explorer's friends. Washed down from that gentle, uninspiring mountain slope and concentrated by those two quite ordinary-looking creeks, the first of the gold of the Cassiar had lain through the ages, awaiting discovery. In the years 1873 and 1874 Dease and Thibert Creek yielded placer gold to the value of $1,000,-000, and that was not the end of the story by any means, for mining continued for years afterwards with gradually diminishing returns.

Slowly the population of Laketon dwindled till, by the late twenties, it was reduced to four. There was Barney McHugh, a recent arrival then, and there was Tom the Packer with his Indian wife, and a fourth character who lived further north along what had once been the main street of the old ghost town. Tom the Packer was an Indian from the Kamloops country who had come north with a drive of beef cattle in the

Cassiar gold rush of the seventies. He had married one of the girls of the town and had stayed on in Laketon, moving into better and better quarters as the old houses became vacant, until now he and Mrs. Tom lived in roomy comfort in what had been the old courthouse building.

One Christmas Eve of those far-off years Harper Reed came down the lake from the south, driving his dogs against the north wind. It was around thirty below zero and a light in some window in Laketon beckoned like an unattainable star. The dogs were tired, the sled pulled hard in the dry snow, and, even moving as he was, with the snow squealing and protesting beneath his snowshoes, Reed was most ungodly cold. He was empty, too, which was the main reason why he was cold—and for ages the light had seemed to be getting no nearer. . . .

The light was in Tom the Packer's window, and at long last, when Reed was just about at the end of will-power and endurance, his dogs climbed up the bank off the wind-swept lake. The barking of Tom the Packer's dog greeted them and fetched Tom himself to the door, which he threw wide open. Reed's dogs never hesitated: they shot straight through the doorway into the blessed warmth of the old courthouse, sled and all. Reed followed on his snowshoes and the door closed behind him.

"It was one of the most marvellous things that have ever happened to me," Reed said. "It was like getting straight out of hell into heaven. Tom and Mrs. Tom took my mitts off and they each took one of my hands between theirs and rubbed them till the circulation came back. I couldn't even thank them: my lips were so stiff that I couldn't speak properly. You know how it is, sometimes?" And he paused in his tale and looked at me.

I nodded; I didn't want to stop him even by one word.

They gave Reed a cup of coffee, and slowly the warmth flowed back into him and he limbered up and his brain began to tick again. All this time he had half-consciously noticed a table standing against one wall. It was beautifully set out for six or seven people and covered with all the Christmas cheer that the Cassiar of forty years ago could provide. From the stove and the oven came the smell of more good things, hot and all ready to be eaten. Reed asked his hosts if they were expecting a party—but, no, they said, they always had things fixed like this on the feast days of the year, so that if one man or a party should happen to be on the trail and make their house for the night all would be ready for them. And now, here was Harper Reed, straight out of the night and the black, frozen wind—he would be their Christmas guest this year. Barney McHugh was away, and that left one other citizen of Laketon; he might be over or he might not, and in the meantime there were the dogs to see to, and *then* . . .

It was a wonderful dinner, Reed said. And he was able to add to it, for in his load were two or three "permits"—bottles of rum destined for McDame Creek, away down the Dease, and for the Lower Post on the Liard. He might be the Indian Agent and there might be strict regulations regarding the sale and distribution of firewater; but there was a time for everything, and now was the time for breaking the law: soon a bottle of rum was gracing the festive board—rum that really *was* rum, for it was still a dozen years or so before Mackenzie King got at it and diluted it with the Ottawa River.

"Do you know," Reed said to me, "it's an amazing thing, but we drank that bottle of rum clean up!"

"That doesn't surprise me in the least. . . ."

So sleep was sound that marvellous Christmas Eve at Tom the Packer's, and it was late and a brilliant sun was shining when Reed hitched up his dogs and made ready once more to buck the north wind. Good-byes were said and Reed drove his dogs along the trail that had once been a street—past the empty Gold Commissioner's office, winding through the encroaching trees. Suddenly the lead dog stopped and reared up.

Hackles flew up and the team just stood there, balky, snarling and suspicious. Round the corner Reed could see something black in the trail, and his first idea was, a bear that had unaccountably emerged from hibernation. He started to pull out his rifle—but nothing seemed to be happening so, instead, he investigated.

The black object proved to be a pair of felt boots, and in the boots were the extremities of the fourth citizen of Laketon. A half-empty bottle of rum lay beside him in the snow. He was very well wrapped up in good winter clothes and did not appear to be dead—yet. He had evidently celebrated his Christmas Eve in true hyperborean fashion and had then set out to bring a friendly drink to Tom the Packer's but had found it very comfortable where he had fallen and had slept there.

Reed threw off his load and slung the "body" onto his sled. He hauled it back to Tom's, and there they slowly thawed the fellow out—*unharmed!* God knows what miracle of circulation and alcohol and Christmas dinner had kept that lonely reveller alive through that sub-arctic night!

Six miles or so further north down the lake, out of sight behind the curve of the cliffs and on the eastern shore, there is the site of an old Hudson's Bay Company's fort. Dawson's map, which I had with me, shows it to be at the mouth of a small stream, on the point that today is called Sawmill Point. Dawson marks it thus: *"H.B. Co.'s Post (abandoned 1839.)"*

There is a world of drama and adventure in that brief notation, for the fort was built only in 1838. I spread the map out on the grass and put rocks on the corners of it to keep it from blowing away. Then I opened the *Report* and turned over the pages till I came to the *Discovery and Exploration of Cassiar District. . . .*

They were persistent and determined men, those old fur-

traders. They were convinced that to the west of the mountains, somewhere beyond the furthest sources of the Liard,
there lay a rich, untapped fur country—perhaps even "a
second Caledonia . . . There only wants a road to make these
riches available to the Trade." [1] This road that Chief Factor
Edward Smith was writing about to his friend James Hargrave
was not a road as we understand the term today; it was a road
that could be travelled only by canoes—a river road—and the
only way west from Fort Simpson on the Mackenzie lay up
the Liard. That river, with its rapids and its dangerous canyons, its powerful floods and its difficult low waters,[2] when
the reefs rise to the surface and the channels are constricted,
can be almost as much a barrier as it can be a means of communication. Still, the fur-traders probed away at it, establishing their forts and exploring the tributaries.

The North Westers had a fort up the Fort Nelson River
by 1805. By 1824 Fort Liard was where it is today. In 1823
and 1824 a young Hudson's Bay Company clerk, John M.
McLeod, was exploring the South Nahanni River country,
antedating the self-styled "explorers" of the present day by
some 140 years. In 1824 Chief Trader Murdock McPherson
was away up the Beaver River, another northern tributary of
the Liard; and that same year there was compiled, under his
direction at "Fort de Liard," a map [3] showing the rivers and
the mountains as they were then known. They are surprisingly recognisable. Across the south-west, in a straight line
and looking just like a crenellated wall, runs the line of the
mountains with the Liard cutting through it. West of the
main range and on the Liard there is a little star marking
the furthest known point on the river. That was reached in
August 1823 by a party of seven Fort Liard Indians under the
leadership of one, Niltsitaibeta. These men had been sent out
by McPherson in June of that year to search out "the source
of the West Branch of this River." Another star, far up the
Beaver River and marked *"July 19th 1824,"* marks the fur-

thest point reached by McPherson himself. Beyond these two stars, to the west and to the north, all is a beautiful, unsullied blank—a boundless wilderness in which the fur-traders of McKenzie's River were free to imagine strange new tribes of Indians, vast populations of beaver, and great rivers running towards the setting sun.

While McPherson, personally, was always of the opinion that the Liard was too dangerous a river to afford a practicable way into these new countries, there were others who believed that the thing was possible, and their tenacity of purpose and pride of achievement drove them on. Already by 1829 the Nahannis of the South Nahanni River were bringing in to Fort Simpson furs that had come to them in trade from Indians whose hunting grounds were around Frances Lake and the upper Pelly River—though these names were not yet in existence and ten years more were to pass before any white man would set eyes upon these places. In that same year of 1829 Fort Halkett was established on the Liard in the heart of the canyon country, about seventy miles above Hell Gate though still a good hundred below the mouth of the Dease. A clerk, John Hutchison, was put in charge.

In 1831 J. M. McLeod went far up the Liard, "to its source in the Icy Mountains." [4] He arrived back at Fort Simpson that September with a mixed tale of achievement and disaster. When he and his party were already far on their way home their canoe was swamped in a rapid and broken into three pieces. Two men were drowned and all the small gear was lost, and the survivors got ashore with but one portion of the canoe. "In such cases the commander has nothing to depend on but the resources of his own imagination, and Mr. McLeod, with the means he had, made a shift to repair the wreck to bring him home." [5] That set the affair of the West Branch back a year or two, but it was impossible to stop men of that calibre and in 1834 John McLeod was at it again.

In that summer, and using Fort Halkett as a base, McLeod,

a Chief Trader now, made his final effort to find a route to the western sea. He went up the Liard as before, over Portage Brûlé, over Mountain Portage, avoiding the dangerous whirlpools, lining or portaging the bad rapids, till he reached the mouth of what he called the Nahany River, which has since become the Dease. Can he have heard something, perhaps from Samuel Black regarding the Trading Nahannis, that he was moved to give their name to this new river?

A hundred and eighty miles up this stream brought him into the long, beautiful lake which he named Dease's Lake in honour of a man he much admired: Chief Factor Peter Warren Dease, who had taken part in Sir John Franklin's explorations in the far North. Following the lake to the head, he left his canoes and took to the old Indian trail over the Pacific-Arctic Divide—the trail that we have followed. With the exception of Samuel Black, he was the first white man to cross the Divide in all the many miles between the Skeena River country and the Arctic Ocean. It was a red-letter day for John McLeod, and it must have been one of life's supreme moments when the trail led him down into the softer climate of the Stikine and he first set eyes on the big river that flowed towards the west.

McLeod and his eight men went on, and they came to the Tuya, the Second North Fork of the Stikine. But there, bridging the Tuya at the foot of what was later known as Thomas' Fall, a horrifying structure met their eyes. This was one of the Indian "improvements" on the old trail of the wild game—a bridge of such appalling design, poised so delicately above the Tuya torrent, that it seemed utter madness to attempt it. Robert Campbell came to this same bridge four years later and has left a description of it: it was, he writes, "a rude, ricketty structure of pine poles spliced together with withes and stretched high above a foaming torrent; the ends of the poles were loaded down with stones to prevent the bridge from collapsing . . . It inclined to one side which did not tend to strengthen its appearance for safety."

The longer McLeod's party looked at this nerve-shattering contraption, the less they liked it. Probably other factors, also, were involved; but in the end, taking everything into account, they decided they had come far enough. They turned back; and always afterwards they thought and talked of that bridge of the Trading Nahannis as Terror Bridge.

It was in this same summer that Ogden was arguing it out with Zarembo down at the mouth of the Stikine and, later, with Etolin at Sitka. The Hudson's Bay Company was indeed pressing hard on the overextended Russians.

That fall a new man came to Fort Simpson. His name was Robert Campbell and he came from the experimental farm at Red River. In the early winter Murdock McPherson came down from Fort Liard to take over Fort Simpson, and with him, as a visitor, came John McLeod. Thus, through the dark winter days, Campbell, the future explorer of the Yukon, was able to pick the brains of the explorer of the South Nahanni and the Upper Liard countries. What he was told set his imagination on fire, and it was with regret that he saw McLeod, "a most genial man," depart in December for Fort Halkett— a five-hundred-mile trip on snowshoes, but only a pleasant country walk compared with the trips the future held in store for Campbell. . . .

The next attempt to do something about Dease Lake and the fur-trade of the Stikine (which, for a time, they called the Pelly after McLeod's naming) took place in 1836. Dawson had the story from Robert Campbell himself and gives an outline of it in the *Report*. The elements of comedy are not lacking.

John McLeod left McKenzie's River in the spring of 1835, never to return, and Fort Halkett was once more placed in the charge of John Hutchison, who had been absent for a while at Fort Resolution on Great Slave Lake. Hutchison, in 1836, was instructed to establish a post on Dease Lake and from there to extend the Company's trade down the Pelly— or Stikine, as it was soon to become. With this in view, and with doubt in his heart, he left Fort Halkett in June with a party of men and two large canoes carrying an ample provision of trade goods.

Nobody took at all kindly to this venture, and it seems that both leader and men were ready to jump at shadows. They got all of twelve miles up the Liard, and then, when they were engaged on the two-mile Portage Brûlé (the trail being on the north bank), something happened: some strange sound was heard or somebody thought he saw something.

Panic swept through the brigade. Down went every load, and the whole outfit, leader and all, hit for the river, tumbled into the canoes, and shoved off downstream. They abandoned Fort Halkett altogether, worked with unnatural speed on the Devil's Portage,[6] paused for a few days at Fort Liard, and arrived, to everybody's amazement, in late July at Fort Simpson with a harrowing tale of Indian attack. McPherson wrote to Hargrave, as usual, that November: "Mr. Hutchison met with a very formidable Party of Indians who gave him such an alert as to abandon the West Branch altogether and lost the whole of the Furniture of the Fort—Nets, utensils, etc. etc.—which put it out of my power to re-establish the place in the fall. But we will give it another tryal next spring. I never had a good opinion of the West Branch as a channel for extending the Trade . . ."[7]

Robert Campbell wrote in his journal: "An alarm was got up that hundreds of Russian Indians were advancing on camp to murder them all . . . and of course, for some time, their narrow escape was the engrossing topic of the day."

It took a year or so before they found out what had really happened. Hutchison, after his fortunate escape from the Russian Indians, showed little desire to return to the upper Liard. On the contrary, he seemed quite anxious to leave McKenzie's River, and since that could not be done without leaving the Company's service he took that step. It attracted little attention—at the time. In the same year, 1837, Robert Campbell was instructed to re-establish Fort Halkett. He accomplished that in the face of considerable difficulties. His crews were afraid of the Upper Liard and also of the strange Indians who had attacked Hutchison. Campbell had to turn back once on account of desertion. Valuable time was lost and, as a result, coming again, he met the Liard flood before reaching Hell Gate.

Somehow they got through the Gate—probably by the high-water channel on the north side of the island rock. Then came four miles of plain tracking, and then the next constriction of the Liard, a short distance below the Ile de Gravois. How they got through that I do not know, for that is as far as I have ever been by canoe. But in time they came to the Devil's Portage.[8] There, when they had the stuff scattered all along the portage trail, one of the men sought to stampede Campbell by slipping out of camp early and moving and cutting open one of the bales. He then raised the alarm and pointed to the ripped bale as a sign of hostile Indians; but Campbell also had been up early that morning and was ready for him. No more bales were tampered with and the work went forward.

"When the river is in flood," Campbell writes, "no boat could ascend from the Devil's Portage as the current is not only strong but is full of rapids and whirlpools, and rushes between perpendicular walls of rock two or three hundred feet high. Our progress was slow and I was kept in constant anxiety lest the men would lose heart, as the croak of a frog or the screech of a night-owl was immediately taken as an enemy's signal."

Eventually they reached Fort Halkett, where it was plain to see that no man had been since the flight of Hutchison and his party. The men took heart, the place was put in order, and Campbell installed himself there. It was too late in the season by that time to venture on up to Dease Lake.

The Alaska Road runs past the site of Fort Halkett today, but in 1837 it was one of the loneliest places in the North.

The fort stood on the north bank of the Liard, just above the inflow of Smith River. The setting is plainly shown in a sketch map of Campbell's of 1847, and the name "Smith's River" dates from the founding of the fort during Chief Factor Edward Smith's time at Fort Simpson. There were worse places than Fort Halkett. It was a good garden spot, Campbell says, and a wonderful place for wild fruit—raspberries and strawberries, blueberries and cranberries. In winter they relied on their fisheries, which were on lakes thirty miles or more up Smith River. Nearby were warm springs—cold as ice in summer but warm (though not hot) in wintertime and keeping a channel open all winter for miles along the river bank.

That autumn Campbell went up to Portage Brûlé, and there, scattered along the two-mile portage trail, was the evidence of Hutchison's rout. Not a thing had been touched by any man. The provisions had been eaten by wild animals, the fabrics were spoiled by the weather and useless, and the only things that could be salvaged were the balls and shot. All that effort and expense thrown away—and perhaps the alarm had been nothing but a black bear met with in the portage or a bush-partridge whirring through the trees!

The story did not get down the river till the fall of 1838. In his November letter of that year to Hargrave, McPherson, whose wrath had simmered down a bit by then, writes Hutchison's epitaph: "Have you seen Mr. Hutchison, and what was he going to do for himself? There can be only one opinion of his unprecedented story of his shameful flight from the West Branch. He was affraid of going to pass a Winter in such a Country and invented a story to avoid that . . ." [9]

The gale was blowing harder than ever and the lake was like a stormy sea. Barney McHugh had stopped hoeing and had gone in to get his midday dinner: a puff of wood-smoke appeared from his stove-pipe, only to be torn away in shreds and vanish on the north-west wind. As for me, even wrapped in my eiderdown and sitting in the sun, I was hardly more than warm. It was plainly a temperature that I had—and that would be the flu that had come up on the *Hazel B* and which, when I passed through, was laying low the denizens of Telegraph Creek. And here was a great place to have flu: stuck on Dease Lake with a hurricane blowing and still seven or eight miles from sheltered water. Oh, well—at least the sun was shining. And I turned again to Dawson's *Report*. . . .

In the spring of 1838 a young apprentice clerk, a Mr. McLeod (*not* the John M. McLeod who first crossed the Divide and found Terror Bridge), together with some extra hands from Fort Simpson, joined Robert Campbell at Fort Halkett. And as soon as possible after McLeod's arrival Campbell started for Dease Lake with two canoes and eight men.

The river had risen almost to flood stage and every rapid was a dangerous stretch of furious, tossing water. There were many portages—Portage Brûlé, Mountain Portage, Cranberry Portage, and all the lesser ones that might not have been necessary at a lower stage of the river. Their way took them through the mountains, which were then and for many years to come a natural game sanctuary, so difficult of access was this country. They lived well, meeting with many "moose and reindeer [caribou], grizzly, black and brown bears, and beaver whose cuttings of poplar trees along the river looked like clearings made by axemen." They came, after much toil, to a more level, open country and then "to the forks of the Liard and the Nahany River. We followed the Nahany." This was the Dease of later years, and they were now at least a hundred and twenty river miles above Fort Halkett, having passed around the northern end of the Rockies.

They went on up their Nahany River and it led them into and through the Cassiar Mountains, "some of them capped with eternal snow." And at last they emerged from the grass-bordered lagoons at the head of the river into the long, narrow sheet of water that they called Dease's Lake. That was in early July, and they lost no time in picking the site for the new fort and starting the work of building.

July 20 came, and by that time the ground was levelled, the sill-logs were laid on rock foundations, and the walls of the fort were rising. On that day Campbell left with two pine-bark canoes for the head of the lake. With him were Hoole, his interpreter and a skilled hunter and maker of canoes, and two young Indians, Kitza and Lapie—all of whom were to accompany him on many a long journey in the years to come. The little party of four reached the head of the lake, beached the canoes and hit the trail. For food they intended to trust to their guns. That night they slept by water that flowed to the Pacific.

The next day they saw, far below, "a river that looked like a thread, running through a deep valley." That was the Tuya, and by evening they had made their way down to it, having experienced in one day the four seasons, from winter snow "to the ripe strawberries of autumn." They followed along the river till they came to Terror Bridge.

In the course of their descent to the Tuya and the bridge they had seen, on a rocky shelf on the far side of the valley, an Indian hut with smoke curling up from it. Campbell decided to cross and try to make a contact. Hoole balked at this —he was worried about the strange Russian Indians, and the bridge itself was no inducement—but Campbell, who had about as much idea of turning back as Samuel Black had, ordered him to cross. One by one they got over. Then they climbed up the zigzag path to the hut. They found the place deserted; the Indian owner had fled, but it seemed that he could not be far away, for a bright fire was burning on the hearth and around it stood three metal pots, in one of which salmon had been cooking. From the rafters hung split salmon, drying in the smoke. They took some of that for their supper, leaving some tobacco and a knife in payment. Then they crossed back over the bridge and made their night camp.

The next morning a small party of Indians came to Campbell's camp. The chief advanced, holding out a pipe of peace, which was passed around and smoked by everybody. Then several of the young men made ready the traditional Stikine salmon-gaff, tightly binding large hooks onto long, light poles. Soon a number of freshly caught salmon were lying on the bank and the whole party breakfasted on them.

The owner of the hut in which Campbell had found the Russian cooking pots and the salmon had returned when it seemed safe to do so and had found the knife and tobacco. He had then run the fifteen miles or so to the great encampment on the Tahltan to bring the news to his people, the Trading Nahannis, that strange white men had arrived on the Tuya and that they had come in friendship and not in war. The Nahannis had kept this news to themselves, not sharing it with the Tlingits, and the chief had come secretly with this party to Campbell to warn him against venturing on to the rendezvous.

The great chief from the sea, Shakes, was there, and though the Nahanni chief and his band would be willing to protect Campbell, they would be unable to do so. "Shakes will kill you," he went on, "and his men are many, even as the sands of the beaches." He said that Campbell was the first white man he had ever seen, that they had smoked and eaten together and now he did not wish to see Campbell's blood spilled. He and his people, the chief added, had always been told that if they ever met with white men from east of the mountains they were to be sure to kill them. . . . That sounds like the careful, far-sighted policy of the Tlingits, who had threatened to fight Ogden only four years previously in defence of this same monopoly—and now, to Campbell, it was relayed as a friendly warning. It had no effect. "But I was not to be moved. All their arguments were thrown away. I was determined to go on."

So on they went—meeting, every now and then, with more parties of Nahannis bent on turning them back. Things were beginning to look serious, and Campbell decided to send back Hoole and one of the two Indians to the other side of Terror Bridge, there to camp and wait for a couple of days. If he, Campbell, did not show up by then, they were to assume that he was dead. In that event they were to destroy the bridge and make for the fort at Dease Lake, bringing the news to McLeod.

That seemed a sensible arrangement, and Hoole was delighted with it—but it foundered on Kitza and Lapie. Their fathers had told them that if ever they deserted Campbell in the hour of danger, they need never return home themselves. So now they would go on and die with him. This they said with tears in their eyes, and nothing would dissuade them. Finally Campbell took them on and Hoole with them, much to the latter's disappointment.

From the top of a hill about thirteen miles from the Tuya they first set eyes on the great encampment "of which we had heard so much, and indeed the description given us was not exaggerated. Such a concourse of Indians I had never before seen assembled. They were gathered from all parts of the western slope of the Rockies and from along the Pacific Coast. These Indians camped here for weeks at a time, living on salmon which could be caught in thousands in the Stikine by gaffing or spearing, to aid them in which they had built a sort of dam across the river." In the crowd of Nahannis, Campbell became separated from his companions and from the chief. Another Indian who could speak some broken English attached himself to the explorer, and together they went down into the throng below. "Every word I said in reply to the numberless questions asked me was taken up and yelled by a hundred throats till the surrounding rocks and the valley re-echoed with the sound."

Meanwhile a lane was being cleared through the crowd so that Shakes could come forward and meet Campbell. This title of Shakes was not necessarily hereditary. It passed of right

to the most capable of the family—if he was man enough to
hold it and to use it wisely. Otherwise it might be fought
over and pass into some other family. But no matter how it
went, it had to go to a strong and kingly man—and such a man
Campbell now saw approaching.

"Shakes was a Coast Indian," Campbell writes, "tall and
strongly built . . . He ruled despotically over an immense band
of Indians of different tribes, and he came up the Stikine every
year, with boats and goods, to the splendid rendezvous where
I met him. Here he traded with the Indians of the Interior
for the Russians, who supplied him with goods at the mouth
of the river. He shook hands with me and led me to a tent . . ."
They entered with others of the chief men and sat down, and
whisky and a cup were produced. Campbell merely tasted the
liquor, but all the others in the tent drank. "Meanwhile the
din outside was something fearful."

Suddenly the tent lurched and heaved; the walls were lifted
from the outside—and then the whole thing was torn loose
and swept away amid loud shouts. This was done, Campbell
discovered later, by the Nahannis, who were afraid that Shakes
was planning to murder their guest under cover of the tent.
So by this alarming onset they fetched the drinking party out
into the full glare of noonday, crying out as they did so: "If
the White Chief is killed much blood will flow here."

"I was well armed," says Campbell, "having pistols and a
dirk in my belt, and a double-barrelled percussion gun which
was a great source of wonder to them as the only guns they
were familiar with were single-barrelled flintlocks. Shakes
wanted me to fire so that he might see how the gun went off.
I took the precaution to have ball, powder and cap in my
hand, ready to slip in after firing a shot. At every report the
whole camp yelled, clapping their hands on their mouths at
the same time, and the noise was frightful."

Some of the Tlingits present, Campbell found, had been
on long sea voyages to the south in their great canoes—even

to Fort Vancouver on the Columbia River. There they had met the famous Dr. McLoughlin and also James Douglas. Campbell wrote notes to these officers, informing them that the so-called Pelly and the Stikine were one and the same river and asking them to forward this information to York Factory. He entrusted the notes to the seafaring Tlingits, and in due course they reached Fort Vancouver.

"I remained in camp for some time, the object of much curiosity, till at length I got clear of Shakes and the crowd on the plain [we should call it a flat] in safety, which was more than I expected when I first went among them. I found my small party also all right on the top of the hill, where I forthwith hoisted the H.B.C. flag and cut H.B.C. and the date on a tree, thus taking possession of the country for the Company."

Here on the hill Campbell met a very remarkable woman— the Chieftainess of the Nahannis. Campbell must have seemed equally remarkable to her, for he was the first white man she had ever seen. This woman, with her aged father, ruled directly over this tribe of nomad hunters, then about five hundred strong. She also commanded the respect of the tribes with whom she and her people had dealings. "She was a fine-looking woman, rather above the middle size and about thirty-five years old. In her actions and personal appearance she was more like the Whites than the pure Indian race. She had a pleasing face lit up with fine, intelligent eyes, which, when she was excited, flashed like fire. She was tidy and tasteful in her dress. To her kindness and influence we owed much on more than one occasion; in fact, in all probability, we owed our lives to her more than once."

Some things had been stolen from Campbell during his stay at the rendezvous and this woman immediately recovered them for him, simply by sending two young men back to claim them and bring them. After that display of authority she accompanied Campbell's party on the trail towards the

Tuya, urging them not to rest till they were across Terror Bridge, warning them that Shakes might send some of his young men in pursuit to kill them. When they parted she and Campbell exchanged gifts: "my handkerchief and all the loose nicknacks I had about me, and I received in return her silver bracelets. We walked hard and late and got across the bridge in safety, much elated at the result of our trip . . . ."

Campbell wasted no time at Dease Lake: he and Lapie left the new site there immediately in a pine-bark canoe for Fort Halkett. There they changed the pine-bark for a birch-bark—in which they were all but swamped and sunk at Hell Gate—and drove on down the Liard at full speed to Fort Simpson. There Campbell brought the news of the new venture to McPherson, only to meet with disappointment: McPherson refused to give supplies for Dease Lake. They would have to hunt and fish and winter themselves as best they could. The posts of McKenzie's River were almost permanently short of everything in those early days; but what carried even more weight was McPherson's lack of faith in the Liard as a way to the West.

So back they went, Campbell and Lapie, up a hill of water over two thousand feet high and seven hundred miles long, over the miles of portages and up the many rapids, the first of which begins only twenty-three miles above the Mackenzie and the last of which ends only thirty miles below Dease Lake. The banks of the river and the mountain slopes of the Cassiars were aglow with the last reds and golds of autumn when they passed by. They reached Dease Lake on October 11 at night in a blinding snowstorm, and the new fort the next day.

The men scattered out, hunting; but, with all they could do, the party—one might almost say, the garrison—spent a miserable winter. They lived, Campbell says, on such animals as they could kill and, failing meat, on *tripe-de-roche*—the lichen *umbilicaria* which could be scraped from exposed rocks and cleaned and cooked, a stomach-filler rather than a

food, and a diet which, if too much indulged in, could bring
about the most unfortunate results. Several times they were
helped by the Nahanni Chieftainess; and on one of these occasions a dangerous riot almost accounted for their lives.

The Nahanni lady had arrived that February day and had
brought with her an ample provision of salmon and caribou—
just when the larder was particularly bare, too. She had immediately set her people on to cooking—and now it was night.
Peace and contentment prevailed and all was quiet. But something happened: some insult must have passed between the
Indian retainers of the Chieftainess and the white and half-
breed servants of the Company. "Yell after yell suddenly
broke the silence and the now furious savages rushed into the
room where McLeod and I were sitting, loading their guns.
Some of them seized our weapons from racks on the wall, and
would assuredly have shot us had not the Chieftainess, who
was lodged in the other end of the house, rushed in and
commanded silence. She found out the instigator of the riot,
walked up to him and, stamping her feet on the ground, re-
peatedly spat in his face, her eyes blazing with fury. Peace
and quiet reigned as suddenly as the outbreak had burst forth.
I have seen many warrior Chiefs with their bands in every
kind of mood, but I never saw one who had such absolute
authority, or who was as bold and ready to exercise it, as that
noble woman."

What with one thing and another and, according to Campbell, "the constant danger from the savage Russian Indians,"
it was a winter they would not forget in a hurry, and they
were very glad to see the spring. But still the game avoided the
long-frozen lake for the warmer valleys, and at last the end
came. The larder was more than just low: it was cleaned right
out and there was nothing for it but to abandon the place.
"As we were now ready to start and our snowshoes were no
further use to us, we removed all the netting off them, and
that, along with our parchment windows, was boiled down

to the consistency of glue. The savoury dish thus prepared formed the 'menu' of our last meal before leaving Dease's Lake on 8 May, 1839.

"Wild fowl of all kinds being plentiful, we soon killed enough, as we drifted down the river, to make a good meal, a luxury to which we had been strangers for a long time . . ."

McPherson had the last word. In November 1838, in his yearly letter to Hargrave, he had written: "We made a small advance in our very tardy business of the West Branch this last summer. Dease's Lake was established; that is to say—the Establishement of Fort Halkett was moved to the very *ridgepole* of the Rocky Mountains, a region of eternal snow and barren rocks, and, I do believe, of nothing else . . . If we could convey Goods and Provisions enough to that Country I have no doubt but we might get some Returns out of it—but by the present route up the West Branch, I do think *that* impossible. If we make anything of it it will be from the Westward." * [10]

McPherson was right. The fort on Dease Lake was never again occupied. Fort Halkett was re-established, and Campbell used it as a steppingstone on the long trail over Campbell's Portage to the Pelly and the Yukon. The faithful three —Hoole, Kitza and Lapie—made those journeys of discovery with him. Then, that very year of 1839, the Russian Coast Strip was leased to the Hudson's Bay Company,[11] and all further dealings with the uplands of the Cassiar were carried on, as McPherson had foretold, from Fort Stikine (Wrangell) and the trading posts up the Stikine River. The Tlingits continued their age-old trade with the Trading Nahannis at the rendezvous by the Tahltan, and the Dease Lake country slept again, almost forgotten by white men, for over thirty years.

The noonday hours slipped by on that sunny bank un-

* See also Appendix F.

heeded by me, for I fell asleep, wrapped in my eiderdown and dreaming a weird, feverish dream of a starving fort by a frozen lake on which moose fled past, pursued by packs of wolves. And, as always happens with me in dreams, no gun would fire. When I woke, the sun was already in the south-west and the wind was as strong as ever. Nothing could be done, so I got up, picked up the *Report* and my diary, and went back through the trees to the camp on the little bay. There I made supper—there had been no midday meal—and after that I piled the outfit in good order so that, if the chance came, I could load the canoe and get out in a hurry. By a pure fluke I found, in with the camera outfit, a forgotten bottle of aspirin. Bonanza! And I swallowed two tablets and went to bed early.

I woke in the first, grey light to an unearthly stillness: not even a ripple was lapping on the outer shore. Convinced that the wind was going to blow again (which it did), I rolled out of bed, bundled up my camp and loaded the outfit into the canoe. Then I ate a bit of bannock and a square of chocolate, took a good drink of Dease Lake and got going, heading due north along the line of cliffs.

It was cold at first and I drove as hard on the paddle as my swollen wrist would let me. I kept close under the cliffs; it was encouraging to see the rock wall slipping past, whereas out in the lake there was no sense of movement at all—only of thrusting away at an infinity of water. Soon a gorgeous red sunrise spilled over the ridges to the east, flooding the lake and the western slopes with a soft, rose-coloured light. That meant wind later; it was lucky I had got going early. The glow of the sunrise lasted for only a little while; soon the lake, still unruffled by any breeze, was taking on the hard blue of day. . . . Now the cliffs had eased off; and here was the little stream coming into the lake across the flat that today bears the name of Sawmill Point: it was here, then, that Robert Campbell had lunched off boiled parchment windows and the filling of his snowshoes just over a hundred years ago. Dawson's map was handy, stuffed in between the big tarpaulin and the rear thwart of the canoe. I took a look at it to refresh my memory and then I stepped ashore, feeling "like death on a raft" but determined to see. The site of Campbell's fort should be, it seemed, on the north side of the stream and a bit away from it, close to the lake shore.

I waded around in the long grass and the heavy dew, searching among the trees. Soon I came to ground that seemed to have been disturbed and then on a mound of stone that was half-buried in the drifted leaves and the humus of a hundred and ten years. That would be a hearth and a chimney; and these mounds and hollows and scattered stones were all that was left of Campbell's fort—all that remained of the white man's first desperate venture to the Cassiar—a venture that was before its time, and one that could not hope to succeed with the wild waters of the Liard as its only line of supply. I wished there had been time to make breakfast on that spot, but a small ripple was beginning to show on the lake and I wanted to get on and into the shelter of the river before the wind rose. So I went on, slipping along the east shore, looking across to Porter's Landing, where there seemed to be no sign of life—but whence I was observed and noted, George Dalziel told me later. Then onward into some lagoon-like stretches of the lake with what looked like water-meadows of tall, waving grass on the far shore. And then at last there was a current and the canoe quickened and came to life in the clear, shallow water. What Samuel Black would have called an "eligible" gravel point offered itself, and I landed to make the breakfast fire. . . .

Where it leaves the lake the Dease is a beautiful small river, clear, swift and winding, little more than a nice trout stream. Dawson puts it at a hundred to a hundred and fifty feet in width, "rather swift" and around three feet deep in the middle. He passed by in June, three days after the lake opened.

Kirkendale puts the Dease at thirty to fifty feet for the first few miles, but he came in July after a long dry spell. I came in August after a good hot spell and one thunderstorm: my estimate, therefore, would be nearer to Kirkendale's than to Dawson's.

Anyway, it was an enchanting little river and the day was perfect. Furthermore, the wind, which had risen again and was probably kicking up another sea on the lake, made little difference to me here. I shifted the load a bit, putting more weight in the nose of the canoe so that it rode almost on an even keel, and that took care of the wind. It also enabled me to run down the small, shallow riffles without ever touching a stone. In fact, all was as it should be except that I was feeling very queer. All my actions seemed to be so far away that it was as if another person was handling the canoe. The paddle rose and fell, reaching forward, driving back—and it was some other man who was doing all this. Trout, remote and dimly seen in the sun-dappled water, flickered away from the canoe's shadow—and it was somebody else who fitted the little steel rod together and found the right spinner, and fished in dark, clear pools and at the foot of dancing riffles till the canoe was littered with lovely fish. It was this other man (who seemed to be reasonably capable—enough, anyway, so that one could have some confidence in him) who avoided the frothing drift-piles into which the river set so strongly and towards which it tried to draw the canoe; and it was this same fellow who beached the canoe and waded out into the stream, axe in hand, to cut the lower branches off a tree that had fallen across a narrow chute, barring the way. He made no mistakes or slips —which was as well, seeing that pencils could be sharpened with these axes. Quivering in the racing water, the branches fell one by one and were swept away downstream, leaving a channel beneath the tree that was safe for the canoe, provided one knelt low and kept one's head down.

In F. S. Smythe's *Camp Six* I have read his tale of "the pres-

ence" who climbed with him above that camp on his lonely
bid for the summit of Everest. This was different. Here I was
the disembodied presence, and it was from outside that I
watched this strange, remote personage who was dealing with
the small hazards of the river. Twice I saw him draw the canoe
up on a gravel point and splash away downstream to cut the
top off a fallen tree that blocked the channel. He seemed to be
a careful sort of fellow: he would put the axe away exactly
where it ought to be, with the shining blade safe in its leather
cover; then he would let down the canoe by hand, easing it
past the foaming, decapitated tree in perhaps three inches of
water. Once, in a calm reach of the river and after a particularly stabbing shoot of pain, this half-familiar stranger
sat and let his canoe drift, wiggling his swollen left wrist close
to his ear . . . and—yes—it actually did: it squeaked quite
audibly and creaked, as some damaged surface in it scratched
roughly over a nearby bone. Noises, by God! Well, at least
that was something new!

Canyon Creek came in from the west and the Dease grew
that much larger. There were good camping places around
the mouth of Canyon Creek, but I passed them by, for it
would have been a shame to waste an afternoon like this,
huddled in an eiderdown in meek surrender to some malevo-
lent germ. I would go on—for a few more miles, anyway:
something would be sure to show up, and very likely something better. But a little below Canyon Creek the Dease
enters the Cassiar Mountains, through which it cuts, almost
at right angles, for about seventy river miles. The summits
rise higher and come closer and the river slows down. In
place of the swift and shallow trout stream one is faced with
a slack current and a calm, meandering river, flowing silently
between low, steep banks. For some miles it is almost impossible to land, owing to the dense jungle of willow backed with
the tall, slender spires of the northern spruce. Once embarked

on a stretch of river of that description, there is no point in stopping.

Few people travelled this river, and the wild-life seemed unafraid. Canada geese lingered until well within gunshot; moose tracks showed on every patch of silt, and once a cow moose, with only mild interest, watched me pass within a few feet of where she stood, browsing on the willow tops. As the sun sank into the west the beavers came out about their business, and even they could be passed close by if one kept quite still and drifted, without using the paddle. Ducks with heads of russet-brown colour (mergansers?), accompanied by large broods of ducklings that spattered over the water like handfuls of flung stones, swam frenziedly with zigzag course ahead of the canoe. Sometimes they flew with scuttering flight, almost touching the water, downstream ahead of me for miles. It was all very peaceful, and that was just as well, for I doubt if I could have coped successfully with any serious emergency.

I made camp on a little bar where Anvil Creek flows into First Lake. The evening was perfect, as the day had been, and Dawson's Skree Mountains to the east of the river were splendidly lit with the glow of the sinking sun. Soon trout—several trout—and bacon were sizzling and spitting in the pan. The tea-pail sang and a savoury smell pervaded camp. A blue wraith of wood-smoke crept out, low down on the quiet lake water, and a family of loons, somewhere by the far shore, broke the silence with their wild laughter. To me, later, sitting on the grub box, warm at the bright fire and pleasantly full, there returned for a while a clear head and a blessed unity, and I no longer saw myself from afar as a stranger. Realising that this happy state of affairs might not last forever, I rose and tarped up the outfit, for the sun was down behind the mountains and the dew was beginning to fall. Then I rolled into my eiderdown, though not yet to sleep, for the last rays of the sun still touched, with lingering fingers, the tops of the Skree Range. Then those stony summits became cold and grey and the laughter of the loons ceased. Only the beavers still worked and played in the lake, coming sometimes close to the canoe, attracted as always by the dying flicker of the fire.

A blanket of mist lay on the lake the following morning and everything dripped with the heaviest dew I have ever seen. It might just as well have poured with rain. Rivulets ran down the lean-to tarpaulin under which I had slept— water both inside and out. Let it run, I thought; and I turned over to sleep again, or at least to put off the evil hour of getting up. The pain from my wrist was spreading up my arm, the flu had returned in force, and I had a red-hot head on me the size of a Halloween pumpkin. Something would have to be done about this.

I got up late. I tried the trout, bacon and tea cure. It didn't work. I sat by the fire—almost *in* the fire—and wrote up my diary: weather, birds and beasts seen, difficulties of the river, and so forth. Then, to pass the time, I got the maps out and did some careful figuring of distances, finding out, incidentally, that here at the mouth of Anvil Creek I was a bare five miles to the westward of that famous pencilled, 270-mile air-line between Rothsay Point and the Lower Post.* Having ascertained this valuable piece of geographical information, I then had to dry the maps before folding them again, for they had become damp and limp in the saturated air. Next I sat down by the fire and carefully cleaned my old Mannlicher. And finally, in desperation, I shaved. Suddenly the mists lifted and a patch of brilliant turquoise showed—but only to vanish again. Then came a small breeze from the south-west, driving the fog-bank before it, and the full glory of the sun burst through. For the first time I noticed that there was a touch of autumn gold coming on the cottonwoods.

Awkwardly and painfully I loaded the canoe and shoved off. I was feeling decidedly ill, and the only sane thing to do was

* See page 32.

to travel on till a good, dry, comfortable camp showed up. And then fix everything up so that it would be just like home—and go to bed and stay there till the germs were defeated. . . . Very well, then; so be it! And the canoe slid easily across the calm water.

At the sight of it the loons started up again. They appeared to be a complete family—two adults and two young birds— and the noise they made in the dead silence of those mountain lakes was something to remember. Followed at a distance by the loons, the canoe, after a mile or so, slipped through a narrows into Second Lake, a beautiful sheet of water, a bit over a mile long and with a trapper's cabin at the south end of it. Canada geese got up and flew, and in the distance a large duck with what seemed to be a yellow head—a stranger to me —took off. Mallard rose, and the place became alive with the sounds and the flight of waterfowl. I landed and waded through the long grass to look at the cabin; and, as I walked around, the loon family made it through the narrows and swung towards my canoe, which they seemed to recognize. Once more they burst forth into their wild, hooting cry that we call laughter. Second Lake was a place of echoes, and I have never heard anything in bird song to equal that concert of the loons on that silent lake beneath the Cassiar Mountains.

I went on. In the north-west, about three miles away, rose the queer, anvil-headed mountain that Dawson had named and from which came the ice-cold creek where I had camped. Anvil Mountain is well over seven thousand feet, and so, also, was another mountain in the south, two or three miles behind the trapper's cabin, for it was still streaked with the previous winter's snow. Robert Campbell wrote of the Cassiar Mountains as being, some of them, "capped with eternal snow." The northern world was colder in Campbell's time than it is today: the higher summits may then have been completely covered.

There followed a three-mile stretch of river, mostly slow. Kingfishers were much in evidence there, and twice I saw

Steller's jay with his long blue tail and cocky crest. In came a big, clear creek from the east, from a coulee in the Skree Mountains. The eddy below its mouth was alive with trout; that was something I could eat, flu or no flu, so I took two and then went on towards Third Lake. A mile or so below the creek mouth the trees fell away on either side and the Dease flowed into the lake through a delta of fine silt and tall grass. All was peace—and then, in one instant, the whole place seemed to explode. Up got everything—mallard, Canada geese, pintail, widgeon: they circled and swept over me and then headed back upstream. And there I sat, with one .375 Mannlicher in the canoe and no shotgun. Even blear-eyed, fat-headed and dry-throated as I was, the idea of a nice fat mallard still had some appeal.

I made camp on a point on the west side of the lake, about a mile down from the delta. The point was dry and open: one could see up and down the lake and across to the Skree Mountains, which rose straight up from the east shore. The breeze here would hamper the activities of any wandering mosquito, while the open situation would lessen the dew. There was a good sandy beach for the canoe and, judging from the maze of tracks, every goose in the country thought highly of Goose Point. And if a gale got up and blew from the south, it would be just too bad, for I had set up my lean-to, tightly stretched between two trees, facing in that direction.

As I worked, feeling most peculiar and a bit dizzy, I made tea and sizzled some nice trout over the fire. And when they were disposed of I went to bed in the bright afternoon sun-shine and fell immediately into a blessed sleep.

When I woke it was towards sunset. I crawled out and made more tea, which I drank thirstily. Supper was one carefully rationed aspirin tablet—and so to bed again. From where I lay the view was perfect: a line of spruce in the west, black against the evening sky; to the south the lake, then a tree-clad, pointed promontory, the green line of the delta, and the snow-streaked mountain beyond Second Lake; and to the east, across the water, the high, still-sunlit Skree Mountains. A fine view from any hospital window, and I lay and enjoyed it for a while. Then I pulled down the mosquito net and slept again.

Waking that night in the darkness and the utter silence and wondering how much longer it was to dawn, I switched on a small flashlight to look at my watch. Instantaneously with the light there came a tremendous roar of sound, as if the water of the lake were boiling into eruption. Then wing-beats came through and I knew what it was—but still the sleepier, slower birds went on thrashing at the water, gaining flying speed. Then that, too, ceased and the whistle of a thousand wings passed overhead and faded away into the darkness, leaving me amazed and wondering. All the birds of the four lakes must have settled in around this point after I had gone to sleep. It was evidently their usual place, for the same thing happened again two night later. A flashlight switched on under the mosquito net and beneath a thin, light-green tarpaulin must have appeared to the startled birds as if a church had suddenly been illuminated on that lonely point. Never before or since have I heard like that the thunderous roar of innumerable wings.

I hate having to admit defeat, but Goose Point was my home for four days and nights. Most of the first full day I slept, tottering forth about twice to make tea and eat one orange, one square of chocolate and one aspirin. Under the circumstances, a well-balanced diet. That was the day the first goat appeared, high up at timberline on the Skree Mountains. He must have found a bit of country that he liked, for he was still there when I left Goose Point. A second goat joined him on the second day and that pair of old billies (they had good heads on them) barely moved half a mile in two days, coming back each noonday to the same rock ledge to rest and look down on the lake. Judging from the growth, there seemed to be a spring up there, and so the goats had everything they wanted: water and their pick of the alpine herbage. I could see those two from my lean-to, and in my waking moments I lay and watched them through the glass till I began to think I knew a thing or two about mountain goat.

The place seemed to be a favourite haunt of birds. Jays and whisky-jacks visited me, and once a flight of bluebirds lit the camp with their flashing, turquoise wings. But that was only once, for summer was almost over and the bluebirds were already on their way. All the waterfowl were to be seen. Plainly they regarded the point as their own, but by day the camp kept them at a little distance. And then the loon family turned up. They must have come on down the river, fishing by the way, and I watched them coming across the water, heading straight for the point—where, incidentally, I had noticed, as I dipped water from the lake, numbers of small fish darting across the sun-warmed shallows. The loons came on majestically and strangely silent. They observed the camp, which lay open to the south. Then they passed round the point to the north side, where the canoe lay on the shelving, sandy beach. The sight of it seemed to touch some responsive chord, for all four of them burst into a wild chorus of applause (I like to think it was applause; it may well have been disgust) and then, still laughing madly, they passed out of sight, hidden by my tarpaulin shelter. But they remained in the lake and often they would return to the point to pass a few remarks regarding that inoffensive little grey canoe.

So, one way and another, there was plenty to see without even taking one's aching, outsize head off the pillow. With the sun pouring in on my eiderdown, and the birds and the goats, and one moose that spent an afternoon browsing around in the delta, this free nursing home that I had established on Goose Point beat any civilised one that I ever heard of for entertainment value. There were books, too. I had Crosbie

Garstin's *The Owls' House* and Donn Byrne's *Messer Marco Polo* (both old friends and light to carry) and the *Report* and the maps—and the most carefully entered diary of all time: every bird that came found a place in it.

The diet and the skilled treatment took effect, and on the third day I felt better. As it proved, that was something of a false dawn; but at least it *was* a dawn and no longer just a dismal twilight. That morning it turned grey and blew and rained, but I dealt with that (being now empty as a drum) by eating hot-cakes and maple syrup. Then the day became warm and dry, though still sunless, and I slid the canoe into the water and paddled it a couple of miles down to the north end of the lake, where, at the outlet, Dawson marks a little rapid. I looked that over, but there was nothing to it, though I did get myself a nice trout out of it. Then I poled the canoe west along the shore to a big, well-built cabin that stood, facing south up the lake, among tall pines. It was a trapper's cabin, judging by the traps and stretchers that were hanging under the big eaves. It was only seven or eight miles from the other main cabin on Second Lake: that was getting to be pretty close quarters for main cabins in a trapping country, and close quarters can be productive of dangerous feuds. I wondered who these two men were and which way their lines and out-cabins ran. Between the cabin and the lake there lay on skids a large, strongly built scow with the name *Otter* painted on it in big letters. Now how on earth, I wondered, did they get that thing down that little, winding river? And would that be somebody's winnings from the wartime freighting operation on the Dease? It looked enormous, sitting up there on dry land among the tall trees.

Around the cabin, wherever the sunlight could get down through the pines, were all the wild fruits of late summer: there were red and black currants, low-bush and high-bush cranberries, raspberries and blueberries. I never saw so many blueberries or such large ones. I ate there like a bear till I could eat no more. Then I poled the canoe back along the west shore to my camp—poling to save my left hand for paddling on the morrow. And back in camp I had barely got the fire lit when something told me that this would not be the night to sup off trout—or, indeed, off anything at all. I downed instead a mug of tea and the last aspirin and then, sweating but at the same time shivering, I hurled myself into my eiderdown and knew no more till morning . . .

That was the end of the flu. A vicious bug, that one—and I heard afterwards that mine was not the only stricken camp. Scattered all over the wilds of the Cassiar were fellow sufferers—groaning and aching guides, hunters, packers and cooks—not many, but one or two here and there, and all cursing, feebly but fluently, the Unknown Passenger on the *Hazel B* who had brought the plague into the country.

I woke, clear-headed and well, to the sound of rain. Later the day cleared a bit and I broke camp in splashes of sunshine and squalls of rain and west wind. Then the day changed and the sun came through and I got out. I took a trout and a grayling out of the little rapid for my supper, and then I ran the canoe down it without any trouble and went on down the five-mile stretch of river that lies between Third and Fourth Lakes.

This, the last of the lakes on the Dease, is also the smallest. Like the others, it is a beautiful little lake; and like them, too, it is an obstacle to travel, for they all freeze earlier and open later than the river. Immediately below the outlet of Fourth Lake Cottonwood River comes in from the west, flinging across the path of the Dease the stony barrier that has backed the water up and created the lake. Down that slope of scattered boulders and detritus roars the Dease, and the hill of white water so made is known as Cottonwood Rapid.

Back in Telegraph Creek they seemed to have some respect for this rapid, and Steele Hyland, Marrion and George Ball had all told me of incidents that had taken place there: canoes holed, men drowned, scows run up and stuck on the boulders, scows upset and forty-five-gallon drums of gasolene bobbing serenely on towards the Liard on their own—or, alternatively, getting stuck in drift-piles and shallow snyes. It might be as well, I thought, to take a look at this lively bit of water, so I landed at the head of the rapid and walked a little way down the west side. Warburton Pike had run Cottonwood Rapid with ease in 1892, ending up on the east side, where "the waves at the foot of the rapids are small." I had a note of that in my diary, along with several others under the heading of *"Sailing Directions."* Dawson said it was "not at all dangerous to run, with ordinary care." Still it was best to have a look; fifty or sixty years of June floods and spring break-ups might have changed the place completely.

The bush by the bank was thick, and shoving through it on a sultry afternoon with thunderclouds looming in the north was an exercise that soon palled. From the furthest point one could see what appeared to be an eddy, away down the opposite bank and beneath an overhanging cottonwood. Now if one could get into that eddy it would be a safe place to check the canoe and then pick a way down the rest of the slope to the big waves at the foot of the riffle. Supposing one were to start at the top in midstream and work over to the right, to the east bank, and so to the eddy . . . and as I walked back to the canoe I picked out a channel between the boulders.

I hit the head of that rapid plumb in the centre, riding into it on the long tongue of unbroken, dipping water. The canoe rose and fell and a rock raced past—and then another. Then one loomed up straight ahead and I swung to the right of it, only to put myself in line, head on, for a larger one. Luckily that rock rose above the surface, so that the piled-up water and the wash from it helped to sweep me clear without touching. What next? A straight, fast run and the overhanging cottonwood coming at me like a low-flying plane. I let the paddle trail for a second or two, and then, at what seemed to be the right moment, I swept the canoe into the eddy. I hit that eddy, which was more powerful than I had expected, too hard and at too sharp an angle and the canoe gave a wild lurch. However, it was too heavily loaded to tip and it came gently to rest just where I had wanted it—beneath the cottonwood.

I stood up and grabbed a branch of the tree, steadying the canoe with my feet. Downstream lay a slope of tossing water, with here and there a rock showing—but with the sun dancing on the waves it was difficult to pick any definite trail for the canoe; in fact, it was impossible. One could always walk down and see, of course; but the mere thought of ramming a snail's way through the jungle that clothed this bank of the Dease was repellent. If there's one thing I hate, it's tangled undergrowth and dense bush. Anything would be better than crawling like a wounded animal through half a mile of that stuff. So to hell with looking! And I let the canoe slide out of the eddy into the current.

Down we went, close to the right bank. I say "we" because in fast water a canoe seems to become a living thing and a partner in one's efforts. I know also that in times of stress I have found myself talking to my canoe, urging it on, perhaps, or telling it to go easy and not make such a damn fool of itself. And I know that I am not alone in this. There is a story about Albert Faille frogging his canoe up a riffle on the Flat River * and holding a long conversation with it. The story is well authenticated, for his partners in that season's prospecting happened to be watching, unseen by Faille, from the top of a high cutbank. . . .

The impression that remains of the rest of Cottonwood Rapid is one of bright, flashing water; of black rocks that come surging upstream like destroyers; of a strong eddy narrowly avoided; of leaping over the standing waves at the foot

* South Nahanni River country, N.W.T.

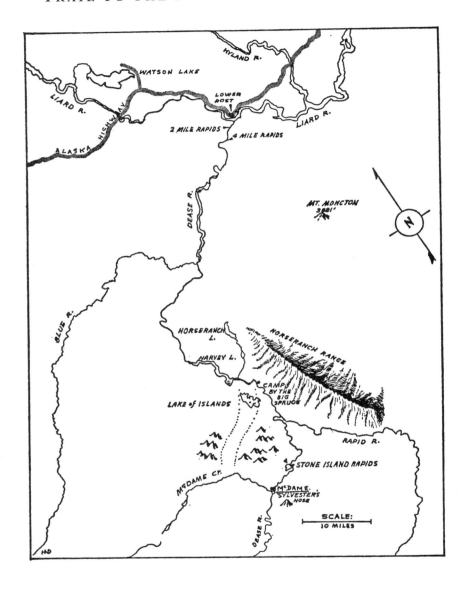

—and then, once more, the uneventful peace of a quiet, meandering river.

Kirkendale, whom we last saw back-packing over the trail near the Tuya, has a word or two to say on the Dease and the Cottonwood Rapid. He must have had quite a lively passage. "When we arrived at Dease Lake," he writes, "we found a great crowd of men there, most of them busy building boats. We had intended building one ourselves but we were fortunate enough to find a party who had built a couple of boats and were willing to sell one for $80.00. The boat was a 21 foot skiff, with square stern, and three planks high on the sides. Three other men who wanted to go down the river offered us a good figure to take them, so we all piled in. With the seven of us and our blankets and grub we were pretty well loaded, in fact the waterline was up to the top plank, but we started off in good spirits.

"Dease Lake is narrow and about 25 miles long. We were fortunate to cross without meeting any heavy wind, but of course we followed the shore in case it did come on to blow. About 20 miles down we stopped at Porter's Landing, where an old man named Porter had kept a trading store since the time of the early Cassiar gold strike, about 25 years before. The store was nearly empty and we crossed the lake in a day and camped that night at the outlet of the Dease River. Next morning we prepared to run the river. As I appeared to be the only one of the crowd who had ever had anything to do with boats, they elected me steersman. I lashed an oar over the stern for a rudder, and trimmed our ship by putting one man in the bow, and four men in pairs on the thwarts each pulling an oar, and old Darkey Smith and myself in the stern.

"The river was only from thirty to fifty feet wide for the first few miles, full of twists and turns, and with a current of about six knots most of the time. I had to keep shouting to the boys to unship their oars to avoid the fallen trees lying in the water, and this happened so often that they soon got trained to act on the second. Coming around one of the bends I saw a huge fallen tree lying across the river from bank to bank about 50 feet ahead. There was no chance or time to stop in the swift current, so I yelled to unship the oars and duck their heads. The trunk of the tree was about three feet above the water and I had just time to shoot the boat through a gap in the branches before the rest of the crew knew what had happened. Then the river widened out a bit, but for the first twenty miles or so it took careful watching to keep clear of the snags and boulders . . . Our worst experience was running the Cottonwood Rapids, about a mile long and full of boulders, with a current of about 20 knots. More by good luck than by good management we came through safe, and reached McDame Creek, 80 miles down the river, three days after leaving the head of the lake . . ."

I wanted to arrive at McDame in the late afternoon of the following day, so I made camp early where Eagle River meets the Dease. Down came a thunderstorm while I was making camp, and then, when that excitement was over, I fished till I could see supper and breakfast in the form of trout and arctic grayling lying in the canoe. Many flights of geese and ducks passed over that evening: the current of the Dease had slackened and all along the twenty-five river miles between the mouth of the Eagle River and McDame the channel did nothing but loop and twist and coil back upon itself. Sometimes one found oneself heading south-east or even due south, and on either side of the Dease there were pools and lagoons and old horseshoe snyes—just a mallard's heaven.

Always having made a point of coming into a post clean-shaven and in full war paint, I devoted some time the next morning to a bath and a clean-up. Then I hit the river. Thunder was in the air and heavy banks of cloud hid the high mountains. The sun, when it shone, was scorching. Twice I sheltered from rain beneath overhanging trees—once in a deluge with a tarpaulin over my head, the lightning blazing and the raindrops hissing on the quiet water, throwing up small fountains as they fell. Slowly the winding Dease stalked, like a coiling serpent, a spectacular, six-thousand-foot peak that I knew was just three miles to the south-east of the post. The clouds cleared from it as the day wore on, leaving it a grey-green knob of mountain against the blue. That was Sylvester's Nose, and by degrees I got it on my right hand. Then it fell behind me and I came to McDame. Mr. and Mrs. Glenn Hope gave me a kindly welcome. They were living in what had been the trader's house of the old Hudson's Bay post, now abandoned by the Company. I carried mail for them and a letter for Mrs. Hope from her sister, Agnes Ball. . . .

McDame was originally known as Sylvester's Landing. Gold was discovered on McDame Creek in 1874, and the rush down the Dease swept some of the incoming miners clear on down to the Liard, which name they corrupted to Deloire. Reports of a rich strike—the better of the McDame diggings paid from six dollars to one hundred dollars to the hand per day—soon attracted the attention of the traders. In 1876 an American, Rufus Sylvester, took an outfit down the Dease to the Liard. On the north bank of that river, hidden from the mouth of the Dease by an island, Sylvester built a trading post. On completion of the work he placed a Mr. Egnell in charge—and of him and his troubles with the Indians we shall hear later. Then Sylvester and his crew tracked and poled the balance of the outfit a hundred miles or so back up the Dease to the mouth of McDame Creek, where they built another trading post and living quarters. Hence the names—Sylvester's Landing and Sylvester's Lower Post. Later on both these posts, together with the outpost mentioned below, passed into the possession of the Hudson's Bay Company. Goods and provisions at these two posts were—and, indeed, had to be—very expensive, what with sea freight, Stikine River freight, fifty-cents-a-pound freight over the portage, and finally freight down the Dease. It was the cost of supplies that finally put all but the best claims in the Cassiar out of business; and, equally, it was hard for a trader to carry on except by running his own pack train and doing his own river freighting.

It was McDame Creek, incidentally, that gave its name to the district of Cassiar—the Indian name for the creek being (as I have seen it written) "Casheahr." This name was adopted by the miners. It was soon corrupted to Cassiar and applied to the whole country.

Sylvester kept horses at McDame, using them both up and down the Dease and also to reach an outpost that he had on the Turnagain River—Samuel Black's river—some seventy miles away to the eastward. These horses he used to put out to winter and rustle their own feed on the Horse Ranch Range, an isolated range of mountains lower down the Dease, where I hoped to put in a few days hunting. Being an easterly outlier of the Cassiar Mountains, the Horse Ranch Range had a much lighter snowfall than the country around McDame. Sylvester was still at the Landing when Dawson went by in 1887; but in 1898, when Kirkendale landed there, a Mr. Emerson was in charge for the Bay. And, since no boatload of supplies had yet got down to him, Emerson's shelves were bare except for tobacco and one box of dried apples. So Darkey Smith's little party—which consisted of himself, George Kirkendale, George Murton and George Fenn—started out on the eighteen-mile trail up McDame Creek to Smith's claims with what remained of the grub in their packs from Telegraph Creek and no more. However, their hearts were light and they had a rifle, while Kirkendale had brought a good supply of fishing tackle and old Smith had a couple of rods and reels.

The gold was there, right from the grass-roots down, coarse but in no great quantity. It petered out at about three feet. They put the flumes and the bridge over the creek in order and went at it for about six weeks, averaging about five dollars a day. That was low-average mining—but the efforts to keep the larder supplied must have absorbed many of the working hours.

McDame Creek teemed with "Arctic trout" (would this mean arctic grayling?), and they varied a diet of unlimited fish with porcupine and the odd groundhog—"but when you put in a few weeks eating fish and porcupine, especially without salt, you begin to wonder if life is worth living." And then Kirkendale got a moose. Every Sunday he would walk the eighteen miles down to the Landing and back just to see if Emerson had got his load of grub down from Dease Lake yet. On one of these occasions an Indian boy told him of moose at a lake "about twenty miles down the Dease," * and so off the pair of them went—probably in the skiff, though that is not definitely stated—and Kirkendale got a young bull. Somehow he got back to camp at the gold claim with seventy-five pounds of the meat *that same night.* Now, what with skinning and cutting out the meat for himself and the Indian, poling upstream again to the Landing, and *then* packing his load eighteen miles uphill to camp—all this, remember, on top of the morning's walk of eighteen miles—that day in Kirkendale's life might fairly be called a full one. He says he always wore Indian moccasins when on the trail; there is nothing like them for getting over the ground when one is used to them, and Kirkendale by this time must have been completely hardened to the trail and inured to heavy packs.

Sylvester's Landing itself was something of a garden spot, but up at the claim the four men were without any kind of vegetables. There were the wild berries, of course; but also, to be on the safe side and to counteract the straight meat and fish diet, they used to chew the inner bark of the jackpine. "When the outer bark is taken off," Kirkendale writes, "there

* River miles in the old days were very often overestimated.

is another layer around the tree which is sweet and juicy and very nutritious."

He then continues: "We stayed with the mining until September, but as our takings were getting less and less we decided to throw it up and try something else. We went down to the H. B. Post and my two partners and two other men took our boat and went up the river bound for the outside. I stayed with Mr. Emerson for another week as he was trying to persuade me to take charge of the H. B. Post on the Liard River, about 350 miles further down. Being at a loose end I had some notion of trying the job but after thinking it over I gave it up and decided to come out. Mr. Emerson said there were some signs of a trail out along the Dease River to the Lake eighty miles away. As no grub had yet arrived for the Post all I could get to carry me out was five pounds of flour and one pound of bacon. My pack consisted of about 40 pounds of clothes, blankets, gumboots, leather boots, rifle etc. For cooking I had a tin plate, tin cup, tin spoon and my sheath knife. I used to put a split stick on the tin plate to make it into a frying pan, grease it with a bit of bacon, mix my flour and water in the cup, and fry my flapjacks, or the fish I caught along the way. In places I could pick up signs of a dim trail, but the first 20 to 30 miles I was most of the time wading in muskeg, with mosquitoes, blackflies and bulldogs in swarms. The little blackflies are worse than mosquitoes, as they dig a hole through your skin before you feel them, and when you smash them another comes along and crawls in the same hole and continues to bore. The bulldogs strike a person like a shot out of a gun, bite out a chunk of hide, and away before you can hit them.

"In the valley of the Cottonwood River I came on the finest patch of red currants I have ever seen. They were as large as cherries, and very sweet. I gathered and ate handfuls, and mixed some with my flour to make flapjacks. It is surprising, the growth of berries and currants in the North. I have seen black raspberries so thick on the old diggings that a person could fill a bucket without moving from one spot.

"Crossing the Cottonwood River gave me my biggest thrill in the North. The river was about thirty yards wide where I struck it, deep and very swift. I went up a bit until I found a spot a little wider but shallower, where I could see a clear gravel bottom all the way across. I got a long pole to brace myself, left my pack, shirt and pants on the bank, and waded in in my underclothes. About half way across when the water was up to my armpits the current swept me off my feet in spite of the pole. I dropped the pole and swam back to the bank about a hundred yards below where I had gone in. I knew I had been in the deepest part when I lost my footing, so I got another pole, lashed my pack on the top of my head to give me more weight, and started in. By good luck I made it this time without slipping, but I have often wondered what would have happened if I had fallen in the water with that pack lashed on my head.

"I had two other rivers to cross but they were small and did not give me any trouble, and in four days I reached Porter's Landing on Dease Lake . . . Here I met Mr. Mathison who was in charge of the H. B. supplies. He told me he had a scow load of provisions ready to send down to McDame Creek, but that one of his Indian boatmen had failed him and he asked me if I would go in his place, with wages $3.00 per day and every thing found. I took the job, and the next morning we started off. The scow was an open one, 40 feet long, and eight feet beam, with a load of two tons of provisions, and a crew of three Siwashes, myself, and a little Chinaman for cook. We pulled four sixteen foot oars and had a twenty foot oar on a swivel on a bit of deck both at the bow and at the stern, for steering through the rapids. As we had a good fair wind across the lake I rigged up a mast out of a pair of oars, and made a sail of a tarpaulin, and we made good time scudding before the wind. This tickled the Siwashes, and put me in their good books for the rest of the trip. Going down the river we had an easy time of it as we had very little pulling to do in the strong current. The Siwashes with the big sweeps on the bow and stern, ran the rapids without any difficulty, and we reached McDame Creek in two days. Mr. Emerson was certainly thankful to get his supplies as they were six weeks behind time.

"We stayed at the Post two days and then loaded up the skins Mr. Emerson had ready to send out, and started our return journey. If anyone wants to know what real hard work means let him have a spell of poling and lining a forty-foot scow up a swift current. We could never use the oars, but it was pole and line all the way up. Into the water on the towline twenty times a day, sometimes up to our necks in water, and alway slipping and sliding on the wet boulders. At night we would build a good fire, cook and eat our suppers, and turn in in our wet clothes, and sleep like a log. Up again at daylight and repeat the same routine. We used to eat five times a day and were always ready for the meal. Poling requires every ounce of weight a man has in him, and the quicker he handles his pole the better he can keep his headway in the swift current. Every once in a while one of the Siwashes would yell, 'Porkpine! Porkpine!', and the boat would be shoved into the bank and tied up, the porcupine despatched with a club, and while one man skinned it, another would build a fire and get the pot boiling. As soon as the water boiled the carcase would be dipped in with a handful of salt, left to simmer for a few minutes, dumped out and devoured. I cannot say I relished the almost raw flesh. Now and again we would come to deep holes in the river and in looking over the side we would see sometimes half-a-dozen big lake trout swimming around. Lines would be thrown over the side, the hooks baited with a piece of the white belly of a fish, and sometimes we would hook two or three before the sinkers reached the bottom. As these fish weigh anywhere from ten to thirty pounds you can imagine the excitement when the lines would get tangled in the struggle to land the fish.

"We reached the head of the lake in five days in a flurry of snow, so I decided I had had enough of river boating for one season. I bought a ten pound sack of oatmeal and started to tramp out to Telegraph Creek. The first day I caught up with an old man going out who said he had started ahead of his packtrain but expected them to overtake him that evening. I shared my oatmeal with him that night, and the next day, as no packtrain had appeared, we still had to fall back on the oatmeal. The third day we came to a ranch kept by an old Mexican named Lopez who had been there for 25 years, and he said he would give us a meal for a dollar. He had caught a salmon in the river that morning, and with potatoes and carrots we had a real blowout. They were the first potatoes I had tasted in nine months, and I never enjoyed anything more. In fact I peeled a potato and ate it raw while waiting for the meal to cook. The next day the old man's packtrain caught up to us just as we reached Telegraph Creek."

From there, with various adventure, Kirkendale went down the Stikine to Wrangell and the sea, eventually reaching Victoria early in December, almost a year after he had sailed from there for the North and the Trail of '98. He would never return to the Cassiar, but the memory of it would remain with him always, becoming greener with the slow descent of the years.

The clouds came low that night I spent at McDame, and a cold wind blew. I slept in the screened-in veranda of the trader's house, and it was not without pleasure that I lay there and listened to the roar of the rain on the roof: not for me next morning a sodden camp and the making of porridge in a deluge. Rather would there be breakfast in a warm room with a table to eat off and a real chair to set one's back-end on instead of cowering under the lean-to on a rolled-up eiderdown. And so, with these pleasant thoughts, to sleep. . . .

The morning broke wet and windy and we spent it mostly in talking. The Hopes warned me of several rapids that lay ahead, and it seemed, from the tales they told, that rivering and freighting on the Dease had a pretty lively history behind them. Not wishing to add to the record by any ill-judged frolics of my own, I made a few more notes in my diary under *Sailing Directions,* such as "watch out for big sand-cliff—then run to right of island . . ."

Towards noon the rain eased off and I went up McDame Creek a way—far enough to get some idea of the mining upheaval that had taken place there in the seventies. Most of it seemed to have occurred on the benches on either side of the stream—Dawson says "in an old high-level channel"—and a tremendous upheaval it was: it looked as if platoons of giants had been hurling rocks around. And with the prizes at stake, and in view of the high cost of merely existing at McDame, one can well understand the frenzied work that was put in. Men were not there for their health: all they wanted to do was to make a stake and get out, and every boulder that got in the way must have been attacked as a personal enemy—to say nothing of the streaks of frozen ground. The richest claim in all the Cassiar was on Snow Creek near its outflow into McDame Creek some twenty-odd miles up from the Landing. There, in one week's work, seven men got three hundred ounces of gold. McDame Creek gold fetched about $18 per ounce, so that would make $5,400, or slightly over $770 per man. And just figure out what that would have purchased ninety years ago!

On the way down I looked into the old Hudson's Bay store. It had not long been abandoned by the Company, and a large, open box of books was still there, the post's library awaiting removal. I went on down to the canoe and fished out *The*

Owl's House and one other. The Bay fell heir to these, and in exchange I took a couple: Evelyn Waugh's *Black Mischief* and Norman Douglas' *South Wind:* a bit of luck finding those two here. And in the early afternoon, with the library re-stocked and a good lunch under my belt, I said good-bye to the Hopes and to McDame and slipped away down the Dease.

The clouds were still low. They were the colour of ink and they hid the mountains, and from them, at well-spaced intervals, came the rain. The big sand-cliff hove in sight just where it was supposed to be, and below it was the Stone Island Rapid. Above the island a small, clear creek came into the Dease, and as I floated across the eddy below it, standing up in the canoe to view the rapid, I saw beneath my feet a swarm of trout. That delayed me for a while until four large ones lay on the floor of the canoe—and then, with supper and breakfast in hand, I ran the rapid to the right of the island, as advised by Glenn Hope. It was lucky that I did that fishing by the Stone Island, for the Dease there was breaking out of the Cassiar Mountains and getting into a more level, muskeg type of country: it may have been chance or it may have been lack of local knowledge, but I never got again the wonderful fishing that I had come to regard as a matter of course in the river's upper reaches.

At that stage of the Dease there was nothing to the Stone Island Rapid, though one could see how, at high water, it might be dangerous for a small canoe. Next came Coulihan Canyon, a short narrows between rock walls which, again, could be a problem in flood-time but which I ran with no trouble close to the right-hand wall. The place is so named because on one occasion, when Hyland's boat and the Hudson's Bay boat were racing upstream, an Indian by the name of Coulihan fell off the leading boat (Hyland's) and was swept under it, to be picked up, undamaged, by the Bay boat, which was following.

The inky gloom and the rain of that afternoon effectively

prevented the taking of any pictures on this interesting stretch of the river. But by evening the sun had broken through. The first shaft of yellow light struck the river just as it was making a tremendous detour, running first north-west, straight into the eye of the sun, and then, in a three-mile sweep, turning right back into the south-east to meet, head on, Rapid River, which came in from that direction. There I had intended to camp and fish, but at that point the father and mother of all thunderstorms appeared in the north-east, climbing over the summit of the Horse Ranch Range, which was less than ten miles distant. The mouth of Rapid River was too exposed for a stormy camp: shelter was essential, so I raced on for another mile and found a good camp ground in tall, friendly spruce, off the main river in a snye.

A few more miles the following morning brought me to the stretch of the Dease nearest to the Horse Ranch Range. Almost immediately (as so rarely happens) the perfect camp showed up—on the east bank of the Dease, about three miles from the mountain slope, at the foot of an island and therefore out of the main current. In fact, it was almost into the snye behind the island. It was an old camping place of the rivermen and the ground was clear of underbrush and softly carpeted with spruce needles. The camp was sheltered except from the west, the side that faced the river. A huge old spruce dominated the place; there was a good sleeping place beneath it, and through its thick tangle of branches no rain could penetrate. There was a fireplace of river stones, long unused, between the tree and the landing place. What more could a man want?

I unloaded the canoe and pulled it up on the bank to dry. Later on I laid it, turned over, beneath another spruce, tying it to its tree with the trackline. That, in the last days of August, looked rather absurd, but I had been well taught, twenty years previously, by Albert Faille on the South Nahanni River never to take any chances with a canoe. In two or three days' time I was to be reminded of his teaching.

A good trail ran past this camp, and nearby a trap was set—a Number 3. I sprang it and hung it in a tree where it could easily be seen by its owner; it had probably been lost under the snow and so not picked up in the spring. I wondered if the trap was one of Tom Harvey's, for this was his trapping country. I had last met him twenty-two years back, when he was forest ranger on the upper Red Deer River in Alberta. The ranger station was close to Dick Brown's old L7 Ranch in the high foothills of the Rockies: my God, I thought, what a change from that wide-open, sunlit, bunch-grass country of the forks of the Red Deer and the Panther to this lonely range in the lee of the Cassiar Mountains and so close to the Yukon Territory!

I set up the lean-to so that it would add to the shelter of the big spruce. Then I set to work and made a light ladder and then a cache, a platform about twelve feet above the ground and supported by three trees, so that I could leave my stuff in it in reasonable safety from animals and get up onto the Horse Ranch Range after caribou. It wasn't much of a cache—it didn't need to be for my bit of stuff—but it surely took an age to build; the time taken for anything just then seemed to be at least twice what it should have been, and I see a note for that day: "Arm now exceedingly painful—damn it, may have to give up the trip at the Lower Post." I think the condition was a form of *mal de raquette* (snowshoe sickness), only in the wrist and arm instead of in the foot and leg. It must have been caused by paddling a load all the way down Dease Lake with a too-tight wrist-watch strap bound over an injured wrist under a very hot sun. The only cure that I know for *mal de raquette* is soaking in hot water and rest—and who would waste time here on the Dease doing that? Besides, surely a mountain walk would do it some good?

An end comes to everything, thank God—even to building caches—and I celebrated with a good supper: trout, bacon,

bannock and stewed dried apricots. Then I went north down
the river trail for three miles or so till I came to a strong
creek and a muskeggy bit of country with small, swampy pools
and old river channels. There I disturbed a cow moose and
calf. They swam the Dease; then they climbed out on the far
shore with that deceptive gait of theirs, which looks slow but
isn't, and disappeared into the bush to the westward.

Breakfast next morning was with the first light. Then I
hoisted the outfit into the cache, doused and soaked the camp-
fire, and got going. I had with me grub for a night or two;
the very light, waterproof outer cover and lining of a mountaineer's sleeping bag (but not the bag itself); a light axe,
some long leather thongs, camera, field glass, and the usual
odds and ends. I carried my rifle slung over my left shoulder so
that the butt of it made a rest—in effect a sling—for my left
hand. In my right hand I carried a strong staff of seasoned fir
with a ribbed hand-grip that I had cut and rasped into it the
night before. The day was cloudy but fine and the prospect
pleasing.

I crossed the little creek above camp, followed the river
trail upstream for half a mile, and then turned into the trees
towards the mountain. The idea was to get up to timberline
by way of a long spur of the range that I had observed from
the canoe and, after that, to play it by ear. This worked well
for a time, and my way took me up bench after bench through
pine and poplar bush so dry and open that one could have
ridden a horse through it with ease. Then came a series of
ridges, up and down with muskeg in between them—not so
good. Then the slope became steeper and the small brush
thicker and more tangled. The Dease at camp was a little over
two thousand feet above sea level, and by this time I was
nearly four miles away from the river and over two thousand
feet above it. So this horrid jungle would be what had looked,

from the canoe, like a smooth and verdant lawn. Decidedly one would be better out of it—and I edged over to the left, to a deep coulee, now becoming rock-walled, that held the head-waters of the little creek that ran down to camp. I climbed down into this and followed up the watercourse for some distance, scrambling over boulders and rock ledges. Down in there, at the foot of a waterfall, I boiled the tea-pail and ate some bannock, raisins and cheese. One could see from there far into the south-west—beyond the Dease to a big lake that was full of islands, and beyond the lake again to a dark cleft in the Cassiar Mountains. That cleft, though miles from the present-day river, must once have been a prehistoric channel of the Dease. Through it went the winter trail from the Lower Post to McDame—the "cut-off" that avoided the wind-ings of the river. Through it today goes the road from the Alaska Highway to the Cassiar Asbestos Mine.

Warburton Pike passed over that winter trail in February 1893. He had spent the latter part of January hauling his outfit and canoe with dog-teams up the Liard from the Lower Post and as far up the Frances as he could get towards Frances Lake. He then found it necessary to make a trip back up the Dease to Sylvester's Landing to haul down additional supplies for the coming summer. A great part of the road he took was visible from this lunch-time fire of mine, and some of his comments on it and on the Horse Ranch Range may be of interest here. Pike made that trip in company with two In-dians, Beavertail Johnny and Secatz, and he made it in the coldest days of that winter of seventy-odd years ago. On the second of February it went to sixty-eight degrees below zero at Dease Lake, and in that sort of cold—even at midday, when it has warmed up, perhaps to forty below—danger dogs every movement. Dog-sleds drag heavily in the powder snow, and there may be overflow lurking between the snow and the river ice. Put a foot through into that stuff in the extreme cold and it's a case of hit for the bank and make a fire with all possible speed. It was that condition that had forced Pike to cache his loads for the time being near the mouth of the Frances and to return to the Lower Post. Yet almost immediately he was on the trail again to McDame Creek.

"The usual winter road," he writes, "follows the Dease for thirty miles, and then strikes off to the eastward, passing through an open, grassy country with numerous lakes, and skirting the foot of a high range known as the Horse Ranche Mountains. It is here that the horses used for packing provisions to the outlying mining camps in the summer pass the long winter, scraping away the snow in search of the bunchgrass, usually coming out in good condition in the spring—although once or twice things have gone wrong, and many of the band have been missing when the snow went off. . . . The Horse Ranche Mountains used to be a good place for caribou, but they were so much hunted when meat could be sold for a big price to the McDame Creek miners, that they are now [1893] only to be found here during the spring and autumn migrations . . .

"At the end of the long portage we crossed the Dease again, having cut off its big westerly bend, and immediately dived into the woods on the west side; and, crossing seven or eight lakes that lie in a narrow pass between high mountains, reached the hard-beaten track from the Landing to McDame's Creek mining camp. Another 8 miles took us to the fort. The total distance by the winter trail from the Lower Post to Sylvester's Landing is not more than 75 miles—a great saving on the circuitous course of 110 miles pursued by the Dease . . ." [12]

I went on up the stream bed into the sunny heart of the mountain. Then the cliffs began to close in on either side. Fearing that there might not be a way out at the head, I climbed out of the coulee to the north and then made my way upwards along the rim. Here there was a clear game trail for a while; but then the brush thickened and the deeply incised

game trail turned into it. It was a most devilish jungle—
willow, alder, black birch and every other cursed thing that
could possibly delay a man—nothing had been forgotten. The
growth came just above my head, and it was so thick and
springy that a man, hampered by pack and rifle, could raise
a foot and move it forward and then be unable to set it down.
May I never get into the like of it again! It grew even *in* the
game trail—which, itself, was clearly marked and quite recently used. But no game was using that trail now; that was a
dead certainty. And why not? Was this because the wolves had
murdered off all the moose and all the caribou? Or was it
rather the march of the trees up the mountainsides that is
taking place in so many areas owing to the slow warming-up
of the North during the last hundred years?

I got out of that jungle in the end—out on to clear, open
slopes of gravel and broken rock with a sparse growth of grass
showing on them and the dry seed heads of the summer flowers. Now at last one could see and move freely and the time
had come to make a plan. So I moved over to the edge of the
cliff, heaved the pack off, and sat down.

My idea had been to make a camp as high as possible and
then to devote the next day to hunting; but, to do that, two
things were essential: wood and water. And neither one was
here: there was not even one straggling, stunted fir, while
down below, in the deep cleft of the stream I had been following, no water splashed or sparkled, nor could any sound of it
be heard. There was only the rustle of the north wind in the
grass, and the head of the coulee was a silent, piled-up scree
of shattered rock with the water underground.

That left the mountain ridge ahead of me and the long, open
slope leading up to it as my only road. And the afternoon was
getting on. . . . The Horse Ranch Range is about twenty-five
miles long, running north-west and south-east. I had hit it
well north of the centre. To the south of where I sat the crest
of the range (though I did not know it then) is more rugged

and broken, rising to a high point of 7,300 feet. To the north
the crest is gentler with big, unbroken slopes, and does not
rise much over 6,500 feet. I had contrived, by pure chance, to
hit the main ridge almost at the boundary of the two zones.
Isolated as it is from other mountains, the Horse Ranch would
be a fascinating range to explore; and no doubt, if one did
that, one would find several good high camps. But, blundering along like this, from hand to mouth as it were, the best
I could hope to do was to make a sensible guess.

It seemed to me, remembering the Rockies, that the strong
south-west winds, sweeping over these treeless slopes, must
drift a tremendous amount of snow over the crest on to the
north-east side of the range. There, sheltered from the afternoon sun, the snow would be in huge drifts, lasting well
into summer, letting out its water slowly. So there should be
more water on the north-east slope; and where water was,
and shelter, there should be trees. Therefore (since I was sure
that this was sound reasoning), my next move would be over
the top and down to the comfortable camp that I could already fondly see in my imagination: tarpaulin set up, fire
burning brightly, tea-pail boiling. . . . It was nice to have it all
settled. The gift of prophecy is a wonderful thing.

I finished off a square of chocolate and a handful of raisins
and took one last look south along the range with the glass
before starting to climb. Something light-coloured was moving just above timberline and about two miles away—beyond
the next coulee after the one at my feet. It was a peculiar
shape, and sometimes a shaft of sunlight would catch it—and
then again it would be almost lost in deep cloud shadow. It
was hard to make out what it was. And then, suddenly, a
small moving object detached itself from the main body—to
caper uphill and back again. Then I saw: it was a grizzly bear
with her cub. I watched them for a while. They might well
have been much closer before I saw them; they had probably
winded me and so been disturbed. And now they were head-

ing south. I earnestly hoped they would keep that idea in
mind and stay with it.

The crest of the ridge was narrow where I crossed it and far
rougher than I had expected. And now—where were all the
trees that should have greeted me? And the flowing streams?
Something somewhere had gone sadly wrong with the arrangements I had made.

The north-east side was wild and barren: slopes of tumbled
rock, stretches of grass, no trees. Far below lay three little
lakes, no more than mountain tarns: in all that vast emptiness
and in the evening light they stood out like three blue staring
eyes. But the first had no trees and the second had no trees;
only the largest and lowest seemed to have a fringe of dwarf
firs on its eastern side. And that was the one I had to get down
to; it meant dropping about two thousand feet from the ridge
and climbing it all again on the morrow. And as I looked I
picked out a way: round the head of this cirque below me,
then down over the rocks and the open grass slopes and out
on that spur to the lake. A pity to lose all that height, but that
was the only camp to be seen. So much for the mantle of the
prophets! And I sat down and pulled out the glass to see what
I could see.

In the south-west, across the shining loops of the Dease,
lay the lake of islands, a sheet of glowing copper beneath a
wandering shaft of sunlight. Beyond it and far into the south
the view was closed by the dark wall of the Cassiar Mountains.
There was no view to the south-east—it was blocked by the
nearest summit of the Horse Ranch Range—but elsewhere,
all around from the north-west into the east, lay the blue
immensity of the Liard plain, shadowy and unshapen, fading
with no horizon into the dim half-light of the cloud-dappled
evening sky. Only in the far north was there any break in
this pattern of green and dark blue. There a bank of grey
cloud seemed to hang motionless between earth and sky, and
from it there came, whispering among the crevices of the

rocks, the same small, cold north wind. That wind was steady and persistent; and as for the line of cloud—I had seen that often enough in the southern Rockies, and never had it been the sign of anything but storm.

In the foreground, in the immediate north, one shaft of yellow light moved slowly, like the beam of a searchlight, across the range. I followed it idly with the glass, and as it passed over a high spur three distant objects which before had been unnoticed sprang to sudden life: three bull caribou. For less than a minute the sunlight gave them form and shadows: I could see distinctly the whitish bands of neck and shoulders and what appeared to be three splendid sets of horns. Then the light moved on and the caribou became once more a part of their background. Knowing where they were, one could just see them still—but only just. They were surely easy to overlook.

These would be Osborn's caribou: they were larger than the ones I had seen years before in the Mackenzie Mountains, which now seemed to me to be a halfway house between these and the Barren Lands caribou. So George Ball was right and there *were* caribou here. Elated, I started down towards the lake and camp. Now if that grey line of cloud would just stay where it was for a day or two (as I had often seen it do in the Alberta Rockies) all would be well. . . .

Camp after a long day's scramble always looks like home. It looked more so than usual that night as I walked along the shore towards it after supper, carrying an armful of dead fir. The lean-to was set well into a clump of green firs and the branches I had cut now made my bed. The lakelet was no more than three hundred yards across and the fire, which was burning cheerfully, flung a pathway of rippling flame across the water. A star or two shone through the clouds and one could feel, rather than see, the rim of the basin high above. And the north wind still rustled gently through the grass and the little trees. That was as it should be—a steady wind. And tomorrow the caribou!

Darkness blanketed the basin when I woke, and there were no stars. I reached out from under the lean-to with a handful of kindling and set the fire in a blaze. Then I wriggled out of the sleeping-bag contraption, which, minus its eiderdown portion, was little more than a windbreak. There was no need to dress: I was dressed already—everything I had with me was on, including a faithful old Balaclava helmet of heavy wool, veteran of many a cold camp and stormy day. The north wind, I was glad to see, was as steady as ever: the ripples on the lake still passed from right to left in front of camp, and the smoke was headed south. That was well, for the caribou were to the north.

I concentrated on breakfast. I made tea and grilled two or three slices of bacon—but the main thing was the porridge. I made a big cooking of it, and the prescription is as follows: to a fifty-fifty mixture of cracked wheat and large, unbroken rolled oats add what butter can be spared and a handful of raisins. Simmer this in the frying pan in which the bacon was cooked, and when ready serve in the pan, red hot. (You have no plate with you, anyway.) Lay on top of the porridge a large pat of butter and a slice of cheese—and don't skimp on the cheese. Sprinkle the whole as liberally as circumstances permit with brown sugar. Then eat. And when you have that concoction under your belt, you've got something. Cold days become soft and balmy and mountain slopes as little hills. That is, after the first mile or so they become as little hills. A bit windy, sometimes, that first mile. With the exception of good pemmican, Indian-made,* that brew is the handiest, quickest form of dynamite that I know of when it comes to

* One can no longer get that today, and the stuff purveyed commercially in cans, and miscalled pemmican, bears no resemblance to the real thing.

propelling a man over the trail. It can be quickly made, it gives instant warmth and energy, and it can be eaten even when one is exhausted. I gave that recipe once, in gratitude for hospitality shown to me, to the R.C.M.P. at Fort Simpson, N.W.T. They adopted it down there on the Mackenzie, and they called it "Patterson's Porridge," and I heard that the police indent for raisins and cheese rose considerably. How long the tradition lasted I do not know.

Slowly and reluctantly, as I packed up camp, a grey, dirty dawn appeared. Then I saw what the trouble was—why it had stayed dark so long: the clouds were down on the Horse Ranch Range. They were not coming down into the basin, but they lay level with the tops of the cliffs; and every now and then the grey mist would come tumbling down over the rim like a drift of spray from a waterfall, only to be flung back up again by some warmer air from below. That would be the grey line of cloud that only last night had seemed so far away— perhaps beyond the Liard. Borne on that north wind, it would be unlikely to clear as summer mist would do, beneath the heat of the sun. Still one could always hope, and in any case it was no use waiting here. And I doused the fire and started to climb. . . .

Where I crossed the hump of the range I never knew; but, judging from what followed, it was probably rather to the north of where I had crossed it the evening before. I had no compass with me, so all I could do was to keep the wind on my right cheek and walk blindly on. Sometimes the mist would thin a little and one might think it was going to clear. And then another wall of it would roll along out of the north, blotting out everything so that one could hardly see two paces ahead. The furthest that could be seen was twenty yards, and at the worst it was unsafe even to walk fast for fear of taking a header over a cliff. Of all the useless days to try to hunt any- thing! And as for that grizzly and cub—had they been in the country, nothing would have been easier than to walk right on top of them.

Something large and dark loomed up. It was a rock, having a little overhang on the south side and a dry space scuffed out there with old droppings in it and a few strands of fine, creamy wool among the stones. So there were goat on the Horse Ranch Range—and I settled myself into the hollow they had made in the lee of the big rock. I would give it an hour and see if, perhaps, the mist would clear. . . .

But the luck was out, and the only change was that it seemed to get colder. And after I had sat there for nearly an hour, nibbling at a square of chocolate and getting slowly colder myself, a snowflake came spinning and twisting into the eddy behind the rock. And then another and another, till the misty air was full of them. This was getting serious. If the wind switched, with this snow, into the north-west or the west, I could mill around here for hours and then, perhaps, end by getting down on the wrong side of the range. As for the caribou hunt—that was hopeless. The smother on the mountain was at times as thick as a London fog, and the only thing to do now was to get down out of it and hit for camp by the Dease.

I set off downhill, going slowly. It then occurred to me that I could swing left and intersect the coulee of the creek that flowed down to camp, and then follow that down more or less the way I had come up. So I turned half left and went down across the slope, keeping the wind behind my right ear. That got me nowhere: either I had turned too soon, before I was far enough down, or else I had been already to the left of the coulee when I turned. There was also a third possibility, and that was that I had crossed the divide much further north than I had intended. So I decided to let coulees and landmarks go to the devil and just head straight down.

That very soon brought me up with a jerk on the edge of a cliff. I looked over, but the bottom of the cliff was hidden in the mist; it looked most unpleasant, with the black, snow-streaked rock vanishing into nothing in particular; and, any-way, it was sheer. So I followed the edge to the left—which I think was to the south—till I had below me a smaller cliff with an easy way down. That was all right as far as it went; but what, I wondered, came below it? There was nothing to be seen but a scree of broken rock sloping down at a steep angle into the mist. And what did that lead to? The edge of another cliff and a slide over it to perdition in a cascade of tumbling stones? And while I crouched on the edge, trying to figure it out, the snow was getting wetter and heavier. Nothing was getting any easier, and the longer one hesitated, the worse it got. So down I went, carefully, hand and foot—and then on down the scree, hoping for the best. And there was no other cliff, and the scree turned to grass and the jungle came up to meet me, dripping with wet snow from every twig. I rammed my way down through that, and the snow changed to sleet and the sleet to a cold rain. . . .

Somewhere on that horrible trek I got into a level stretch of old forest, sodden with rain and with wisps of grey moss dangling from the branches like old men's beards. No moun-tain, no landmark of any kind could be seen, but now and then the north wind (at least I hoped it was still the north wind) would come snuffling through the ancient trees, tweak-ing their beards for them as it passed by. That gave me my west and I went on, lining up tree after tree, through swamps and down benches—on and on for ages and rain-sodden ages till I came to the bank of a river that flowed from left to right. And that was the Dease, and close by it was the river trail.

I stared at the river, hunting vainly for some feature I could recognize. If this was upstream from camp, then I must have seen it before, from the canoe. If it was far downstream from camp, it would be new to me. But the Dease gave no sign: it just looked like a thousand other northern rivers, and if somebody had come along and told me it was the Turnagain or the Hyland I couldn't have argued with him. Finally, balancing up the probabilities, I turned to the right—downstream.

I must have been a long way off course to the south, for it was almost another hour before I slopped across the creek and into camp. Off went pack and Mannlicher under the dry old spruce, and I got out from among the branches the kindling I had cached there and set it in the fireplace. But my fingers would not hold and strike a match; I was soaked through with snow and ice-cold rain and my hands were numbed. So I swung my arms furiously till the life came back into my fingers and the flames leapt up at my touch—oh, what a blessed sight! Then the stuff from the cache and a great scalding mug of Ovaltine, and dry clothes, and potatoes boiling for supper—and that was the end of round one with the Horse Ranch Range.

The morning came grey and cheerless. A thin rain was falling and there was a flake or two of snow in it. Clouds lay low on the mountains, covering even the green jungle of black birch and alder at timberline. Up on the caribou range there would be snow and zero visibility, and down here the Dease was rising. I chored around camp, finished drying yesterday's wet rags, baked bannock, cut wood and stacked it by the fire, and wrote up my diary.

Towards midday an Indian family passed by: a young man, an older man, children, dogs carrying packs, and one led packhorse. There were no women visible. If any were there (as was probable), they had slipped past in the bush, unseen by me. The older man, I thought as I looked at him, might well have been the model for any one of the pictures of the Mongol horsemen who once conquered the known world. These people all looked healthy and well and they spoke good English. They were going up into the Horse Ranch Range to hunt; there were caribou and goat up there, they said, but no sheep. The young man added that about four miles south on the river trail a good packhorse trail turned off to the eastward and ran right up the mountain—and no doubt, I thought, to a good high camp. Just one more example, I told myself, of the way in which a stranger to a bit of hunting country can waste his time fighting his way through the bush when, only a few miles away, there exists a perfectly good trail.

The Indians went on and I had lunch. Then the day, poor to begin with, went completely to pieces. A cold rain fell steadily and the north wind roared in the tree tops, driving a series of snow squalls up the river. In this sheltered hollow, walled around by protecting trees, and with the shelter of the big spruce and the lean-to, I was warm and snug. I just sat there and read *Black Mischief* and laughed and occasionally fed the fire. After a late supper I read on by the firelight, having set aside for that purpose some dry spruce branches that could be counted on to burn with a bright flame. The afternoon and evening were enlivened by occasional bangs from the heart of the fire, accompanied by whining, humming sounds as small projectiles flew through the air. Somebody had evidently once upset a box of .22 cartridges here—"longs." Several years of spruce needles had buried them and no fire had burned here since then. Now, as my fire reached down to them, one by one they were exploding. Several bullets fell in the river; others hummed past me on either side. But there were no casualties, nor did the fusillade interfere with my enjoyment of *Black Mischief*. Even as I was dropping off to sleep the bangs still continued, and the snow squalls still came roaring up the Dease.

By morning the river had risen three feet and was lapping at my upturned canoe. With Albert Faille in mind I carried the canoe to higher ground and tied it to another tree. As for the day, it promised well. River and mountains were invisible, hidden in dense mist, but the north wind had dropped and one could feel that the sun was trying to break through. Sure enough, in an hour or two, the mist rolled away on a puff of south-west wind, the sun blazed down, and the mountain range stood revealed, clear and sharp in the rain-washed air. The timberline country was snow-covered, but much of that snow would be gone by evening, leaving enough on top so that even I could pick up any tracks with ease. Conditions were ideal. Now for those caribou—if they were still there . . .

I took my time over breaking camp so as to let the bush dry up a bit. Then once again I took a two-night camp with me, slung the outfit into the cache, and hit for the mountain. The camp I planned to make was on the south side of the creek coulee and high up. It would be in the shelter of some big old forest trees close to a small, trickling spring; and from there, staying on the south side of the coulee, the way up to the open country through the scrub jungle might not be so bad. Anyway, it was worth trying: it would give me one whole day on top, and if I got anything I could stay up there for two nights.

All went as planned. I found the camping place, dumped my load there, and went on with my rifle to pioneer a better way through the jungle. That went well, too, and I got up to the summit of the range, keeping well to the south of my first crossing place on account of the south-west wind. From there I searched the range to the north-west with my glass, but I could see no sign of the caribou. That meant little, however, for there were so many small depressions and low cliffs that could easily hide them. The only thing to do would be to go and see on the morrow.

Camp in that grove of old and bearded trees was an eerie sort of place. The south-west wind, the most cheerful of all the winds, had dropped and a dead silence reigned except for the trickle of the little spring. The fire burned on a patch of gravel in the watercourse, and the heat of it rose straight up and set the beards of moss quivering and shaking, as if a bunch of wise old men were deep in argument up there. I read a few pages of *South Wind* by the light of the fire. Then I

put on another log for company's sake and dropped off to
sleep on a bed of deep moss, leaving my old greybeards to
pursue their ghostly discourse beneath a pale aurora and
the glittering stars. . . .

Climbing in the first faint light by the south wall of the
coulee, I noticed that the waterfall was frozen. Frost whitened
the jungle of black birch and light cloud veiled the open
country above timberline. The wind was shifty, veering from
north-west to north and back again. I climbed easily, having
only my rifle to carry. I had left my packsack at camp, slung
from a branch of the old fir under which I had slept, with
everything packed away in it. So in case the clouds thickened,
and to help in finding that group of old trees again, I built,
at the very head of the coulee, a cairn of stones. Into it I
worked a six-foot stick that I had brought up with me, and
to the stick I tied an old red handkerchief. As a landmark on
that barren upland it looked quite impressive. You couldn't
call it foolproof by any means, but it did give an added
chance, in a light mist, of finding the right place to go down.
And even in heavy fog like the first day one might stumble
on to it.

I turned north and angled slowly up to the crest. There
was no visibility to speak of: over the rocks and the sparse
yellow grass the clouds came scudding, now thick and woolly,
now thin, but never letting the sun break through, though
soon one could feel the warmth of it. All one could do was
to keep going on through this pearl-grey mist, in which rocks
took on the shapes of animals and animals, one could be certain, would look just like rocks. As the sun climbed higher,
things loomed up in a vague radiance that was almost a halo,
only to vanish again and give place to some other mysterious
feature—a low, dark wall of outcrop or a level plain of snow,
trackless and already softening in the warmth of the morning.
Over all lay the feeling of loneliness and isolation that strange
country shrouded in mist alone can bring. One moves, as

though in a transparent sphere of mother-of-pearl, towards a yielding curtain of silver-grey that is always just ahead, yet ever in retreat, unattainable like the rainbow's end.

Only by keeping track of time was it possible to guess whereabouts one might be on the Horse Ranch Range, and I must have come about seven pretty rough miles almost due north from camp when I first saw the tracks. Four big animals had come up the slope from the south-west, walked across a patch of fine gravel, and entered a wide expanse of snow. The tracks were very fresh. Where they first hit the shallow, melting snow they were absolutely distinct: the two crescent-shaped marks of a caribou's hoof with the dew claws showing behind. They were also very large: four bulls, I thought they might be. This was early September, still not too late for them to be alone and apart from the cows. My knowledge of Osborn's caribou was book knowledge, and I was now doing my desperate best to recall what I had read from Bryan Williams and other authorities.

Caribou, Bryan Williams had written, were great travellers, so these might be the three I had seen the other day, together with one more that had been hidden from me, or they might be another bunch entirely. They were also very curious and would approach an unusual object; and, above all, they had a keen sense of smell. That being so, it was no use following them straight down wind; so I turned off to the right, planning to make a long detour and then to swing back and intersect the tracks again. I did that, and for a long time I saw nothing at all. That puzzled me, for it was now possible to steer by the vague glow of the sun through the mist, and I began to wonder if I had miscalculated. However, the circle was correctly made, and when next I cut into the tracks they were heading straight north. That was better; and for half an hour I followed them, over patches of gravel and patches of snow, till I lost them on some rocky ground.

I went forward over that as quietly as possible and into a

thick patch of cloud towards some rocks. Suddenly the rocks appeared to move: where there had been two, now there were four. The clicking sound of feet came to me, and a questioning, challenging snort. I stood stock-still for perhaps thirty seconds, peering through the mist. The vague outlines of shadowy, wide-branching horns looked gigantic; but it was impossible to *see*, impossible to distinguish a good head from just an average one. I took a careful step forward, and the movement scared the caribou and they ran—but only for a short distance, for then they wheeled and stood in line, watching, just as a bunch of cattle would do. They were further off now, but no less and no more distinct than at first, for, momentarily, the mist had thinned. Then it began to close in once more, but before they could vanish completely I tried a trick that I had read of somewhere: I put my hat on the muzzle of the Mannlicher, raised it slowly and evenly above my head, and began to move it from side to side. That, to a caribou, may convey the impression of a rival bull; anyway, helped by the mist, it worked and the four bulls came closer, step by step.

Slowly they became more distinct, and it became clear that one head of the four (and *not* that of the largest animal) was far larger than the other three. The bull that owned it was coming up half-hidden by a larger bull—just, of course, what he would do—and my heart began to beat like a hammer with excitement. This was far more exciting than any stalk and—but then, in one disastrous second, everything happened.

The caribou were less than fifty yards away and reasonably visible. I began slowly to lower the rifle (which still had my hat on it) hand over hand. Simultaneously there came a vagrant, malicious puff of south wind. It cleared the thinning mist even as it took my scent to the animals, and for a fraction of a second they stood revealed: three heads that anybody might have been pleased to own, and the outstanding one that I had set my heart on. As they wheeled to run the beast with the big head remained sheltered by the other three, only the splendid antlers showing—and then a bank of cloud rolled over them and they vanished into it and the sharp click of their feet died away with their going.[13] Slowly I lowered the half-raised rifle and reached down to pick up my hat.

That moment of the wheeling caribou is something I shall never forget. It was perfect and it was complete: out of the mist they came in their strength and their splendour, unveiled by the south wind—only to vanish again, enfolded in the clouds, gone like the sudden ending of a broken dream. Nor have I ever been sorry that I didn't shoot. I didn't need the meat and, having once set eyes on that splendid set of horns, there would have been no satisfaction in trying for the second best. And as for the hat trick—that was a useful bit of knowledge acquired and stored away. I worked that one again three years later in the North-west Territories. A bull caribou stood quite close to us, on the crest of a rock ridge, silhouetted against the evening sky. He was on the point of flight, but at the same time he was curious. My companion was fumbling madly with his camera and beseeching me to perform a miracle for him. "Oh God," he was muttering, "please let me get this damned camera out! Ray, hold that beast there till I get its picture! *Do* something, can't you? Don't just stand there . . ."

I made big medicine for him. I didn't bring the Mannlicher into play that time, but slowly, and "in a very gentlemanly way," I took my hat off with my right hand and raised it in salute above my head. That did the trick. The caribou gave no further signs of restlessness: he stayed on his ridge, fascinated, regarding us with great interest; and my friend had plenty of time to get not just one treasured picture of him but two. Not till we moved on did that caribou depart.

I followed the caribou tracks for a way, but very soon they dipped down on the north-east slope of the range, where, in the thickening cloud, I had no intention of following them.

Instead, I turned back and headed for the south-west slope. The fog was dense over the crest, thinning a little when I reached the far side. Then for three hours or so I travelled south-east, keeping the dim glow of the sun on my right hand. When I thought, from the time taken, that I might be coming near to the cairn I began to go slowly, stopping every time the mist thinned a little and looking back. It was during one of these halts that I thankfully saw, well behind me and barely visible, the brave little red flag fluttering in the breeze. I had passed it by when it was hidden; and had it not been for that slight thinning of the mist when I looked back, what a hell of a night *that* would have been: traversing up and down the Horse Ranch Range in the clouds with the light failing, hunting for a pile of rocks, a flagpole of alder, and an old red handkerchief.

Even so it was very late when I came into camp by the Dease and lit the fire. Everything was in order, and once more the place looked just like home.

Two days' travel from that good camp by the Horse Ranch Range saw me down to the Liard. Two islands lie just off the mouth of the Dease: one upstream and one downstream, and both out into the strong current of the Liard. I made camp on the upstream island, facing south-west on to the snye—the small channel of the Liard that cuts through behind the island to meet the last few yards of the Dease. There one could camp in peace, sheltered and hidden by the trees, separated by the Liard from the old buildings of the Lower Post, from wandering dogs and curious Indian children. As for the modern Lower Post of the Alaska Highway—that was well out of sight and sound. The Highway here ran almost a quarter of a mile back from the Liard, and the life of the place, except for some Indian cabins and gardens and the old Hudson's Bay Company buildings, had abandoned the old highway of the river for the modern road.

That suited me perfectly. And the camp was a good one. It was sheltered from the north-east by the woods of the island; the clear water of the Liard ran past it, rippling through the snye; and the late-afternoon sunshine came pouring down on the lean-to and the cooking fire, warming the sand and the river stones. There was not a cloud in the sky. Could it be that the weather, after all its vagaries of the past couple of weeks, had decided to mend its ways?

All the small hazards of the river had been repeated in those last two days of travel down the Dease: sweepers, drift-piles and shallow riffles. Then there had been long stretches of quiet, slack water with flights of Canada geese coming low over the canoe, patterned in V's against an inky sky that made noonday into twilight and the taking of photographs useless.

In the early morning of that first day the Horse Ranch Range lay blanketed in heavy cloud. But as I drew further away from it the clouds slowly lifted, and for a little while the sun shone. I beached the canoe and got out the glass for a farewell look. . . . And a simpler-looking range of mountains, I thought, it would be hard to find. In fact, the whole thing— or, at least, all that I could see of it from down river—looked like a long, low hill, one that would present no obstacles or hazards to the hunter: just a perfect picnic if ever there was one. Who would ever imagine that there were lakes concealed up there—and rock-walled amphitheatres and dangerous cliffs? And a view that seemed to reach beyond the confines of the known world—and caribou with wide-branching, majestic horns?

A mile or so above the mouth of Blue River (the "Caribou River" of Robert Campbell) Dawson had marked a rapid on a bend of the Dease. The last rapid marked on his map had been at the Cottonwood River, so I approached this next one with caution. But there was nothing to it at the September stage of water, whatever it might be in flood-time. I ran it on the right side, and I see in my diary the contemptuous remark: "Just a hill of lumpy water." I made camp soon afterwards, somewhere below Blue River; and it was there, while climbing a small hill after supper, that I came across a tall, four-inch, white poplar, covered with the marks of bears' claws, bent over in a great hoop and with its head resting on the ground. Around and about lay the wreckage of a wasps' nest the size of a Rugby football. It must have been a small bear, for the tree was not overlarge. I should like to have seen that bear up that poplar, hanging on for dear life and swinging in the top of it till he loosened the roots and bent the tree down. It was a recent effort: had the performance, I wondered, taken place on that afternoon of the snow squalls when the wasps would all have been at home and torpid with the cold?

There are no contemptuous remarks in the diary about the last two rapids of the Dease, the Fourmile and the Twomile— so named from their distance from the Liard. Dawson marks both of them on his map as "Strong Rapids"; and if Dawson, who had seen and run so much wild water, says that of a rapid, it is as well to approach it warily. And that is not the only warning of danger. About a mile above the upper rapid (the Fourmile) and on the left bank of the Dease, Dawson marks on his map "Sylvester's Cache." At that point Sylvester, if he was running an outfit down the Dease in the fall and found the water in the last two rapids to be at a dangerously low stage, could land the stuff and cache it in safety, returning to Sylvester's Landing (which today is McDame) without ever taking his boats or scows down to the Liard. Later in the year, after freeze-up, it would then be an easy matter for the post manager at the Lower Post to send teams and sleighs across the frozen Liard and up to the cache to bring the trade goods home—a simple haul of five miles or so through the bush. Or, if the outfit was urgently needed, it could be brought down to the Liard on packhorses and ferried across.

Dawson ran these rapids on June 23, 1887, and he describes them as "strong rapids, which at certain stages of water are reported to be dangerous, and in which all our boats shipped more or less water."

Warburton Pike had a bit of trouble at the Fourmile. "Near the mouth of the Dease," he writes, "are two rapids, each with a clear open channel, but a heavy sea which cannot be avoided; and if the canoe is at all heavily loaded, it is advisable to portage part of the cargo, especially in the second rapid. A short way above the upper rapid we met a boat-load of prospectors who were coming out after an unsuccessful summer's cruise. Among them was Henry Thibert, who gave us an interesting account of his three years' expedition with McCulloch from Minnesota to Dease Lake, in the course of which they made the first discovery of gold on the Arctic Slope. After we had done yarning we inquired about the rapid below, and were told it was good and that we should have no difficulty in running it on the right side. So, without landing to pick out a course, I ran my canoe into the right hand channel and found that we had entered a shallow rapid with a strong current, absolutely choked with boulders and no room for the canoe to pass. We bumped two or three times at the upper end, but luckily the crash did not come till we had nearly reached the foot of the bad water. Then a sharp stone tore a hole in the thin planking, the water rose over the bottom boards immediately, and only a hasty landing and discharge of cargo prevented a serious catastrophe. After we had effected repairs I took a look at the rapid, and I found a straight, deep channel on the left side, through which we could have run with perfect ease if we had not taken the precaution to ask the way beforehand. We took the next rapid cautiously enough, and early on the morning of September 1st reached the Lower Post, a most unpretentious establishment situated on the far side of the Liard, half a mile above the mouth of the Dease. A small store, a log hut for the man in charge and a few rough buildings belonging to the Indians make up the last outpost of civilisation in this direction." [14]

That was in 1892. I came to the head of the Fourmile about noon on September 4—fifty-six years later in time and three days later in the season than Pike. Reefs of schist cross the Dease at these last rapids, and the water above the Fourmile is, in consequence, damned back into a sort of eddying lagoon with high, sandy beaches. On one of these I landed to make tea and have lunch, the idea being that, if I should happen to upset the canoe in the Fourmile, it would be nice to have a good meal inside me to get ashore with. There was a bend in the river where I had landed, and from where I sat one could look straight downstream. But that didn't help very much: all that could be seen was the calm water of the lagoon and then a line of white where the river dipped over the first of the reefs and vanished from view downhill. I could see nothing of the rapid itself, owing to the sudden drop down the slope; a steady roar of water could be heard and irregular spouts of foam and spray kept shooting into view above the creaming line of the reef. And that was all. The longer I looked and listened, the less I liked it: it was the sort of place where one should definitely walk ahead and look—precisely what I felt most disinclined to do on a hot, sunny day and after a good lunch.

I had the details of Pike's performance written into the front of my diary. Thibert had told Pike to run the rapid on the right, and Pike had done that and made a mess of it. Pike had then looked things over and decided he would have done better on the left, or west, side. From where I sat that didn't look too good either—not for a small canoe. There were spouts of spray rising and falling, as much uproar as anywhere else, and there was also a sheer cliff, so that in the event of a wreck it would be impossible to get to land. The right-hand bank was densely wooded but low . . . Suddenly I knew what I would do: I would run it as Pike had run it—close to the right bank. It might be that, after all this rain, I had more water than he had and, anyway, I could probably turn my fourteen-foot canoe, even overloaded as it was, more easily than he could turn his eighteen-footer. And that canoe of Pike's weighed a hundred and thirty pounds against the sixty pounds of mine.

There is something beautifully final in approaching, over calm water, the rim of a rapid that one has never seen—all decisions made, everything snugged down, jammed in, strapped on and tarped up. There is a feeling of peace, perfect peace, of complete relaxation now that the moment has come. One is committed and there is no turning back and all un-certainty is gone. Two or three frantic minutes and the canoe will either be safe in the eddy at the foot of the rapid or else jammed under a sweeper halfway down or bumping along the bottom with a hole in it and a sodden load doing its best to fall out.

The line of the reef was coming closer. The canoe was quickening a little; then it slid over the drop into a welter of white. . . . I have no detailed recollection of running that rapid—only of the bank flashing past, of avoiding rocks and urging the canoe by word of mouth to do its damnedest—and of one rock that came upstream at me like a killer whale. With a heave and a twist of the paddle I missed it, but only just; and I can hear now the long, caressing scrape of it as it hissed along the side of the canoe, scoring the canvas. Then came the reassuring slap of the big waves, and the pace slack-ened and the canoe rode gently into the quiet waters of the eddy. Victory—and I owed it to Henry Thibert, that far-travelled man who found the gold on Thibert's Creek up at Dease Lake in 1873.

The next rapid, the Twomile, was an entirely different proposition. I landed just above it on the left shore of the river and walked ahead to have a look. Here the Dease, run-ning almost due north-east, comes slap up against a cliff and tumbles over a reef. Where the riverboats take the rapid I am not certain. My affair being with a small, rather overloaded canoe, it seemed to me that the best place was a gap in the reef close under the cliff. There was quite a drop there, but the way looked clear; that is, it looked clear enough (which is not quite the same thing) so that I did not bother to climb up the cliff and make certain. Had I done so I would have seen that, beneath the little fall and plumb in the fairway, a stray rock or a fang of the reef was lying in wait. But from the shore all that could be seen were two very powerful eddies, almost whirlpools, just below the drop, having a very narrow pathway of smooth, fast water running between them. That was the trail the canoe would have to take.

I rammed the canoe at the gap in the reef at full speed. It leapt over the drop in splendid style—and just as it did so I caught sight, down through the clear water, of what lay waiting for it. Then the tail of the canoe, just beneath where I was half sitting, half kneeling, came over the fall and landed plunk on a point of the rock, and I could feel the stout cedar planking give as it took the shock. There was a protesting scrunch of splintering wood—but the canoe was immediately flung up again by the water and it raced on its way, only lightly damaged,* straight down the narrow tongue of current between the two whirlpools. And that was all there was to it; the remainder of the Twomile was straightforward and simple.

Years afterwards I was talking with Harper Reed about this spot, and he told me how he once had a bit of trouble there. At the time when he got into this particular jackpot he was Indian Agent for the whole of the vast area of the Cassiar, plus the Yukon as far north as Frances Lake and Campbell's Portage, and his headquarters were at Telegraph Creek. The time of the year must have been early September, for he was travelling up the Dease with a cargo of Indian children, taking them

---

* The canoe was close-ribbed—which means that the wood could splinter and crack from a blow but the damage would not necessarily spread and, if the canvas was not holed, the water still could not come in.

back to school. The weather was perfect, a capable and intelligent Indian was running the kicker, and Reed was in the bow with a big paddle handy, ready for action and signalling the course and the speed to the Indian. And, from the children's point of view, what could be better than a two-hundred-mile trip by river and lake to Dease Lake Landing, followed by seventy-four miles in the white man's skunk-wagon over the portage trail to school at Telegraph Creek on the Stikine?

All was going merry as a marriage bell and Reed signalled to the Indian, now with his right hand, now with his left, till he got the nose of the boat laid exactly at the gap in the reef through which I came with the canoe. Then, with both hands, he gave the signal for full speed ahead. The response was immediate action, but not precisely the kind of action Reed desired.

They were using an old model of kicker, having a grip-control with which it was not too difficult to go, without warning, straight from a forward speed into reverse. Add to this the fact that the boat was poised in a narrow channel of current with, on either hand, a powerful, whirling eddy—and you will readily understand that the Indian was keyed up and tense and watching every move on the part of Harper Reed. He had, however, forgotten, in the excitement of starting out, to see to one routine, though very important, chore: he had not made certain that the kicker was firmly clamped onto the transom of the boat.

When, therefore, the signal came, and the Indian, flustered in his over-eagerness, shot the kicker straight into reverse from a forward speed, that long-suffering piece of machinery not unnaturally rebelled: it did its best to execute a somersault and, failing in that, tore loose from the transom and plunged into the deep water below the reef, to be seen no more by men. That left Reed in charge, at the bow end, with the big paddle. Somehow he got the outfit clear of the big eddies and down to a place where he could get ashore and climb up the cliff. Having seen to the safety of the boat and its occupants, he scrambled up and then cut through the bush to Sylvester's old portage trail from his cache to the Lower Post. That brought him in short order to the bank of the Liard—and fortunately, in those days, the Alaska Highway was still only a dream of the future and the Lower Post had not yet turned its back on the river. Reed managed to attract the attention of the Hudson's Bay Company's post manager across the water, and the latter promptly came to the rescue. He ferried Reed across, lent him a spare kicker, and then conveyed him up the Dease to where the castaways were waiting, more or less patiently, under the cliff. Soon the Indian Agent's boat was on its way again, carrying its lively cargo towards Dease Lake and the portage road to school by the far-away Stikine.

It was safe, by that time, for those Indian children to go nearly three hundred miles through the wilds of the Cassiar, all the way from the Liard to Telegraph Creek. Yet only some forty years previously there had been Indian trouble at the Lower Post—in the early summer of 1888, the year after Dawson and McConnell passed through. Those two arrived there from Dease Lake on June 23, 1887, and Dawson writes of their welcome: "Mr. Egnell, in sole charge, received us on our arrival here with all distinction possible, displaying his Union Jack and firing a salute from his fowling piece. Before leaving we were indebted to him for many other courtesies . . ." This was the same Egnell whom Rufus Sylvester had placed in charge when he founded the post in 1876.* In 1888 he had, as his assistant, Herbert Hankin, nephew of the Philip Hankin who had been a superintendent of the Vancouver Island Colonial Police in the days before the Island became a part of the province of British Columbia. . . .

It was evening at the Lower Post, the end of a long day's trafficking with the Indians. The two men were tired and Hankin was preparing supper—cooking some beaver meat that

* See page 169.

an Indian had brought in—while Egnell checked and piled the pelts of the day's trade. The Indians who traded at the Lower Post were Cascas and Tahltans—good hunters and peaceable, and well disposed towards the white traders: it was they who gave the alarm. Egnell and Hankin heard running feet and a hammering on their door—and a girl's voice with a note of fear in it calling out: "Takus on warpath. Come down Rancheria River. All Cascas going away." Then the girl fled and there was a barking of dogs, and then all was quiet again.

This was the old enmity, dormant for years but now breaking out afresh, of the Coast Indians for those of the Interior—of the Tlingits for the Déné. It had always existed. Only at such rendezvous as that at the Tahltan, where Tlingits and Nahannis suffered each other for the purposes of trade, had there been an uneasy truce.

The term Déné means "The People" and covers a widespread linguistic group of tribes of Athapascan stock. This group includes the Nahannis, Tahltans and Cascas of this book, and the territory of its tribes stretches from the Yukon eastward almost to Hudson's Bay and south (with gaps) into Arizona and New Mexico, where the Navajo and the Apache are the spearheads of the Déné advance, now halted by the white man. In the North-west the nearby hunting tribes of the Interior were in an almost constant state of enmity with the more settled tribes of the Coast, who differed from them in race, culture and language—or languages, for the Coast Indians themselves are divided there. The Taku Indians are a Coast tribe from the Taku River, which flows into the sea by the Taku Inlet, not far from Juneau. . . .

Egnell and Hankin made what preparations they could. They carried up plenty of water from the river, saw to it that food was handy, and loaded every gun in the place, including old trade muzzle loaders—guaranteed, with their black powder, to produce much flame, smoke and noise, if nothing else.

They then cut two loopholes in the north wall of the store. That was the side on which an enemy could approach unseen under the cover of stumps and bushes and second growth. On the south side there was the river, and on the east and west there was little shelter save from the other buildings. When all was done they settled down for the night, one man on guard and one sleeping.

The Takus came in Egnell's watch. He was alerted by the growling of his dog, and that woke Hankin. Through the loopholes they could see two Indians creeping through the bush towards the post. Egnell decided to take the bull by the horns. Leaving Hankin to cover him with his rifle, he threw the door wide open and walked boldly round the house to the north side, his rifle in the crook of his left arm, his right hand raised in salute.

The two Indians rose to their feet and Egnell greeted them. "We come in peace," they said. "We wish to trade." And they walked towards the white man, each one of them producing a silver fox from out of his shirt and holding it up in token that he spoke truth. But by this time Egnell had seen that there were many Indians concealed in the bush, every man armed with gun or bow—a peculiar method of approach for people whose object it was to make a peaceful trade.

"I do not wish for your trade," Egnell replied. "I trade only with Cascas and Tahltans. Return to your own country or I may be forced to fire on you."

The Takus backed sullenly away. Egnell once more barricaded himself in the store, and he and Hankin fired over the heads of the raiders, who slowly withdrew into the bush. But they remained camped, some two hundred of them, all through that day by a snye of the Liard about a mile upstream, arguing, debating and making warlike speeches. And all day Egnell and Hankin maintained their watch in the store, prepared for a sudden change of mind and an attack. But nobody came. . . . And that same evening the Takus broke camp and hit the trail—westward up the Liard, and then south-westward up the Rancheria River, and so to the headwaters of the Nisutlin, where some prospectors caught a sight of them. From there they went by Atlin Lake, and onward through the passes of the Coast Range to their homes on the Taku Inlet of the sea.

A few days afterwards, when they had made quite certain that the Taku Indians had departed, the Cascas returned to the Lower Post and the trade for their spring hunts went forward as though nothing untoward had ever happened. The trade, in fact, proceeded rather more briskly than before, since the spring outfit had arrived shortly after the departure of the Takus—the first boat of the season down the Dease from Lake House, the Hudson's Bay post at the south end of Dease Lake.

A month or more went by before word of this affair came to the ears of the Provincial Police constable at Telegraph Creek, and by that time the scent was cold and to take any useful action would have been hopeless. And so ended, as far as concerned the Lower Post, the age-old war between Tlingit and Déné—not in one last heroic fight that would be immortalised in song and story, but ignominiously, with the Cascas fled and the Takus wavering, "letting 'I dare not' wait upon 'I would.' "

Part Five

Combined Operation

FROM 1888 to 1935 is but a step in the endless march of time. Yet in those forty-seven years the Lower Post, the only trading establishment in one of the most isolated areas in Canada south of the Arctic Circle, emerged from the age of Indian warfare to meet the full impact of the twentieth century.

Up to the 1930's the little outpost still stood on the edge of nowhere. To the west and the north-west lay the vaguely known sources of the Liard; and, except for the short-lived gold fever, nothing took men into those remote places, unless it was an expedition of the Geological Survey, such as Dr. Dawson's, or some lone prospector-trapper, or a restless wanderer and sportsman like Warburton Pike. To the north and to the north-east lay the unknown Mackenzie Mountains and the country of the South Nahanni River. But Robert Campbell's adventures with the Trading Nahannis and their chieftainess had somehow got themselves transferred, in garbled and embellished form, from the Stikine to the canyons of the South Nahanni, with the result that an absurd legend, enhanced by one or two fatalities, had grown up around that lovely river. There was a *mystery* there, men said in the hushed, impressive tones of complete ignorance; it was a good country to keep out of—and further nonsense to that effect. And so the semi-circle of untravelled wilderness around the Lower Post was extended to the north-east and the Nahanni country became, for many years, a sort of preserve for mad, devoted wanderers like Pike or for men like Albert Faille— heirs, in this crowded century, of the *coureurs de bois* of French Canada and of the Mountain Men of the American South-west—men for whom the solitude and the search in the mountains that have become home to them are the only way of life. An excellent arrangement, and there ought to be more places so protected.

To the eastward the dangerous canyons of the Liard formed a sufficient barrier in an age that still travelled by river and reckoned accessibility by the performance of a canoe. And so the Lower Post remained throughout those years, as Pike truly said, "the last outpost of civilisation in this direction." It was linked with the outside only to the south—only by the two rivers and the portage over which we have come.

But in the twenties a new factor began to make itself felt in the development of the North: the aeroplane. By 1929 mail by this method of transport was reaching the lower Mackenzie, the planes landing on the open water in summertime and on skis on the frozen lakes and rivers through the winters. In this way no airports were necessary, but to balance that there were disadvantages. During the two seasons of freeze-up and break-up (which were always liable to be prolonged by change-able weather) no planes could come in at all; and also, on certain rivers, such as the Finlay and the Liard, flood-time could present a dangerous hazard. Then, usually in the month of June and in early July, an armada of drift would come driving downstream on the high water: great trees complete with roots and branches, waterlogged spars drifting almost sub-merged—sometimes the surface of a river would be covered with the floating debris of the forest. That sort of thing could interrupt a plane service for two or three weeks at a time, simply by making it too dangerous to come down on the water. Sooner or later airports were going to be needed.

By the mid-thirties the demand was growing for an air-mail service to the Yukon and Alaska. Accordingly, in the winter of 1934-35, the Canadian Post Office Department decided to make experimental flights to the Yukon. The requisite experience and skill were available from among the ranks of the bush-pilots, a new type of man that had come into being in the years following the Kaiser's War. These young men, many of them with years of wartime flying behind them, were by this time familiar with all the hazards of the North as seen from the pilot's seat of a plane. When anything happened they could cope. They had a splendid record of accident-free flying. And they flew (as, indeed, they had to fly, for there were few aids to navigation) "by the seat of their pants." They blazed the air trails of the North-west and their names have become legendary in the story of Canadian flying.

They flew to the Yukon, on those pathfinding flights, northwards on the east side of the Rockies and then west up the valley of the Liard via the Lower Post. Punch Dickens flew the 1935 flight and Grant McConachie that of 1936. The reports seemed to indicate the eastern route, as given above, as practicable, and it was decided to establish a limited postal service. An air-mail contract was let in 1937 to Grant McConachie's company, later to be known as the Yukon Southern Air Transport, and in that year the flights started.

For the foregoing reasons it was evident from the outset that the Liard at the Lower Post was not going to serve as more than a temporary landing place. What the Y.S.A.T. needed was a sizable lake, not too far away from the junction of the Liard and the Dease, and, adjoining it, a good stretch of level land on which a landing strip and, later, an airport could be constructed. And such a lake existed twenty-six miles north-west of the Lower Post: Watson Lake.

This lake is about five miles in length and nearly two miles across at the widest. At its north-west or lower end it comes within two miles of the Liard, and from that same end a winding creek drains it by a circuitous route to the river. The creek is eroding its bed and cutting down, draining the lake as it cuts. Already, therefore, when the airmen first began to estimate the lake's possibilities as a base, a large and level shingle bar lay exposed along the northern shore. This seemed to offer at least the beginnings of a landing strip, and the level land beyond would make further extension practicable. So there they had the site of an airport, roughly where one would be needed: a little too far to the north-west, perhaps, but good enough. It had been hoped to have the major airfields on this Edmonton-Yukon flight about 200 air miles apart, with emergency landing fields halfway between. Watson Lake, however, would be 248 air miles from Fort Nelson to the south-east, but only 162 miles from Whitehorse to the north-west. Nevertheless, that would still average out at about 200 miles and it was the best that could be managed while still maintaining access from the Lower Post and the Dease.

The man after whom Watson Lake was named was an Englishman from the county of Yorkshire who had set out for the Klondike from Edmonton in 1897. Like many another who took that long, roundabout trail to the gold-fields, Frank Watson had had to give it up. But, unlike most of the Klondike stampeders, he did not go out: he stayed with the country, married an Indian girl, and built himself a home at the head of this lonely lake in the south-eastern Yukon. There he raised a large family, and from there he trapped and hunted for nearly forty years.

One reason why Watson chose to settle by that lake may well have been the amazing quantities of whitefish in its waters: a never-failing supply of food, he must have thought. Yet fail it did in the end, for some parasite—a worm of some sort—got into the fish, causing their numbers to decline and rendering them unfit even for dog feed. For the rest, the

Lower Post was not too far distant, and there a reliable and likable man such as Watson could always count on getting a certain amount of jawbone * from the Hudson's Bay post manager.

Watson was a well-educated man, being, amongst other things, a qualified surveyor. He did a good deal of prospecting in the mountains that rimmed what topographers have come to call the Liard Plain, the very centre of which is Watson Lake. But a more dependable source of income lay closer to hand. Some miles above the Lower Post the Liard passes through a three-mile canyon. Some distance again above the canyon and on the south side of the river there is a bar—Watson's Bar. There was gold in that bar—not in vast quantities but, equally, not too fine or "floury." And Watson staked it.

I have a photograph of the man here, undated, taken by Harper Reed when the latter was Indian Agent. The photograph looks north across the Liard, roughly towards Watson Lake. It shows, according to Reed's caption, "a home-made, placer-mining water wheel, working on Watson's Bar. His clean-up was around $400 every fall." And to this is added, in blue pencil, the cryptic remark: "And Jaw Bone H. B. Co.—see their books."

The interesting thing about this perfectly practical, working water wheel is that there is not a single nail in it. Nails cost money by the time they reached the Lower Post, and Watson had by-passed them completely: this contraption of his is held together by pegs and sinew and straps of moose hide. The whole thing is on a sort of float made out of hewed logs. As Watson shovelled the gravel into the sluice-box the paddles of the water wheel were turned by the Liard current, the water being raised by a succession of old jam and syrup

---

* By the skilful and persuasive use of his jawbone a man could talk a trader into giving him a goods on credit. Hence the term "jawbone" came to be synonymous with "credit."

tins and tipped into the head of the sluice-box. The gold eventually remaining was trapped in a series of riffles after the dirt had been washed away. This was Watson's bank—and a very reliable one, too. Re-sorted and set in order every year by the Liard flood, it functioned steadily and normally right through the depression years of the thirties—which was a lot more than one could say of many far more pretentious establishments south of the U.S. boundary line.

Seated on the float, in the photograph, is "Dr. E. E. Hildebrand M.D., sometime M.O. for Whitehorse, Y.T., and attached to Stikine Indian Agency." He and Reed were on their way to Frances Lake to vaccinate the Indians there. That is a story in itself and I am only sorry that it has no place in this book. On the left, also on the float, stands Watson, looking like a wild man—as who wouldn't, shovelling wet gravel into a sluice-box and working half in and half out of the Liard? He is smiling, and that, too, is in character, for he was a generous and open-hearted man. Reed tells me a story of two young prospectors who were working their way up towards the head of the Liard. It was a slow progress, what with testing and re-testing river bars and side streams, and by the time they met Watson they had run out of supplies and had exhausted the possibilities in the way of credit at the Lower Post. Watson gave them a good square meal and then introduced them to his water wheel and his bar. "Take $200 out of that," he said. "That'll pay your jawbone at the Bay and give you a little to go on with."

To the affluent society that may not sound like much, but it meant an awful lot to men in need on the upper Liard back in the early thirties. Moreover, it was half of Watson's cash income for the year—half, you might say, of his dividends—apart, of course, from his fur catch and his hunting. And (allowing for the decrease in the value of money from that time to this) how many men could one find today in any Canadian community who, having only the smallest of incomes themselves, would give, unasked, five hundred dollars or more to a couple of passing strangers simply because they were stuck?

I have gone into some detail regarding Watson Lake and its first settler because the lake is known far and wide today as a link in the chain of airports leading to Alaska, while the man, though now almost forgotten, exemplifies in his person one of the major tragedies of our power-driven, fast-moving age. Through all the years of his manhood this Yorkshireman had led a precarious, but apparently satisfying, life in the wilderness, on the very edge of the unknown. The trapping, the hunting, the washing of the gold—each activity came in its proper season: an orderly routine and Watson was content with it. The trails that he had cut took off into the bush in all directions, each one with its purpose: there was the trail that crossed the Liard to his prospect in the Cassiar Mountains; the trail to the Lower Post; the trail that led to the beaver streams (he had travelled that one, now, through so many different springtimes!). There was the trail to his marten country. The moods of the lake and the meaning of the clouds had become as an open book to him. Every shift in the wind was a promise or a warning. He must have known every tree. . . . He had come a long way to find this place and it had given him peace for forty years. If he ever gave the matter a thought, it must have seemed to him that this would continue for all the days of his life.

And now the year is 1937 and (from Watson's point of view) a bunch of roughnecks has come, literally out of a blue sky, bursting into his Arcadia, proposing to set up a permanent camp and a radio station and to clear a landing strip. Raising hell in every direction: that's what it amounted to. There might be jobs going, but he was getting a bit old for that sort of thing, and, anyway, if it had been jobs he was looking for he wouldn't have been here at all. No—this Y.S.A.T. outfit might be a nice enough bunch in their way, but "his" lake would never seem the same again, that was a sure thing. . . .

Whether the end of his time had come anyway or whether it was a case of cause and effect, I do not know. But Watson died the following year, 1938—died in hospital in Edmonton, the starting point, in 1897, of his great adventure. This must have been quite sudden, for a man who saw him in 1936 describes him as being "hale and hearty." But for one whole year prior to his death he had known what it was to be the toad under the harrow, the unfortunate beetle that has got in the way of the bulldozer. A casualty of the times we live in and of Hitler's war. . . .

Things moved on with astonishing speed. In 1939 it was decided in Ottawa to construct a modern airway, with the necessary airfields and facilities, following the trail already blazed by Grant McConachie and the Y.S.A.T. Survey parties were sent out, and in September, while they were still in the field, there came the outbreak of war. Since it was possible that the United States would eventually be drawn into the struggle and that Alaska would become a danger point to the whole of North America, the surveyors were ordered to carry on with their work into winter, if necessary, in order to have it completed. They did so, and the last of them were back by January 1940. It was now possible to prepare the plans.

By August 1940 the military situation was looking pretty grim and the Canada-United States Permanent Joint Board on Defence (a crisp, laconic title, if ever there was one) was set up. In November of that year the Board met and decided that the Northwest Airway, as it had come to be called, should be developed and completed with all possible speed in accordance with the Department of Transport's plans. The problem immediately presented itself: how to get at these remote places with modern machinery and equipment. Whitehorse was easy: it had its W. P. & Y. Railroad. Fort St. John and Fort Nelson could be reached overland, so long as the frost was in the ground.[1] But Watson Lake, away out in the blue—how about Watson Lake? And then men called to mind the old river road of the fur-traders, the Stikine-Dease waterway and the portage trail. As a combined operation on the grand scale this was to be the swan-song of the Wrangell-Lower Post trade route, for the building of the Alaska Highway lay only two years ahead. But it was a notable ending, and the ghosts of all those men who had made it possible—Lieutenants Zarembo and Pereleshin; Sergiev and all the nameless Russian rivermen and fur-traders; John McLeod and Robert Campbell, with Kitza and Lapie; G. M. Dawson with his *Report* and his detailed maps; all the old river captains of the Stikine—all these must have watched, with pride and wonder, the new *voyageurs* of the twentieth century coping with their cumbersome freight, passing with their cargoes of giant machinery where the Tlingits had once passed in their cedar dugouts, or Robert Campbell with his birch-bark canoes, so quietly and with little more disturbance than the rippling wake of a Stikine salmon or of one of Kirkendale's thirty-pound lake trout from the Dease.

One man still remained out of that pioneering company: R. G. McConnell, the man who parted from Dawson at the Lower Post to descend through the canyons of the Liard. To the end, they say, he cursed his fate for that he was now too old to venture forth again on those rivers that he had travelled with Dawson over fifty years before, back in the days of his youth, when he could scramble up and down Nahanni Butte in the course of a long morning.

And, of a younger generation, down at Wrangell there were Sydney and Hill Barrington, with forty years of rivering behind them, over half of that time being on the Stikine. At the end of 1940, the year the decision was taken to complete and equip a modern airfield at Watson Lake, the Barrington fleet consisted of the *Hazel B 3*, built in 1917,* and the more recent *Hazel B 2*, built in Seattle in 1923 and brought north

* See Appendix G.

by Captain Sydney Barrington. The latter was a large boat
that could take in comfort fifty passengers—and more at a
pinch. She was powered by two 135-horsepower *Superior*
diesels and her propellers were designed to be raised into
tunnels when she was in shoal water or climbing up a riffle.
Now, however, with all this heavy freight for Watson Lake
looming up for the season of 1941, something smaller with
more power and less draft was going to be needed. So the
thing was discussed from all angles and then the Barringtons
set Emerson Reid, chief engineer of the *Hazel B 2*, to work to
draw the plans. Reid had been on the Stikine for over seventeen years, and he came up with just what was wanted: a boat
64 feet in length by 23 feet beam, drawing 24 inches loaded
and 12 inches light and powered by two 170-horsepower *Superior* diesels. This new boat, the *Hazel B 1* that was to be,
would carry only six passengers but would be able to take on
board thirty-four tons of freight, while also pushing a scow
carrying fifty tons. The contract went to Ernest Anderson of
the Anderson Marine Ways at Wrangell and work started on
March 1, 1941. They lost no time over that job, since the
freight for Dease Lake was already coming into Wrangell
from Vancouver and the south, and the *Hazel B 1* left Wrangell on her maiden trip up the Stikine on May 7, Sydney
Barrington being captain. For three days the office in Wrangell waited anxiously, and then word came over the air from
Telegraph Creek that the *"Number One"* had made it.

But in spite of her power and shallow draft it must not be
thought that the Stikine was any walk-over for the new boat.
Depending on the stage of the water, there was often a good
deal of winching to be done above Little Canyon. At any
riffle where the *Hazel B 1* tended to hang, a small boat would
be launched to go ahead, perhaps through some minor channel in the bar, carrying a 1,400-foot length of cable. This
would be attached to a deadman or to a strong tree, and the
boat would return by the main channel with the crew paying

out the cable slowly by hand. The cable would then be brought aboard the *Number One* and attached to the drum, and the ship, with her engines running all out, would then proceed to winch herself up on the cable, which was no more and no less than a fixed trackline with power applied to it. Then at really tough spots like the First South Fork—the place where I pulled the *Hazel B 3* up on a willow twig—and in low water in the fall, the *Hazel B 1* might have to relay her load: that is, she would have to tie up her barge and leave it. She would climb up the riffle alone and go on to unload her thirty-four tons at Telegraph Creek. Then she would drop down river empty, pick up her barge with its fifty tons, and climb the riffle once more towards her destination. There was no trick or device that the Barringtons did not bring into play. All were needed, for to raise 84 tons of freight 555 feet above sea level, with a river like the Stikine contesting every mile of the distance, was no light task.

Owing to experience and skill, there were no major accidents. In fact there was no time for the Barringtons to fool around having accidents, since, on the first Watson Lake contract alone, there were 3,500 tons of freight to be taken up the Stikine. That would have meant about forty-two full loads for the *Hazel B 1*—an impossibility in one season between break-up and freeze-up. But, with all their boats steadily on the go, somehow the Barringtons managed it. One can imagine them that summer, coming again and again with load after load, feeling their way through the shallows into the great river. Two men are standing on the foredeck of the barge, sounding with long poles, calling out the depths and at the same time signalling them with a flick of the hand to the man in the pilot house: "Four. Four and a half. Four and a quarter. Five." Their voices travel far over the quiet water.

"We had to be on the job all the time," Captain Hill Barrington said. "A river is no place to go to sleep on."

"Did anybody ever try to?" I asked him.

"Yes," he said. "Captain Harvey Alexander of the steamer *Casca* did, once—though that was on a lake. He went to sleep and he ran his ship head on into a rock bluff in deep water on Lake Labarge . . . No, he didn't sink the *Casca*. But he stove the *Casca's* bow in, and the impact sent him flying clean out through the pilot house window . . ."

In the meantime, things had not been standing still in Vancouver. Material was assembled there for transportation to Wrangell, and in the shipyards a stern-wheeler, three tunnel-shaft, shallow-draft power-boats, and twelve scows were framed. These were numbered and then knocked down and shipped in sections to the Barrington Transportation Company at Wrangell to await the opening of the Stikine. This sounds like a very orderly and methodical process. Actually it was not accomplished without some friction.

Mr. S. C. Ells of the Geological Survey had had some experience of the Dease River back in the thirties and, with that behind him, he had now been seconded to the Department of Transport with instructions to "kick the freight through." With a view to getting boats built that would be well suited to the cramped but very active reaches of the upper Dease, Ells got hold of a Captain William Strong, who had freighted for ten years on that river, and brought him down to Vancouver to help in outlining plans for suitable boats and barges—or scows, as some of us call them, according to where we have worked and handled the things. However, he found that all this had already been decided upon by a group of government officials who had never set eyes on the Dease, assisted and advised by one who had had considerable experience of the Mackenzie. "With," Ells said, "results that can be imagined." This all sounds quite normal for the war effort of a democracy (not that the dictatorships were so much more efficient, as we now know), and what it boiled down to was that, as usual, the men on the spot were going to get just exactly what they were going to get and it would be up to them to make a go of it. They were going to have to get that 3,500 tons of freight, already mentioned, down the Dease *somehow,* even if they crawled over the bars on their stern-wheels and propellers. And probably a lot more stuff later on as well. Incidentally, on a cost-plus basis and on that first deal, the freight on one gallon of gas landed at the Lower Post was $1.50. Later on, when things were running more smoothly, a gallon of gas got down there comparatively cheaply—at no more than $1.25.

One can imagine the whole of the age-old trail to the In-terior coming alive—alive as it had never been before. The stuff piled up in Wrangell and the Barringtons grappled with it and hauled it up to Telegraph Creek. The most awkward loads they handled, Hill Barrington said, were the heavy road-building and grading machinery. But it was essential to move that quickly since, long before it could ever see Watson Lake, all that stuff would be needed to do a job on the portage road to Dease Lake. So the old trail of the wild game and the In-dians and the fur-traders got one more face-lifting and the bridges were once more strengthened and rebuilt.[2] Then the stuff started to roll: sections of boats and scows, lumber and marine engines, provisions and building supplies, trucks, graders, bulldozers, drums of gas and oil—all the thousand things that would be needed to reach and to establish Watson Lake. Among other things that came up the Stikine and over the portage were two magnificent roll-top, lock-up desks and the furniture and filing cabinets that went with them—just exactly what men building an airfield at the back of beyond would need most!

Ells was telling me this, and I, remembering the Dease as I had seen it, after six years of ice and floods and tree growth had wiped out the traces of this tremendous struggle—and

finding it difficult to associate this with filing cabinets—began
to laugh.

"What on earth did you do with them?" I asked him.

"Shot them under cover at the head of the lake and left
them there," he replied. "I had enough on my hands just then
without fooling around with office furniture. Gas and oil were
more use to me than roll-top desks."

A small village of temporary buildings sprang up at the
head of Dease Lake and a shipyard was established there.
There they assembled the sections sent up from Vancouver
and Wrangell, installed engines, and put the finishing touches
to the boats and scows. Ells, noting that time was getting on
and that they were, inevitably, missing the flood of the Dease,
foresaw trouble with these long, heavy scows, forty-odd feet
in length, and with boats that had years of experience on the
Mackenzie built into them. He took precautions. He got one
twenty-four-foot, shallow-draft riverboat built, square-sterned
for a four-horsepower outboard, sweeping up and fining in
to a pointed bow. A "pointer." With this and a crew of experienced rivermen he would be able to supervise the operation, help in re-floating stranded boats, and so forth.

Knowing the Dease as he did, Ells had particularly in mind
its shallow upper reaches as a probable cause of trouble. The
small trout stream that leaves Dease Lake to seek the Cassiar
Mountains, winding around one gravel point after another,
narrowing into fast, purling riffles where the only channel
would be close under the cutbank—that was what worried him.
The type of boat that was being built, plus a scow about forty-
five feet long strained solid by means of ratchets and cables to
the forward end of her, was going to make a unit of something
over seventy feet, heavily loaded. This whole unit was going
to have to take the extreme outside of every bend all the way
down the upper river. Any protruding stump or snag might
cause disaster, to say nothing of the chances of running the
outfit under some fallen or leaning tree and getting the com-

plete works—men, pilot house, trucks, sawmill equipment, whatever might get in the way—swept overboard as by a giant scythe. Something would have to be done about this.

So Ells set the twenty-four-footer and its crew to cutting trail (which is what it amounted to) down the first fifty miles of the Dease. Trees, snags and sweepers were all taken out, and the odd rock was rolled aside as well. That took from four to five weeks with twelve men on the job, and, by the time they had finished, that one source of trouble was practically eliminated. Not absolutely, of course, for there were still such things as winds and there is no close season on the falling of trees. But even without this particular hazard, and after blasting some rocks and reefs in the Cottonwood, Fourmile and Twomile Rapids, running these awkward loads down the Dease was going to be far from dull.

In Dawson's time Dease Lake opened anywhere from May 30 to June 16. The ideal time to pull out with freight for the Lower Post would be right after the melting of this mass of ice, or even on the opening of a navigable channel. Owing to the boat-building and the inevitable delays, due to weather, in the road-making and the hauling of the piled-up freight from Telegraph Creek, it was impossible to catch the best stage of water, and by the time the boats got going the flood of the Dease was over. Nevertheless, all concerned went at it with determination: captains, engineers, and deckhands—the whole crowd. "The Dease," says Mr. Wilson in his article, *Northwest Passage by Air*,[3] "is a shallow, rapid and tortuous stream, and our scows and power-boats bumped merrily down over the boulders which obstruct its course for two hundred miles to Lower Post." Old photographs, unearthed from the files of the Department of Transport and obviously taken from the pilot house, show, in one instance, four men on the foredeck of a scow using a heavy sweep to swing the bow away from a gravel point and submerged bar and over towards what Ells called "the outside of the bend," where the deep water

lay. Judging by the mops of raven hair, at least two of the
men are Indians, and judging by their tense, strained at-
titudes they are putting every ounce of beef they possess into
that sweep. In another picture, taken again from the pilot
house but of a different scow, the outfit is running down one
of the rapids of the upper Dease. This time three men are
standing on the foredeck, alert and watchful and with long,
peeled poles in their hands, ready to swing the nose of the
scow aside from any boulder or piece of projecting reef. A tent
has been rigged up over part of the scow, and underneath
there will be perishable goods, perhaps provisions, and men's
bedrolls laid out on top of them. The tent looks none too
secure, and one feels that the weeks that Ells' snagging crew
put in swamping out a trail down the Dease were far from
wasted. Two further photographs have come to light. One of
them shows the stern-wheeler being assembled and finished
at the shipyard at the south end of Dease Lake, while the other
depicts the stern-wheeler with her scow on the Liard, tied up
at the Lower Post and unloading. Heavy crated stuff is being
shoved ashore over a gangway of planks by three-man power,
while aboard the scow there still remain two big crates and
a tractor. On the foredeck a light skiff is lying—in frequent
use, probably, when getting off some gravel bar or winching
up the Dease.

On the main deck of the boat and below the pilot house
window one can see a power-driven drum with a cable coiled
around it. That is the motive force by which the "fixed trackline"—the cable carried ahead and made fast to a deadman
or a tree—is wound back on board as the ship pulls herself up
a riffle. In the foreground an empty truck is waiting on the
ramp. It, too, has made the journey down the river.

One thing in all this freighting has so far defied accurate
research, and one might entitle it: "What Happened at the
Cottonwood Rapid"—though that rather oversimplifies it.
Having failed completely to reconcile the stories told to me by

Ells and Harper Reed, Hyland and Barney McHugh, George Ball and Marrion and a dozen more besides, I have now come to the conclusion that quite a lot of things happened at the Cottonwood Rapid (and elsewhere) and that each man has told me, perfectly genuinely, either what he saw or what was told to him at first hand—but not necessarily with regard to the same trip or the same load of freight.

One story goes that there was an upset at the Cottonwood: that some scow got loose and broadside on to the stream and spilled its load of gas and oil drums into the Dease. The scow was not wrecked in any way, but it took time to straighten things out, and meanwhile the drums bobbed serenely on down the river. They also got stranded, quite a number of them, in shallow snyes, on the points of islands, or in drift-piles. So a boat crew had to follow them up, extract them from their many hiding places, and herd them on towards the Liard. Most of them arrived, a bit dented but in good order, and were corralled by a waiting crew down at the mouth of the Dease—but, naturally enough, not before every trapper on the river had got himself a drum of government gas cached away in the bush for his outboard. Unfortunately this effort at self-help backfired: this particular load happened to be high-octane gasolene, and so "it wasn't more than two or three months before all the poor devils' kickers seized up. Too bad it couldn't have been the real stuff . . ."

Then the Dease began to drop and the boats bumped and crawled more and more often over the bars. So, to lighten the loads, the men took to throwing the gas drums deliberately overboard in moments of stress, catching them again—most of them—down at the mouth in a kind of glorified fish-trap built for the purpose. I am not putting the names of my several informants to these tales because the various stories overlap or conflict or even expand one another, and it's impossible to disentangle them. But, without doubt, where there is smoke there must be fire.

Drums of gas were, unfortunately, in a class by themelves: one could not, for instance, throw tractors and bulldozers into the Dease—not, that is, to any advantage. But they could, and did, land these things and use them to blade out a channel: that is, to shove aside the rocks and shingle of the bars so that the boats could get through. Or the machines could be unloaded and set to make their own way through the bush across a point, thus allowing boats and scows to be run light down some shallow riffle, re-loading again below. Freighting this sort of stuff was constantly creating new problems, and the problems were solved, as always in the West, with a light-hearted ingenuity that took them in its stride.

The first boats unloaded at the Lower Post on July 1, 1941. From there a twenty-six-mile road had to be bulldozed through the bush to Watson Lake. No time was lost over that, and the first loads reached the airport site on July 9. Meanwhile the boats and scows had returned immediately, fighting their way up the shallow river to the head of Dease Lake. The flow of freight down the river continued, and so also, as we have already seen, did the fall in the level of the water. This was becoming serious; but the Dease rose unexpectedly to the occasion and produced a second high-water. Not a moment was lost, and from that time onwards some pretty desperate freighting was achieved until freeze-up came, late in October. The last trips were downstream, and then both boats and scows were hauled out for the winter at the Lower Post, to await "much-needed repairs."

By that time things were already on the road to completion, though still very much in the rough, at Watson Lake. Men and equipment had been flown in there in the spring, ahead of the Dease River loads, and the site was a level one needing little grading. By late summer a sawmill was producing lumber for the necessary buildings, and on September 2, 1941, a single-engined "Beechcraft," piloted by W. S. Lawson, made the first wheeled landing by the lonely lake where, so recently,

Frank Watson, ignoring the twentieth century, had lived and hunted in the time-lag of a bygone age.

On December 9, 1941, the United States came into the war. Alaska and the Aleutian Islands immediately became an area of strategic concern, and the construction of Watson Lake Airport was immediately justified. Canada's portion of the Northwest Airway was in rough-and-ready working order and the country was in a position to offer to the U.S. the facilities of a chain of airports, "adequately, though not yet completely equipped," reaching from Edmonton to the Alaska border at, roughly, two-hundred-mile intervals.

The existence of this chain of airports was mainly instrumental in determining the route to be followed by the Alaska Highway, the need for which was immediately seen, and which was forced through the twelve hundred miles or more of Canadian territory in the season of 1942. Other, and probably better and easier, routes west of the Rockies were rejected for this same reason, and the new airports came into use as survey bases for the new road. Without them it is doubtful whether the Highway could have been made passable (I will not say "built," for, in certain stretches, it still washes out with almost clock-like regularity every summer) in the very short time of six months.

The wartime use of the airway made necessary a vast increase in buildings and facilities of all kinds, and work proceeded at speed all though 1942. As regards Watson Lake, this was again made possible by using, as in 1941, the old fur-traders' trail, the Stikine-Dease Portage route from Wrangell to the Lower Post. But that was almost the end of the story: a road now runs from the Liard to Dease Lake, passing through the dark cleft in the Cassiar Mountains through which Pike and Beavertail Johnny and Secatz drove their dogs that February of 1893, and the need for the old waterway is gone. Over the greater part of its length the new road does not follow the Dease; and down there, in those quiet reaches to which the silence has returned, the trout still rise and the Canada geese still come over on their evening flight, undisturbed except by some trapper's riverboat or the passing of some wandering sportsman's canoe.

Part Six

End of the Trail

SOMETHING of these events I already knew when I made camp on the island at the mouth of the Dease—but by no means all. Enough, however, so that, when I looked across the Liard that evening towards the old Hudson's Bay Company buildings, I could conjure up the happenings of the past: Sylvester's long reign there; the coming of the Hudson's Bay Company; Egnell and Hankin packing up to those same old log buildings, now glowing in the sunset light, the water for the siege; the arrival, at that ramp bulldozed out of the steep cutbank, of the freight for Watson Lake. A float now rode in the water at the foot of the ramp, and, even as I watched, the sound of a small plane made itself heard on the evening air. Soon the plane itself came into sight, flying low up the river. It lit gracefully, like a bird, on the water and taxied up to the float where the pilot made it fast. Then he walked up the ramp, carrying a dunnage bag, and disappeared behind the trees.

In the morning, shaved and spruced up, I tracked the empty canoe up the snye, jumped in, and drove it across the racing current of the Liard to the far bank. I poled up to the float, beached the canoe, and walked up the ramp. The little plane had already gone and the old waterfront was deserted. The life of the place had taken itself off to the Alaska Highway, and I followed it.

I found the Bay post manager, Mr. Robertson, busy with his accounts in a brand-new store (no log buildings this time) facing on the Highway. I explained who I was and asked if there was any mail for me, and it was then that Robertson realised that I had not come by car.

"You're the man who was coming down the Dease," he said. "Yes, I've got mail for you. Who did you come down with?"

"Myself," I answered. "I was guide, camp cook and river-man, all in one."

"Were you? And what kind of a boat did you use?"

"A fourteen-foot canoe. It's down at the landing now, and I'm camped over on the island."

"A fourteen-foot canoe! And how did that take the rapids?"

"Oh, fine." And I told him about the trip. It never occurred to me that I had done anything out of the ordinary, but I heard later that, in the two days I was around the Lower Post, I was an object of some interest as "the man who came down the Dease in the fourteen-foot canoe." They could well have added "and with one hand."

I mentioned that I wanted to go on up to Frances Lake, going all the way by river—provided Dalziel could fly me out. I thought I could make it, I said, given any sort of weather luck.

Robertson was against it. It was about a hundred and forty miles, he said, up to Frances Lake, with some tough water and some portages. And it could easily snow in the first half of September (as I well knew), and here was the first week already gone. However, he would try to get a message to Dalziel—that is, if Dalziel happened to be at Watson Lake.

We talked, and I commented on the scarcity of moose in the country. Since leaving the Stikine, I had seen only three.

Wolves, Robertson said: that's what it was—wolves. They practically owned the country. The Indians were out of meat more often than not and even the game trails were growing in. I capped that statement with a heartfelt account of the bush obliterating the trails on the Horse Ranch Range, and we went at it hammer and tongs till some tourists wandered in, looking for souvenirs.

Civilization had come to the Lower Post and, as the morning wore on, more and more of it roared up and down the Highway, sending the loose gravel flying. A dust cloud would almost settle, and then along would come another straining, overloaded car from Mich. or Tenn. or Neb., plastered with mud and dust, radiator grille dented, windscreen starred. And the fog of dust would rise again and I would call to mind the talk of the American airmen one wartime winter's night at Watson Lake. Somebody had said: "What the hell do they think they're going to do with all these buildings when the war's over?"

And somebody answered him: "Do? Why, they'll make the place into a fishing resort or something. Tourists'll go any place, you'll see. But, oh boy! Once I've gotten out of this, the golden Yukon'll never see me again!"

Then the whole room chimed in to explain to this mad visionary how any tourist, taking his annual three-week holiday and starting, say, from Minneapolis or St. Paul, the nearest big centres of population, would have to be insane before he wasted all his leave driving to Fairbanks and back. "Three thousand miles and more of mud and dust and flying rocks," they said. "Or else it's frozen tighter than hell, like now." (It was over sixty below that night.) "What the poor guy would need would be another three weeks to rest up in after he got back from a trip like that. And who wants to see the Godforsaken country anyway?"

But he of the fishing resort—who was also a true prophet— stuck to his guns. "You'll see," he said. "Some sucker will."

Idly I watched the passing parade of suckers on the dusty road, thinking fondly of my pleasant camp on the island and of a fool hen that I had knocked over the night before. But I had to wait in case Dalziel came, so I wandered along and found a place to eat. . . .

I was in luck, for Dalziel came down that afternoon from Watson Lake. We discussed the Frances Lake project from all angles and, in estimating my time up the hundred and forty miles of the Liard and Frances Rivers, I had to admit that I had badly wrenched my damaged wrist when avoiding that dangerous rock in the Fourmile Rapid. Scrambling around in the Horse Ranch Range had gone a long way towards mending it. Now it was right back where it had been before.

Also to be considered was the length of the canoe: it was all right for running downstream but not so good for poling upstream. It did not, I had found, have the momentum of the longer canoes: it moved upstream about as long as the pole rested on the bottom of the river, and no longer. This would add appreciably to the time of travel.

Dalziel summed up the situation. "The weather's fine now," he said, "but we've already had a bad August with snow. The way it's been, we could easily be in for a bad fall. It's a tough bit of river in places and when you do get to Frances Lake you'll be higher than Dease Lake and two hundred miles further north. And Dease Lake's around two thousand five hundred feet. Just to slow things up a bit you've got a lame wrist and a short canoe, and if it does put down a heavy early snow in Frances Lake it might freeze hard and make it impossible for me to come down and pick you up. Then you'd have to cache your outfit and make your own way out, and there's no good trail. And the old Bay post at the lake is closed. Better call it a day."

That was something I had not taken into account—the possibility of early ice on Frances Lake. There would be no getting around that one. So, reluctantly, I called it a day; and then we parted, but not before Dalziel had kindly promised to come and drive me up to Watson Lake Airport the following evening. Robertson, too, seemed to think it a wise decision to abandon the Frances Lake venture, and he, with equal kindness, gave me the key to one of the old Bay buildings by the river so that I could pack my outfit there and leave it in safety for shipment to the end of steel. He would see to that, he said. And now, once again, I look back with gratitude and happy remembrance on all the men of the North who so freely and kindly render assistance to the passing traveller. Robertson also said he would take charge of the canoe for me; and eventually he sold it on my account to Dalziel, who, after doing a bit of measuring and thinking, had decided it was just what he wanted: he would be flying it in to some lake where he had a use for it. And so its venturesome life would continue until age came upon it, and its canvas hide, rotten, patched and torn, flapped loosely over its battered ribs—or until some bear, scenting in it, but not finding, the bacon it once had carried, took a disgusted and devastating swipe at its ancient fabric. . . .

Returning from the dusty world of the Alaska Highway and crossing the clear, fast-flowing Liard to my camp on the island was like dropping back fifty years in time. That camp, except for the growth of the trees, could scarcely have altered since the Klondikers passed by, since Watson saw it for the first time. Not a sound reached there from the road: one heard only the murmur of the water as it raced down the head of the snye.

Nothing could have been more perfect than that evening. I enjoyed every moment of it as I sat by the fire, turning and re-turning the fool hen, which was now plucked and cleaned and spread wide open on a forked willow above the glowing embers. My attention was divided, part being given to the roasting bird and its delectable smell, and part to the delicate pattern of the trees against the cloudless glow of the sunset. So tranquil was the close of that September day that it seemed as though autumn must go on forever and winter never come.

Nor, if the truth must be told, did winter come until the last days of October, after one of the finest autumns of all time —thus making a mockery out of all our wise precautions.

But that, unfortunately, I could not possibly know on that last evening; and for the moment the vital thing in my small world was the fool hen, done to a turn and demanding my undivided attention.

Appendix

A

Page 58: This planned and organized hunting of the wolves was new to me. I had never seen it happen, nor had I ever heard of wolves planning a hunt on this scale. I happened to mention it to a friend, Mr. Frank Edgell of Saanichton, who spent his early years near Wilmer in the East Kootenay. It did not come as any surprise to him: the big coyotes, the "brush wolves" of the Purcell Mountains, he said, used to do exactly the same thing. They would round up the deer on the mountain slopes on the west side of Lake Windemere and drive them down Goldie Creek on to the ice of the lake, where they planned to deal with them as the timber wolves of the Klappan dealt with the moose. Things did not always work out as planned, for if there were any Indians nearby they would hasten down to the shore, eager for the coyote bounty, and when the whole pack was well out on the lake ice with the deer the Indians would start shooting. A frantic stampede for the shore and cover would ensue and the hunt would be over, while the deer would either fall to the Indians' rifles or make their escape as best they could.

B

Page 69: Petty, vindictive streak: that needs justification, and it puts me in mind of a story. At the time when I was working on the "Introduction" to *Black's Rocky Mountain Journal* (Hudson's Bay Record Society, Vol. XVIII) my wife was on a visit to England. She was lunching one day at the Savoy with the late Sir Edward Peacock, a very distinguished Canadian, then on the Executive Committee of the Hudson's Bay Record Society, a connection of mine by marriage. The talk turned on the progress of the "Introduction" and on the various historical characters involved in it. My wife, speaking of me, said: "Raymond says he would never have worked for Sir George Simpson."

"I most certainly would not have worked for him," Sir Edward replied. "Let me tell you a story that was told to me by the first Lord Strathcona, who, as plain Donald Smith, took service with the Hudson's Bay Company, rose to be chief factor, and eventually became Governor. When he was in his twenties he was at the post of Mingan, on the North Shore, north of Anticosti Island. He had serious trouble there with his eyes: snow blindness started it and a most painful condition set in which did not seem to get any better. An old Indian made young Smith still more worried by telling him that this could lead to total blindness. Through that summer of 1847 he wrote several letters to Simpson at his house and estate at Lachine, above Montreal, asking to be allowed to make the easy journey in to Montreal to see a doctor. No answer came and Smith wondered if his letters had gone astray. Actually they had been received and Simpson had ignored them. Finally, in November 1847, Smith, afraid for his sight, took a chance and boarded a passing sailing vessel for Montreal. On arrival he thought he had better report immediately to Simpson so he went out to Lachine.

"Simpson was at dinner and Smith was informed by the manservant that he had to wait. Some dinner was sent out to him in a separate room. Finally the Governor appeared, evidently in a very bad temper, and demanded to know on what authority Smith had left his post. The young man explained, and Simpson, ridiculing the idea of blindness, sent for his own doctor, who examined Smith in another room and prescribed a remedy for the eye condition. They then returned to Simpson, who inquired only if there was any danger of total blindness. The doctor said, "No, but—," whereat the Governor, without waiting to hear more, threw himself into a rage and told the astonished young clerk to get out of Montreal immediately for his *new post* of North-West River—a bleak and lonely spot far up the north-east coast of Labrador—the equivalent, in the fur-trade, of being banished to Siberia. And Donald Smith would have to make by far the greater part of the journey on foot."

Here, apparently, Lord Strathcona had looked at E. R. Peacock and said: "That was my welcome. What would you have done?"

E. R. P. said: "I'd have told Simpson to go to the devil and take his Hudson's Bay Company with him."

"Well," said Lord Strathcona, "I said to myself—if the Governor wants to give me an order like that, I'll show him that I am able to carry it out."

Sir Edward then went on: "The weather broke and young Smith had an appalling journey in storm and blizzard. He engaged two guides, one of whom died on the trail from exhaustion and the cold. With the other guide, and with his eyes once more giving pain, Smith just managed to make a halfway post where the trader in charge and his wife brought him back to life and strength and contrived an excuse to detain him through the winter. He came to North-West River in April, 1848, and in charge of that post he remained, rising to be a chief factor, until after Simpson's death in 1860."

That was Lord Strathcona's own story as relayed by Sir Edward Peacock to my wife. The whole thing, arising, as it did, out of the ignoring of Smith's letters, smacks of the inconsiderate martinet, hardened in the mould of success. This hasty and ill-tempered order resulted in the death of one man and might well have caused the death of all three.

From the standpoint of the Hudson's Bay Company's officers the trouble was that, if they didn't like the service, there was no place for them to go. The life of a free trapper was practically barred to them, and all their experience and training was as good judges of fur, hard travellers in the bush and Indian traders. The only thing they could do was to stay with the Company, keep their hard-won seniority and make the best of it—as did young Donald Smith, though with more success than most.

C

Page 77: Simpson-Black-Ogden. In the late 1830's Black and Ogden were still west of the Rockies, each one now a chief factor. Black was in charge of the Bay post of Thompson's River (Kamloops) while Ogden was at Stuart's Lake (Fort St. James). Well over three hundred miles of wild country separated the two friends—and that was as the crow flies. It was more like four hundred miles by saddle-horse and canoe. In spite of that, Ogden was able to write, years afterwards: "We had shared in each other's perils; and the narrow escapes we had so frequently experienced tended to draw still more closely the bond of amity by which we were united. It was our custom to contrive an annual meeting, in order that we might pass a few weeks in each other's company . . . to fight like old soldiers 'our battles o'er again' over a choice bottle of Port or Madeira; to lay our plans for the future, and, like veritable gossips, to propose fifty projects, not one of which there was any intention on either part to realize."

A man is known by his friends. As Black's closest friend we have this lively, intelligent man, "the humorous, honest, eccentric, law-defying Peter Ogden, the terror of Indians and the delight of all gay fellows." * A man of this description would be unlikely to have as one of his warmest friends the tedious, suspicious, calculating demon that Simpson describes in his *Character Book:* "His generosity might be considered indicative of a warmth of heart if he was not known to be a cold blooded fellow who could be guilty of any cruelty and would be a perfect Tyrant if he had power. Can never forget what he may consider a slight or insult, and fancies that every man has a design upon him . . . So tedious that it is impossible to get through business with him."

If we have to believe this and the companion observations on page 70, then we must also believe that the well-educated, laughter-loving Ogden would travel four hundred miles by river and trail specially to pass *a few weeks* in the company of a morose, boring windbag of a man, without heart or human feeling, forever on his guard against his fellows.

It simply does not make sense. Father A. G. Morice, O.M.I., the historian of central B.C., evidently had access in later years to some of Black's private correspondence, and he writes that "Black must have been a good-natured man who saw life through rose-colored glasses and had not a little sense of the ludicrous." It is easy to see that the good Father thoroughly enjoyed what he read of Black's letters and was only sorry that more had not survived. Quite plainly it was the man whom Father Morice could visualise through his minute, slanted handwriting who was the friend of Ogden, and not the scheming, cadaverous monster so ably delineated by the little god of the fur-trade in his secret *Character Book.*

What Simpson was still remembering, of course, was that first Canadian winter of his on Lake Athabasca when even the name of Black, the villainous North Wester, was enough to make him order an immediate inspection of arms. Shuffle it off as he might, that still rankled.

As for Ogden, what he collected in the *Character Book,* in addition to the pleasant remarks on page 70 of the text, was a statement to the effect that he had been thoughtless and much given to coarse practical joking. Now what, one wonders, had the two friends been up to? Simpson visited them at their posts in the course of his peregrinations in the

* *Adventures on the Columbia River,* by Ross Cox (London, 1831).

far West. Had Black received him at Fort Nez Perces on the Columbia with a torrent of words as a form of self-defence against a man he disliked, and had he remained in full spate till Simpson was glad to get away and leave him to his own devices, knowing full well that in Black he had a trustworthy man who could be relied upon to do his duty?

And Ogden? What was his crime? Spruce gum in the saddle is a coarse practical joke and not easy to pin on anybody in camp or on the trail. I have known of such things, and the wilderness has many other possibilities besides.

D

Page 86: George Kirkendale, Senior, was born in Hamilton, Ontario, in 1871. His family had originally come from Holland to the American colonies in the seventeenth century, the family name being then Van Kykendall. In the year 1811 a branch of the Van Kykendalls moved to Canada, and over the years the name was gradually Anglicised to Kirkendale.

George Kirkendale came west and tackled the usual variety of jobs: taught school at Chemainus on Vancouver Island and at Beaver Point on Saltspring Island; fished off the mouth of the Fraser River. Next came his Stikine adventure; and then, in the years that followed, he took to the sea, studying in his spare time for his deep-sea master's ticket, which he obtained. In 1901 he went with an expedition to Cocos Island in search of buried pirate treasure—almost to the equator, where a little of the Stikine ice would have been more than welcome.

In 1907 he became Shipping Master for the Port of Victoria. In 1921, the port traffic having become somewhat lighter, he combined this office with those of Harbour Master and Port Warden, and he performed these various duties until he retired in 1943. Through all these years he was well known around Victoria, and it was to him that many a young seaman, with examinations looming ahead, came to be coached in trigonometry and navigation. No one ever met with a refusal; and, after one has read his hitherto unpublished *Stikine Trail of 1898,* that can be easily understood from the nature of the man.

George Kirkendale was also one of the founders of the Thermopylae Club (of Victoria), an institution devoted to the lore of the sea and its famous ships. He died on January 12, 1945. It was a full life, lived by an outstanding man.

E

Page 118: Moose losing their fear of men.

As Reed talked I was reminded of an experience of Gordon Matthews' in 1961 when, alone in his car, he got into a forest fire on the Hart Highway through the Rockies, in east-central B.C. It was important to him that he should get through on time, and he had taken a chance and gone—and now the fire was across the road behind him and it looked almost as bad ahead. And the road was like a corral—packed with animals and all of them going the same way. The fear of the fire was on them, and all their normal fears and enmities no longer meant a thing. *The greater fear had taken charge.* They were all there, shoulder to shoulder, elk and moose and bear and the rest; and a man in a car to them was no longer an enemy but just another scared refugee like themselves. Along went the cavalcade at a trot, and Gordon told me that several times he had to nudge some wild beast gently with the bumper of his car to get it out of his way. They paid no attention to him as a man.

F

*Page 151: In that same letter of November 24, 1838,** McPherson further states: "Mr. Campbell found a brigade of Russian traders with a very large congregation of Indians who meet at the same Rendezvous twice every Summer . . . The Russian Com. in chief of the Party (a 'Mr. Monrobe') received him with apparent politeness and introduced him to three other ragged Officers like himself, and treated him to a Glass of Whiskey. It was, however, very evident that they were jealous of his appearance in that Quarter."

Campbell must have told McPherson of this when he made his trip down to Fort Simpson in the late summer. Yet no mention of the Russian traders is made in his journal. Was this because he was anxious to avoid providing any evidence that might seem to indicate that the Russian sphere of influence extended up the Stikine east of the Coast Range? I can think of no other reason.

G

Page 221: Epitaph for a river boat. In a letter of January 12, 1950, George Ball gives some account of the demise of one of the principal characters of this book, the *Hazel B 3:*

* *The Hargrave Correspondence,* p. 271.

"Agnes and I thought we had written you about the *Hazel B* sinking: she struck a snag on the 24th of May 1949 during extremely high water and on the down river run. No lives were lost, there happened to be only one passenger, and even the mail sacks were all recovered. It was probably a good thing she went when she did as she was getting pretty old and creaky. I was getting nervous about having the children come back from school on the *Hazel B*. The biggest loss for Al Ritchie on the whole was the good new diesel engine he had put in just a year ago. She sank at Beaver Point at the mouth of the Scud River, the same place where the old *Beaver* sank years ago, before I came to this country— I saw her old boiler sticking up above the water in 1915."

The *Hazel B 3* was thirty-two years old when she sank. Her successor today is the *Judith Ann*.

Notes

PART ONE

1. *Far Pastures,* pp. 51-53, by R. M. Patterson (Gray's Publishing, Sidney, B.C., 1963).
2. The old cabins of the linemen and operators (abandoned after the introduction of radio) were about twenty miles apart.

PART TWO

1. This was written in 1964. Recent mineral discoveries on the Iskut and elsewhere have once more (1966) brought human activity to the Stikine gorge country.
2. *The Hargrave Correspondence,* p. 271. The Champlain Society, Vol. XXIV (Toronto, 1938). Henceforth referred to as *H.C.*
3. There is a good photograph of the *Clifford Sifton* coming through Miles Canyon in *Yukon Voyage,* by Walter R. Curtin (The Caxton Printers Ltd., Caldwell, Idaho, 1938).
4. *Alaska Beckons,* pp. 96-106, by Marius Barbeau (The Caxton Printers Ltd., Caldwell, Idaho, 1947).
5. *Chinese Central Asia,* p. 217, by C. P. Skrine (Methuen, London, 1926).
6. *Through the Sub-Arctic Forest,* pp. 29-34, by Warburton Pike (Edward Arnold, London, 1896). Henceforth referred to as *Sub-Arctic Forest.*

7. A picture of one of these canoes, with the steersman at the sweep, is to be found in *Sub-Arctic Forest* facing p. 72.

8. *Steamboat Days on the Skeena River,* pp. 10-11, by W. J. (Wiggs) O'Neill (Smithers, B.C., 1960).

9. At Petersburg, Alaska, 35 miles north-west of Wrangell, a salmon weighing 126½ pounds is on display.

10. Letter of W. F. Wentzel, clerk in North West Company; after 1821, clerk in Hudson's Bay Company.

11. *H.C.,* p. 184.

12. See p. 50. Could Mr. O'Neill have been mistaken in the year of his trip with Captain Bonser?

13. *The Trail of the Goldseekers,* by Hamlin Garland (Macmillan, New York, 1899).

14. *The Beaver,* Autumn 1962, pp. 4-15.

15. *The Daily British Colonist* (now the *Daily Colonist*), Victoria, B.C., June 12, 1898. Henceforth referred to as *Colonist.*

16. *Colonist,* Oct. 4, 1898.

PART THREE

1. *Colonist,* July 16, 1874.

2. *Colonist,* Aug. 5, 1874.

3. *A Daughter of the Aurora,* by Jack London.

4. *Wrangell & the Gold of the Cassiar,* by C. L. Andrews (Seattle, 1937).

5. The map name is Edziza Peak—not to be confused with the "Ice Mountain" mentioned on p. 43.

PART FOUR

1. *H.C.,* p. 75.

2. The ratio of flood volume to low-water volume is at least as 20 to 1.

3. McPherson's map is now in the Hudson's Bay Company's Archives at Beaver House, Great Trinity Lane, London E. C. 4, England.

4. *H.C.,* p. 84.

5. *H.C.,* p. 84. Chief Factor Edward Smith to James Hargrave. November, 1831.

6. Nearly 40 miles below Fort Halkett—almost 4 miles in length and with a climb, up and down, of 1,000 feet each way.

7. *H.C.,* p. 248.

8. For a good description of the Devil's Portage in wintertime, see

Charles Camsell's *Son of the North,* pp. 66-69 (Ryerson Press, Toronto, 1954).

9. *H.C.,* p. 272.

10. *H.C.,* p. 271. See also Appendix E.

11. See pp. 76-77.

12. *Sub-Arctic Forest,* pp. 110-113.

13. For a similiar experience, see *Dangerous River,* pp. 167-168, by R. M. Patterson (William Sloane, New York, 1954).

14. *Sub-Arctic Forest,* pp. 66-68.

PART FIVE

1. Somebody at the source of supply, away down east, failed to grasp that vital point and, as the result of avoidable delays, certain items of heavy equipment bogged down before reaching Fort Nelson—to be brought on later only with considerable difficulty.

2. See the *Canadian Geographical Journal* for March, 1943, *Northwest Passage by Air,* by J. A. Wilson, at that time in charge of Civil Aviation Development. Among many photographs there are to be seen two that apply here: "The road as we found it" and "The road as we made it."

3. *Canadian Geographical Journal,* Vol. XXVI, No. 3, March, 1943.

Bibliography

BOOKS

Andrews, Clarence L. *The Story of Alaska* (The Caxton Printers, Caldwell, Idaho, 1938).

" *Wrangell and the Gold of the Cassiar* (Luke Tinker, Commercial Printer, Seattle, 1937).

Barbeau, Marius. *Alaska Beckons* (The Caxton Printers, Caldwell, Idaho; Macmillan Co. of Canada, 1947).

Berton, Pierre. *Klondike* (McClelland and Stewart, Toronto, 1958).

Camsell, Charles. *Son of the North* (The Ryerson Press, Toronto, 1954).

Clark, James L. *The Great Arc of the Wild Sheep* (University of Oklahoma Press, Norman, Oklahoma, 1964).

Curtin, Walter R. *Yukon Voyage* (The Caxton Printers, Caldwell, Idaho, 1938).

Galbraith, John S. *The Hudson's Bay Company as an Imperial Factor, 1821 to 1869* (University of Toronto Press, 1957).

Garland, Hamlin. *Trail of the Goldseekers* (Macmillan, New York, 1899).

Lee, Norman. *Klondike Cattle Drive,* The Journal of Norman Lee (Mitchell Press, Vancouver, B.C.).

Muir, John. *Travels in Alaska* (Houghton Mifflin, Boston and New York, 1915).

O'Neill, Wiggs.   *Steamboat Days on the Skeena River, British Co-*
                         lumbia (Northern Sentinel Press, Kitimat, B.C.,
                         1960).
        "   *Whitewater Men of the Skeena* (Kitimat, B.C.,
                         1960).
Pike, Warburton.   *Through the Subarctic Forest* (Edward Arnold,
                         London, 1896).
Rosenberg, Frantz.   *Big Game Shooting in British Columbia and
                         Norway* (Martin Hopkinson, London, 1928).
Williams, A. Bryan.   *Game Trails in British Columbia* (John Murray,
                         London, 1925).

UNPUBLISHED DIARIES AND LETTERS

George Ball.   Letters, various dates.
Robert Campbell.   Journal, 1834-1839.
George Kirkendale.   Diary, 1898.
Janet Patterson.   Diary, 1946.

PUBLICATIONS OF HISTORICAL SOCIETIES

Black's Rocky Mountain Journal, 1824, with an Introduction by R. M.
    Patterson (Vol. XVIII, The Hudson's Bay Record Society, London,
    1955).
The Hargrave Correspondence, 1821-1843, with Introduction and Notes
    by G. P. de T. Glazebrook (Vol. XXIV, The Champlain Society,
    Toronto, 1938).

BIG GAME

North American Big Game, The Boone and Crockett Club (Charles
    Scribner's Sons, New York, 1939).
The Big Game Animals of North America, by Jack O'Connor and
    George G. Goodwin, Outdoor Life (E. P. Dutton, New York, 1961).

CANADIAN GOVERNMENT PAPERS

Geological Survey of Canada, *Report on an Exploration in the Yukon
    District, N.W.T. and adjacent northern portion of British Colum-
    bia,* by George M. Dawson, reprinted 1898 (Queen's Printer, Ot-
    tawa, 1898).

Department of Mines and Resources, Bulletin 61, *Native Trees of Canada* (King's Printer, Ottawa, 1939).

NEWSPAPERS AND PERIODICALS

The Alaska Sportsman, various dates.

The Beaver, Autumn, 1962, pp. 4-15: *The Long March of the Yukon Field Force,* by Arthur L. Disher.

Canadian Geographical Journal, Vol. XXXX, No. 4, April 1950, pp. 174-181, *Indian Engineering,* by A. F. Buckham.

Canadian Geographical Journal, Vol. XXVI, No. 3, March 1943, *Northwest Passage by Air,* by J. A. Wilson.

The Pacific Motor Boat, November 1941, Article on the *Hazel B 1.*

The Shoulder Strap, April–September 1946, pp. 119-122, *The Pioneers of Lower Post,* by Constable Jack Meek.

University of California, Publications in Zoology, 1922, Vol. 24, No. 2, *Birds and mammals of the Stikine River region of northern British Columbia and southeastern Alaska,* by H. S. Swarth.

The Victoria Daily Colonist, various dates.

The Wrangell Sentinel, various dates.